iBT TOEFL LISTENING

NEW EDITION

LinguaForum

기획	링구아포럼 기획편집팀				
지은이	링구아포럼 리서치센터 연구팀				
디자인	링구아포럼 디자인팀				
편집인	최인호				
발행인	이길호				
발행처	링구아포럼				
교재문의	02) 3480-6627	대표전화	02) 590-6900		
등록번호	제2000-000335호	등록일자	2000. 5. 17	ISBN 978-89-5563-682-6 (14740)	가격 21,000원

Copyright ⓒ 2010-2011 by LinguaForum

No unauthorized photocopying.

All rights reserved. No part of this book may be reproduced or transmitted in any form or by any means, electronic or mechanical, including photocopying, recording, or any other information storage and retrieval system without the written permission of the publisher.

이 책은 링구아포럼이 독창적으로 개발하였습니다. 이 책의 내용, 사진 등 일부 혹은 전체 내용을 어떠한 방법으로도 무단 복사, 복제, 전재하는 것은 저작권법에 의해 금지되어 있습니다.

Printed in the Republic of Korea SS1601

R/N(CRmTFLneG): 12281030KB / 03091130KB / 10051130KB

Preface

머리말

TOEFL은 영어가 모국어가 아닌 사람들을 대상으로 영어권 학교에서 영어로 진행되는 수업을 듣고 이해할 수 있는지를 평가 하는 시험이다.

그런데 아는 만큼 들린다고, 익숙하지 않은 발음과 처음 듣는 단어들은 귀에 잘 들어오지 않기 마련이다. 영어 청취 능력의 향상을 위해서는 기본 실력을 쌓고, 꾸준히 연습하는 것이 중요하다. 또한 단순한 청취 능력 외에도 원어민적인 감각이 요구되기 때문에 그만큼의 지식과 노하우가 필요하다. 짧은 시간 내에 실력을 쌓기가 쉽지는 않지만, 이 교재를 길잡이로 꾸준한 듣기 연습을 한다면 영어가 들리는 범위가 점점 확장되어 귀가 트이는 것을 경험할 수 있을 것이다.

이번에 새롭게 개정한 링구아포럼 iBT M TOEFL LISTENING은 새로운 디자인과 구성으로 TOEFL iBT에 보다 철저히 대비할 수 있도록 한 것이 특징이며, TOEFL iBT 문제 유형의 개념 정리, 전략, 그리고 실전용 테스트에 이르기 까지 다양하고 알차게 구성하였다. 특히 단순한 맛보기 식 학습이 아닌 구체적이고 효율적인 내용만 담은 교재가 되도록 하는데 중점을 두었다.

이 책은 TOEFL을 처음 준비하는 학습자부터 청취 능력의 전반적인 향상을 위한 연습과 전략이 필요한 중급 학습자들을 위해 개발되었다. 이 책이 청취력 향상을 위해 고민하고 노력하는 이들의 길잡이가 되어 더 넓은 세상으로의 문을 열어줄 수 있기를 소망한다. 영어에 날개를 달아 더 많은 것을 듣고, 더 많은 것을 경험하며, 세계 속으로 뻗어나갈 수 있게 되기를 기대하며…

LinguaForum Research Center
청취 연구팀

Structure
각 장의 구성

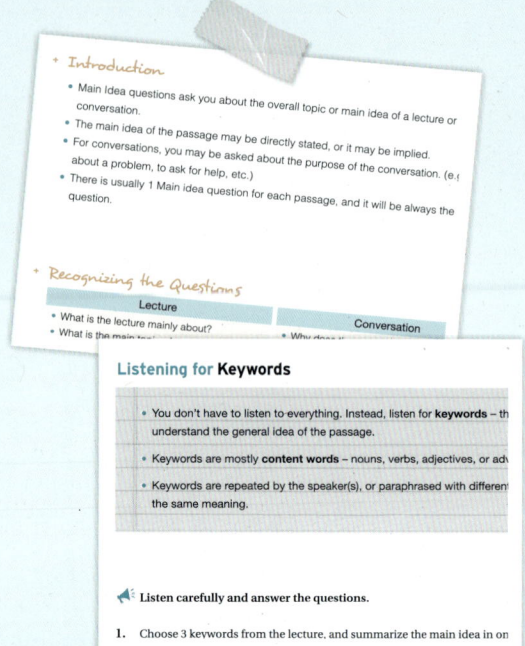

Overview
각 문제 유형에 따른 기본 개념과 접근 방법을 알아보고, 예제를 통해 실제 TOEFL iBT 문제를 경험한다.

Building Skills
각 문제 유형에 필요한 기초 스킬을 익히고, 간단한 연습문제를 통해 이를 점검한다.

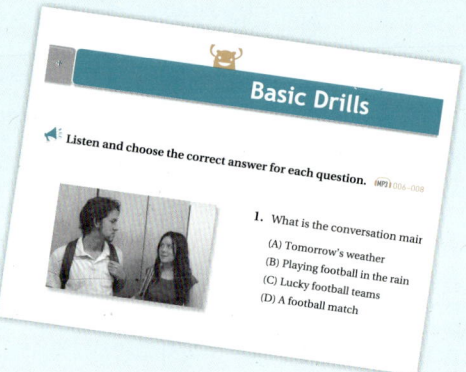

Basic Drills
본격적인 청취 연습에 앞서, 각 장에서 소개한 토플 문제 유형에 대한 기본 개념을 짧은 청취 지문들을 통해 연습한다.

Listening Practice
실제 TOEFL iBT에서 제시되는 다양한 주제의 청취 지문들을 통해 본격적으로 듣기 연습을 해본다.

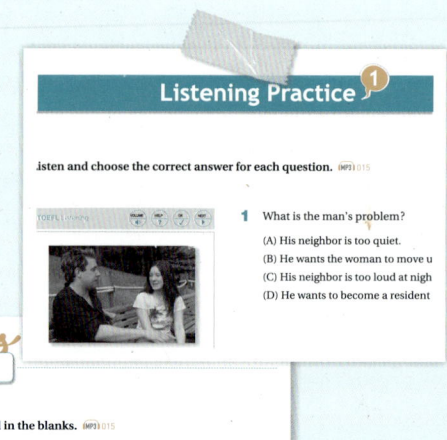

Dictation
받아쓰기는 청취력 향상을 위한 필수적인 연습 방법이다. Listening Practice에서 나온 지문을 다시 한번 듣고 받아쓰는 연습을 통해 들리지 않고 이해되지 않았던 부분이 어디인지를 확인한다.

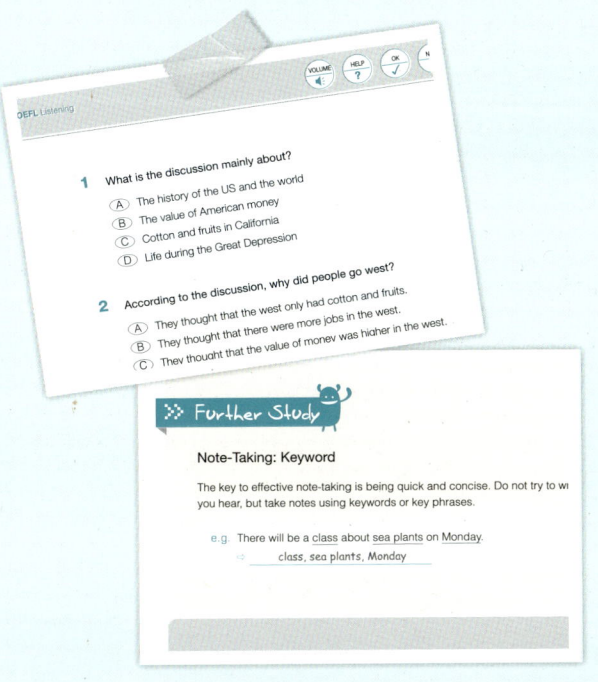

iBT Practice

실제 토플 시험과 같은 상황을 제시하여 좀 더 긴 지문을 듣고 문제를 풀어본다. 각 장에서 연습한 실력을 최종적으로 점검하고 실전에 대비한다.

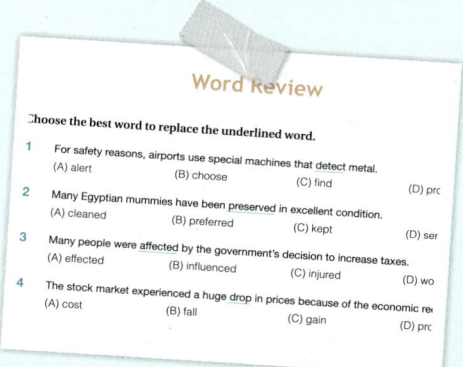

Further Study

TOEFL iBT에서 고득점 취득에 중요한 역할을 하는 note-taking 기술 향상을 위한 팁을 익히고, iBT Practice에서 나온 지문을 다시 한번 듣고 이를 활용해본다.

Word Review

각 장에서 나온 주요 어휘를 문제 형식으로 복습하여 어휘 실력을 튼튼히 다지도록 하였다.

Actual Test

3회분의 Actual Test를 수록하여, 실전에서의 자신의 예상 점수를 가늠해 보고 실전 적응력을 높인다.

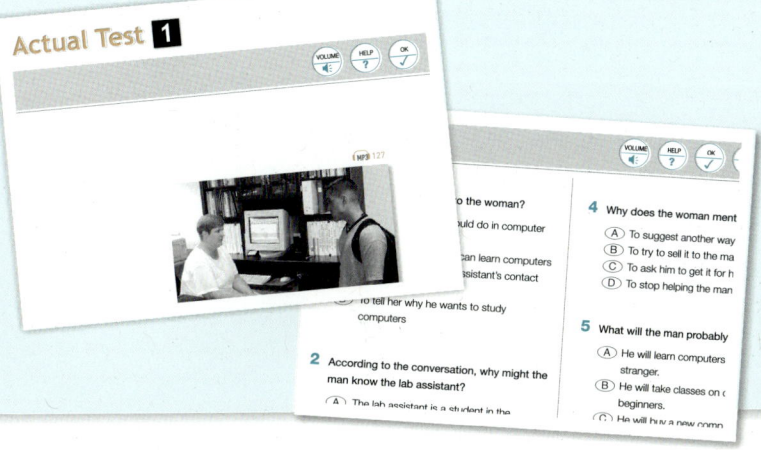

Contents

Part A Basic Comprehension Questions

| Chapter 1. | Main Idea | 9 |
| Chapter 2. | Detail | 27 |

Part B Pragmatic Understanding Questions

| Chapter 3. | Function | 47 |
| Chapter 4. | Attitude | 65 |

Part C Connecting Information Questions

Chapter 5.	Organization	85
Chapter 6.	Connecting Content	103
Chapter 7.	Inference	121

Actual Test 1-3 140

Scripts & Answer Key

Basic Comprehension Questions

Basic comprehension questions test your basic understanding of the overall ideas or important details expressed in the passage. Basic comprehension of the listening passage is tested in two ways: with Main Idea and Detail questions.

PART A

LINGUAFORUM + iBT + mTOEFL + LISTENING

Part A +

Main Idea

Detail

Part B
Function
Attitude

Part C
Organization
Connecting Content
Inference

CHAPTER 1

Main Idea

+ Introduction

- Main Idea questions ask you about the overall topic or main idea of a lecture or conversation.
- The main idea of the passage may be directly stated, or it may be implied.
- For conversations, you may be asked about the purpose of the conversation. (e.g. to talk about a problem, to ask for help, etc.)
- There is usually 1 Main Idea question for each passage, and it will be always the first question.

+ Recognizing the Questions

Lecture	Conversation
• What is the lecture mainly about? • What is the main topic of the lecture? • What aspect of X does the professor mainly discuss?	• Why does the student visit the professor? • What problem does the man have? • What are the speakers mainly discussing?

+ Strategies

1. Listen carefully to the beginning of the lecture or conversation. The main idea is often found there.
2. Pay attention to words and ideas that are frequently repeated or paraphrased. They probably have something to do with the main idea.
3. Do not choose any answer that is either too broad or too specific. The correct main idea must cover all the key points.

+ **Sample Question**

MP3 001

TOEFL Listening   VOLUME HELP OK NEXT HIDE TIME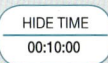

What is the talk mainly about?

- (A) Bad ideas
- (B) Group leaders
- (C) Peer pressure
- (D) Real friends

Script

It is normal for friends to chat and do things together. But sometimes, they can also do bad things, like smoking or stealing things. Although they do not enjoy it, friends in the group force them, not physically but mentally. This is called peer pressure.

Most peer pressure starts with a bad idea from the leader. There is always a leader in groups. If they get a bad idea, then everyone follows. The rest of the group finds it hard to reject the idea. As more and more of the members do it, the rest of the group follows. Everyone knows it is bad, but they do not want to feel left out of the group.

It is not smart to give into peer pressure. Friends don't have to listen to and follow one person, if they are doing something bad. Real friends understand each other, and stop other friends from doing bad things.

Answer & Explanation

The answer is (C). The teacher starts the lecture by explaining what peer pressure is. Then she talks about how peer pressure occurs, and ends the lecture by giving her opinion on peer pressure.

Building Skills

Listening for Keywords

- You don't have to listen to everything. Instead, listen for **keywords** – they will help you understand the general idea of the passage.

- Keywords are mostly **content words** – nouns, verbs, adjectives, or adverbs.

- Keywords are repeated by the speaker(s), or paraphrased with different words that have the same meaning.

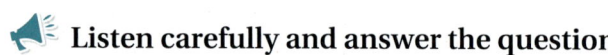 Listen carefully and answer the questions.

1. Choose 3 keywords from the lecture, and summarize the main idea in one sentence. **MP3** 002

| ride | public transportation | choose | buses | taxis |
| popular | subway trains | carry | travel | reason |

Keywords : _____ , _____ , _____
Main Idea : _____

2. Choose the 2 most important keywords from the conversation. **MP3** 003

| English | class | games | funny |
| jokes | lucky | terrible | teachers |

Keywords : _____ , _____

Listening to the Introductory Section

- Remember that the main idea is often stated at the **beginning** of a lecture or conversation.

- Listen for **signal words** that identify the topic or main idea.
  e.g. I'd like to discuss … / we're going to talk about … / I was wondering if …

- Once you identify the main idea, anticipate key points and relate the details to the main idea while you are listening.

 **Listen carefully and answer the questions.**

1. Listen to the beginning of a lecture, and fill in the blank. (MP3) 004

   | In class, the teacher will give ideas on _____. |

   (A) things to learn when you live overseas
   (B) how to make friends in another country
   (C) easier ways of learning a new language

2. Listen to the beginning of a lecture, and guess what the lecture will be mainly about. (MP3) 005

   (A) Finding out what kinds of chemicals are poisonous to the human body
   (B) Knowing the reason why humans get addicted to caffeine
   (C) Knowing how the human body works

Basic Drills

Listen and choose the correct answer for each question. MP3 006-008

1. What is the conversation mainly about?

   (A) Tomorrow's weather
   (B) Playing football in the rain
   (C) Lucky football teams
   (D) A football match

2. What is the teacher talking about?

   (A) How cavemen hunted
   (B) What food cavemen ate
   (C) The weapons of cavemen
   (D) Distracting big animals

3. What is the talk mainly about?

   (A) Musical instruments
   (B) Yellow paper
   (C) Sheep and goats
   (D) Parchment

🔊 **Listen and choose the correct answer for each question.** MP3 009–011

4. Why does the man talk to the woman?

   (A) To make her look for Jack
   (B) To ask her to help him move
   (C) To ask if she knows where Jack is
   (D) To break the promise with her

5. What is the talk mainly about?

   (A) The inventions of man
   (B) Types of wheels
   (C) The early days of man
   (D) The importance of wheels

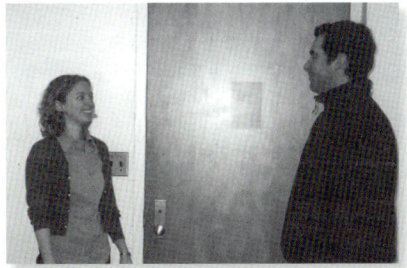

6. Why does the woman talk to the man?

   (A) To ask him if he likes pizza
   (B) To ask him about dinner
   (C) To tell the man about Italian food
   (D) To get the man to buy dinner

Listen and choose the correct answer for each question. MP3 012-014

7. What is the talk mainly about?

   (A) Exercising for health
   (B) Eating healthy foods
   (C) Becoming healthy
   (D) Caring for our body

8. Why does the woman talk to the man?

   (A) To ask him to look for Mr. Adams
   (B) To tell him what subjects she has chosen
   (C) To ask if he has chosen all his subjects
   (D) To get a booklet from the man

9. What is the speaker mainly talking about?

   (A) The instinct of carnivorous animals
   (B) The foods of carnivorous animals
   (C) The homes of wild animals
   (D) The safety of feeding carnivorous animals

Listening Practice 1

🔊 **Listen and choose the correct answer for each question.** (MP3) 015

1 What is the man's problem?

(A) His neighbor is too quiet.
(B) He wants the woman to move upstairs.
(C) His neighbor is too loud at night.
(D) He wants to become a resident assistant.

2 What is the role of resident assistants?

(A) They clean up the dorm rooms.
(B) They make sure everyone is comfortable in the dorm.
(C) They help students in the dorm with their studies.
(D) They turn up the music in the rooms.

3 What will the man probably do?

(A) He will apply for an RA position.
(B) He will talk to the RA.
(C) He will tell the man to be quiet.
(D) He will not sleep in his room.

Dictation

Listen again and fill in the blanks. MP3 015

W: You look very tired. _____ _____ _____?

M: No, I only slept for three hours last night.

W: What did you do?

M: Well, it's _____ _____ upstairs. He turns up his music _____ _____ every night. I know it's a school dorm, but it's still too loud. It's like he has a party every night.

W: Oh, did you tell him _____ _____ _____ _____? He _____ _____ _____ after midnight. That's part of the dorm rules.

M: Yes, I told him to be quiet, but he _____ _____ _____ _____. He says that he will be quiet, but he _____ _____ the music 10 minutes later.

W: I think you should talk to the RAs. They will _____ _____ _____.

M: What is an RA?

W: An RA is a resident assistant. RAs are actually students, too. They _____ _____ _____ _____ in the dorm. They have to make sure that everyone is _____.

M: Oh, why didn't I know about this RA? I will talk to the RA when I go back to my room tonight. I really need _____ _____ _____ _____.

W: Don't worry. I'm sure the RA will _____ _____ _____.

Vocabulary

- **dorm (dormitory)** a building at a college or university where students live
- **resident** someone who lives in a particular place
- **assistant** someone who helps someone else in their work

Listening Practice 2

Listen and choose the correct answer for each question. MP3 016

1 What is the talk mainly about?

(A) Supermarkets in Germany
(B) Barcodes in microchip scanners
(C) Technology in supermarkets
(D) Scanners in cashier counters

2 What is RFID?

(A) It is the name of the bars on the codes.
(B) It is a new technology overtaking barcodes.
(C) It is the name of a supermarket in Germany.
(D) It is the way barcode scanners read microchips.

3 According to the lecture, how do barcodes work?

(A) The cashiers type barcodes into the computer.
(B) The RFID detects the barcodes.
(C) The barcode displays the total price.
(D) The barcode is scanned into the computer.

Dictation

🔊 **Listen again and fill in the blanks.** (MP3) 016

Many people visit supermarkets. Supermarkets have so many things that it is hard _____ _____ _____ _____ everything. This is why supermarkets use a lot of _____ _____. They use technology to make shopping quicker and easier.

Barcodes are _____ _____ _____ in the supermarket. The barcode system shortens cashier lines because fewer mistakes are made. The cashier _____ barcodes through a scanner. The scanner reads the code and adds the total amount. When all the items are scanned, the computer _____ the total price.

Although barcodes have been very popular, there is _____ _____ _____ overtaking barcodes. The system is called RFID. _____ _____ _____, every item in the supermarket will have very small microchips. Large microchip scanners in the checkout lanes _____ the microchips _____ _____ _____ inside the shopping carts. This allows shoppers to walk through the cashier _____ _____ each item. This _____ _____ a lot of time. There are already large supermarkets in Germany that have this system.

Vocabulary

- **keep track of** to know; to stay informed
- **overtake** to become more successful than someone or something else
- **checkout** a counter in a supermarket where you pay for your purchases
- **lane** a narrow way; road
- **detect** to find; to discover

Listening Practice 3

🔊 **Listen and choose the correct answer for each question.** MP3 017

1 What are they mainly discussing?

(A) The number of fossils found in the Grand Canyon
(B) How to tell the age of dinosaurs from fossils
(C) What fossils are and what they can tell us
(D) Differences between plant and animal fossils

2 What are mammoths?

(A) They are animals trapped inside stones.
(B) They are dinosaur bones in the ground.
(C) They are animals in the zoo.
(D) They are large elephants from the stone age.

3 What can we learn from fossils?

> Click on 2 answers.

(A) The number of dinosaurs in the world
(B) The minerals and fuels in the area
(C) The changes in the Grand Canyon
(D) The development of animals and plants

1. Main Idea   21

Dictation

🔊 **Listen again and fill in the blanks.** (MP3) 017

T: Today, we _____ _____ _____ _____ fossils.
Does anyone know _____ _____ _____ ?

M: They are dinosaur bones in the ground.

T: Close, but not really. Fossils are _____ _____ _____ of bones or plants. Fossils give us _____ about the Earth's history.

M: Can _____ _____ of animals become fossils?

T: Not usually. They are usually made by _____ _____ _____, like bones and shells. However, _____ _____ have been preserved in stones. Mammoths have been found _____ in ice. Mammoths are large elephants that lived during the stone age.

M: Oh, when I visited the Grand Canyon, the guide said that there were _____ _____ _____ _____ there. Is this true?

T: Yes. There are many _____ of fossils in the Grand Canyon. Each layer is older than the layer above it.

W: So, can fossils tell us _____ _____ besides how old an animal or plant is?

T: Yes, we can learn other things from fossils: _____ _____ of animals and plants, as well as _____ _____ of each layer.

M: And I think fossils tell us information _____ _____ _____ in that area.

T: Right! We can also find out information about minerals and fuels. Well, that's all for today's class.

Vocabulary

- **fossil** the remains of a plant or animal from a long time ago
- **shell** a hard outer covering of an egg, nut, etc.
- **preserved** kept in a particular condition
- **layer** a single thickness of a material covering a surface

iBT Practice

TOEFL Listening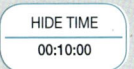

Note-Taking

iBT Practice CONTINUED

1. Main Idea

TOEFL Listening

1 What is the discussion mainly about?

- Ⓐ The history of the US and the world
- Ⓑ The value of American money
- Ⓒ Cotton and fruits in California
- Ⓓ Life during the Great Depression

2 According to the discussion, why did people go west?

- Ⓐ They thought that the west only had cotton and fruits.
- Ⓑ They thought that there were more jobs in the west.
- Ⓒ They thought that the value of money was higher in the west.
- Ⓓ They thought that nobody traveled west to work.

3 When was the Big Boom?

- Ⓐ Just before the Great Depression
- Ⓑ When people went to California
- Ⓒ After picking cotton and fruits
- Ⓓ After the Great Depression

4 According to the lecture, why did the Great Depression occur?

- Ⓐ There were too many people looking for jobs.
- Ⓑ There were too many people moving to the western states.
- Ⓒ There weren't enough people selling goods.
- Ⓓ There was a huge drop in the value of money.

Further Study

Note-Taking: Keyword

The key to effective note-taking is being quick and concise. Do not try to write down everything you hear, but take notes using keywords or key phrases.

e.g. There will be a <u>class</u> about <u>sea plants</u> on <u>Monday</u>.
⇨ _class, sea plants, Monday_

Listen again and fill in the blanks using keywords. MP3 018

Topic: Great _____
- Actual state – during _____
  – whole world was affected including _____
  – just after _____ in the US
  – no jobs & _____
- Reaction – people _____ to find jobs
  e.g. _____ : most _____ to death
                     because too many people came

1. Main Idea

Word Review

Choose the best word to replace the underlined word.

1. For safety reasons, airports use special machines that detect metal.
   (A) alert (B) choose (C) find (D) produce

2. Many Egyptian mummies have been preserved in excellent condition.
   (A) cleaned (B) preferred (C) kept (D) served

3. Many people were affected by the government's decision to increase taxes.
   (A) effected (B) influenced (C) injured (D) worried

4. The stock market experienced a huge drop in prices because of the economic recession.
   (A) cost (B) fall (C) gain (D) product

Choose and write the correct word to complete the sentence.

| assistant | layer | for nothing | rough |
| fossils | resident | instinct | literally |

5. Ancient _____ of Homo sapiens show that humans may have evolved from apes.

6. The ice was too _____ to skate on, so we had no choice but to give up on our plans for ice skating.

7. Don't try to understand the poem _____ – try to make your own interpretation of it instead.

8. In dangerous situations, the best thing you can do is follow your _____.

9. I am a(n) _____ of the United States, but I haven't been granted full citizenship yet.

10. I hired a new _____ to help run errands.

11. A(n) _____ of snow covered the roads, making it very dangerous to drive.

12. The soldier died fighting for his country, so his death was not _____.

LINGUAFORUM + iBT + mTOEFL + LISTENING

Part A +

Main Idea

Detail

Part B
Function
Attitude

Part C
Organization
Connecting Content
Inference

CHAPTER 2

Detail

+ Introduction

- Detail questions ask you about specific information or facts in a lecture or conversation.
- They do not ask about minor details or implied information.
- Some Detail questions have more than 1 answer.
- There are usually 1-2 Detail questions for each passage.

+ Recognizing the Questions

- According to the professor, what/who/which/why/when/where/how …?
- What does the professor suggest to the student?
- What is the difference between X and Y?
- What are the reasons for X? Click on 2 answers.

+ Strategies

1. Take notes on the main points and *related* details. Detail questions always ask about important details that support the main idea, not minor ones.
2. Do not simply choose the answer that repeats a word from the listening passage. The correct answer often paraphrases the information using different words or structure.
3. If you are stuck, eliminate incorrect answers which contain wrong or unmentioned information. That will be easier than just looking for the correct answer.

+ Sample Question

TOEFL Listening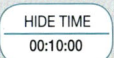

What did the senior science class do in class last week?

A) They only read about things.
B) They did a test on eggs.
C) They did a test on water.
D) They tested the labs.

Script

W: What do you think of our science class?

M: I think it's alright, but it's quite boring sometimes.

W: I agree with you. I think it can be very boring. Don't you think that the class could be fun?

M: Yes. I heard that the senior class can use the labs and do other fun experiments.

W: Yes, I remember that they did a test on eggs last week. It looked like so much fun. I heard that they will test water tomorrow.

M: That's unfair. We only sit in the classroom and read about things.

W: You're right. Let's talk to our teacher and ask her about it. I don't see why we can't use the labs.

M: Yes, I'm sure that our grades will be higher once we see what the teacher is actually talking about.

Answer & Explanation

The answer is (B). They talk about how the science class could be fun, and as an example, the woman says that the senior class did a test on eggs last week. (C) is what the class will do next week.

Building Skills

Focusing on the Important Details

- **Important details** are details that are needed to understand the main idea. Therefore, a clear understanding of the main idea will help you know which details you should focus on.
- Pay attention to **new facts, descriptions, definitions, reasons, results, examples,** etc.
- Listen for **signal words** that identify important details.
  e.g. for example … / the reason is … / that is to say … / to show what I mean …

Listen carefully and answer the questions.

1. Listen to part of a conversation. Put an **O** if the question is answered in the passage, and an **X** if it is not. (MP3) 020

   Q1. What is the largest state in the US? (   )

   Q2. Where is Alaska located? (   )

   Q3. Which country is the biggest in the world? (   )

2. Listen to part of a lecture. Write **T**(True) or **F**(False) after each statement. (MP3) 021

   Q1. Hummingbirds are the smallest birds in the world. _____

   Q2. Hummingbirds are a little longer than 5 centimeters. _____

   Q3. We can see the wings of hummingbirds moving with our naked eye. _____

   Q4. Hummingbirds need to move their wings fast to fly further away. _____

Recognizing Rephrased Details

- **Paraphrasing** or **rephrasing** is when you restate something in your own words without changing the meaning.
  e.g. They know all the rules of this game. → They know how to play.

- The correct answer to Detail questions is often **paraphrased**. Remember that an accurate paraphrase must correctly convey the information from the passage.

Listen carefully and answer the questions.

1. Listen to part of a conversation. Choose the one that best paraphrases the following sentence.
   MP3 022

   > People used white paint to hide the black marks.

   (A) People painted the building white to change the old color.
   (B) People covered the burned parts with white paint.
   (C) People used black and white to paint the building.

2. Listen to part of a lecture. Write **T**(True) or **F**(False) after each statement. **MP3 023**

   Q1. The degree of an earthquake can be expressed in numbers. _____
   Q2. The Richter scale was given the same name as its inventor. _____
   Q3. The Richter scale tells us about how often earthquakes occur. _____
   Q4. An earthquake at 7 on the Richter scale is very weak. _____

Basic Drills

 Listen and choose the correct answer for each question. MP3 024-026

1. What does the man like to watch?

   (A) He likes action movies.
   (B) He likes horror movies.
   (C) He likes family movies.
   (D) He likes the opera.

2. According to the talk, what are killer whales?

   (A) They are dolphins.
   (B) They are whales.
   (C) They are penguins.
   (D) They are seals.

3. What is the man's lucky number?

   (A) He likes number 7.
   (B) He likes number 4.
   (C) He likes number 1.
   (D) He does not have a lucky number.

Listen and choose the correct answer for each question. (MP3) 027-029

4. Why were the soldiers getting sick?

   (A) Because of the dirty food in the army
   (B) Because of flies carrying diseases
   (C) Because of fighting with enemy soldiers
   (D) Because of the screens on the windows

5. How long did the students have to sign up for a room in the hostel?

   (A) One day
   (B) Three days
   (C) One week
   (D) One month

6. How many mini cars does the man have at home?

   (A) He has one car at home.
   (B) He has 13 cars at home.
   (C) He has 60 cars at home.
   (D) He has 180 cars at home.

Listen and choose the correct answer for each question. MP3 030-032

7. What animal stands for evil in many American classic stories?

   (A) The eagle
   (B) The pig
   (C) The rat
   (D) The bat

8. What does the woman usually do in the library?

   (A) She reads and studies.
   (B) She usually falls asleep.
   (C) She steals things from people.
   (D) She catches thieves between classes.

9. Why won't the woman enter graduate school?

   Click on 2 answers.

   (A) She did not get the scholarship.
   (B) She wants to sit around and do nothing.
   (C) She cannot afford the expensive school fees.
   (D) She wants to get a job.

Listening Practice 1

🔊 **Listen and choose the correct answer for each question.** MP3 033

1. What is wrong with the man?

   (A) He wants to see the teacher about his scholarship.
   (B) He has to go to the biology class tomorrow morning.
   (C) He needs to see the teacher about an assignment he didn't hand in.
   (D) He wants to ask the teacher about going on a vacation.

2. Why did the man miss his class?

   (A) He was too lazy.
   (B) He did not wake up in time.
   (C) He did not run to the class.
   (D) He wanted to go on vacation.

3. What will the man probably do?

   (A) He will slip the assignment under the professor's door.
   (B) He will call the professor over the phone to talk about the assignment.
   (C) He will run faster back to his room.
   (D) He will talk to the professor after the vacation.

Dictation

🔊 **Listen again and fill in the blanks.** MP3 033

W: You look worried. Is everything alright?

M: No. I have _____ _____ _____ _____.

W: Oh, tell me what is wrong.

M: Well, you know that I'm _____ _____ _____, right?

W: Yes, I know you are.

M: _____ _____ _____ _____ a B average every semester, or my scholarship _____ _____. That would be a big problem for me.

W: Wow, that's tough. So what is the problem?

M: I had biology class in the morning. I was supposed _____ _____ _____ an important assignment, but I _____. When I finally woke up and ran to class, the professor wasn't there. _____ _____ _____ hand in this assignment, the best I can do in this class is a C.

W: Why didn't you go to his office? I'm sure he would have been there.

M: I did, but he _____ _____ _____ _____ as soon as the class was over. He probably took everyone's assignment too. Oh, I don't know what to do.

W: You can talk to him when he _____ _____. I'm sure he will understand that it was _____ _____ _____. You can't just slip the assignment under his door while he is away.

M: Yes, I guess not. I really _____ _____ _____ faster.

W: No, I think you should have _____ _____ _____.

Vocabulary

☐ **scholarship** money given to a student to help pay for his or her education   ☐ **hand in** to give or bring to someone
☐ **slip** to put something somewhere quickly or quietly

Listening Practice 2

Listen and choose the correct answer for each question. MP3 034

1 What is the talk mainly about?

(A) The California gold rush
(B) The football teams of California
(C) The towns of Alaska
(D) The gold rushes in North America

2 Who were the original 49ers?

(A) The Klondike miners in the gold rush
(B) The San Francisco football team
(C) The miners of the California gold rush
(D) The Native Americans living in Alaska

3 According to the lecture, who first discovered gold in Klondike?

(A) Skookum Jim Mason
(B) George Carmack
(C) White people
(D) Californians

Dictation

🔊 **Listen again and fill in the blanks.** (MP3) 034

The gold rush in California of 1849 is _____ _____ _____ gold rush of North America. Over 80,000 people, called the 49ers, because of the year 1849, _____ _____ Northern California _____ _____ easy money. The football team from San Francisco is called the 49ers, _____ _____ _____. A lot of people died on their way to California. Even when they did reach California, most of the gold spots _____ _____, and there was little land to get gold from.

But there were other gold rushes, mostly in the western regions of North America. They were _____ _____ _____ or hard as the Californian gold rush. The Klondike gold rush of 1896 is _____ _____ _____.

Klondike is a small town next to Alaska, and is part of Canada. A Native American named Skookum Jim Mason _____ _____ gold. Unfortunately, at that time, the white people _____ _____ _____ Native Americans. So a friend of Mason, called George Carmack, registered the land _____ _____ _____. They began to find a lot of gold in the area and built a small place to live.

Soon, more people _____ _____ about this gold. The new gold miners to Klondike were prepared. They made sure that they had enough food and warm clothes. In fact, they were so _____ that the gold rush was very _____ and people _____ got hurt. Klondike still has a gold mining company, but the gold rush is over.

Vocabulary

☐ **rush** to act or move quickly   ☐ **miner** someone who works underground to remove coal, gold, etc.   ☐ **spot** a particular place or area   ☐ **region** a large area of a country or of the world   ☐ **register** to put one's name on an official list

Listening Practice 3

🔊 **Listen and choose the correct answer for each question.** MP3 035

1 What are the friends mainly talking about?

(A) Getting a full-time job.
(B) Playing sports activities
(C) Using a computer in the library
(D) Getting a part-time job

2 What does the coach's assistant do?

Click in the correct box.

	Yes	No
(A) Listen to music		
(B) Manage lots of equipment		
(C) Plan sports activities		
(D) Use the internet		

3 According to the conversation, why will the man NOT like the library job?

(A) The library has too much equipment.
(B) The library is too quiet for him.
(C) The library is too exciting for him.
(D) The library has baseball bats and helmets.

Dictation

🔊 **Listen again and fill in the blanks.** (MP3) 035

W: What are you planning for _____ _____ _____?
M: I'm planning on getting _____ _____ _____ in the school.
W: Really? What sort of job are you looking for?
M: I was thinking about working _____ _____ _____ as an assistant.
W: Hmm, that job _____ _____ _____ for you.
M: _____ do you say that?
W: You are _____ _____ _____ and like music. The library will be _____ _____ for you. You _____ _____ _____ the internet or listen to music in there.
M: I guess you're right. _____ _____ do you think I can try?
W: I heard that _____ _____ team coach is looking for an assistant. He's always very busy with a lot of work.
M: What kind of job do you think an assistant _____ _____? I don't want to just wipe baseball bats and helmets.
W: Now you're just being silly. I heard that the assistant _____ _____ _____ a lot of equipment. The assistant also _____ the sports activities for the whole semester. It's a big job, but it can also be _____ _____ _____ _____!
M: Hey, that does sound like a lot of fun! _____ _____ _____ I didn't think of that. Thanks a lot. I'll _____ _____ _____ right now.
W: _____ _____ _____ and find him fast. _____ _____ students want to work with him.
M: Don't worry, I know the coach very well. I'll talk to him _____ _____ _____ I see him, and _____ _____ _____ _____. I really want that job now.

Vocabulary

☐ **wipe** to rub something to clean it   ☐ **equipment** tools or machines to help do a job or an activity   ☐ **quite a few** many

*i*BT Practice

TOEFL Listening

MP3 036

Note-Taking

*i*BT Practice CONTINUED

2. Detail

TOEFL Listening

1 What is the lecture mostly about?

- Ⓐ Why we celebrate April Fools' Day
- Ⓑ Ancient holidays and April Fools' Day
- Ⓒ The origins of April Fools' Day
- Ⓓ Famous holidays in April

2 What happens on April Fools' Day?

- Ⓐ People try to fool or trick others.
- Ⓑ People celebrate the New Year.
- Ⓒ People switch calendars.
- Ⓓ People attend church rituals.

3 How did the church feel about the Feast of Fool's Day?

- Ⓐ The church accepted it in order to make the people happy.
- Ⓑ The church tried to get rid of it since it made fun of them.
- Ⓒ Church officials joined to celebrate the feast.
- Ⓓ The church tried to change it into a different type of holiday.

4 Why did people make fun of those that used the older calendar?

- Ⓐ They wanted to relieve stress.
- Ⓑ They wanted to set the model for a holiday.
- Ⓒ They found the Julian calendar inaccurate.
- Ⓓ They celebrated a different New Year.

Note-Taking: Organizing Your Notes

You can use different note-taking formats depending on the content and organizational structure of a listening passage. Using the appropriate note-taking format will help you remember key facts and related details better.

e.g.
Introduction
1. Main Point
   1) Detail 1
      - Further Detail
Conclusion

Main Point
├── Detail 1
│   └── Further Detail
└── Detail 2
    └── Further Detail

Detail 1 ┐
Detail 2 ┼── Main Point
Detail 3 ┘

🔊 Listen again and fill in the blanks using keywords. MP3 036

The Origin of _____
├── Theory 1
├── Theory 2
└── Theory 3

- **Theory 1** : _____
  – reserved one day to _____

- **Theory 2** : Middle Ages
  – "_____" : made fun of _____

- **Theory 3** : _____
  – _____ reform
  – the beginning of the year was moved
    : between March 25th and _____ → January 1st

Word Review

Choose the best word to replace the underlined word.

1. I'm feeling under the weather, so I'm not very keen on going to the party.
   (A) afraid of (B) eager about (C) familiar with (D) proud of

2. The students are such troublemakers; they are always trying to trick their teacher.
   (A) assist (B) fool (C) please (D) respect

3. There were so many people at the park that I was unable to reserve a spot for a picnic.
   (A) allow (B) expect (C) offer (D) save

4. France switched its currency from the franc to the euro in 2002.
   (A) changed (B) distinguished (C) prevented (D) prohibited

Choose and write the correct word to complete the sentence.

| scholarship | quite a few | greed | rush |
| regions | ancient | equipment | widespread |

5. After being shown his future by the Ghost of Christmas Present, Scrooge lost his _____ and became generous and kind.

6. Getting good grades isn't the only way to get a(n) _____; many universities also offer them to students who join the student council.

7. Everyone made a(n) _____ for the exit when they heard the fire alarm.

8. South Korea is one of the most densely populated _____ in the world.

9. We store all our office _____ in the supply closet.

10. It began raining heavily on the day of the football match, but surprisingly, _____ people turned up to watch the game.

11. Bowing to your elders is a(n) _____ tradition that started in China.

12. Underage drinking is still a(n) _____ problem in many countries.

Memo

Pragmatic Understanding Questions

Pragmatic understanding questions test your understanding of certain features of spoken English. In this type of question, you need to do more than hear what is said. Pragmatic understanding of the listening passage is tested in two ways: with Function and Attitude questions.

PART B

LINGUAFORUM + iBT + mTOEFL + LISTENING

Part A
Main Idea
Detail

Part B +

Function

Attitude

Part C
Organization
Connecting Content
Inference

CHAPTER 3

Function

+ Introduction

- Function questions ask you about the speaker's purpose or intended meaning of a specific statement.
- These questions ask you to understand not just *what* the speaker says, but also *why* he or she says it.
- Typically, these questions replay a specific statement from the listening passage.
- There are usually 1-2 Function questions for each passage.

+ Recognizing the Questions

- Why does the student say this: 🎧 (replay)
- What does the man mean when he says this: 🎧 (replay)
- What does the professor imply when she says this: 🎧 (replay)

+ Strategies

1. Use the context. The speaker's function is not directly stated, so relate the statement to the surrounding statements. Then choose the answer that is most logical from the context.
2. Distinguish between what is *said* and what is *intended* by the speaker. The intended meaning does not always match what is literally said. Therefore, do not rely on words, but think about what the speaker wants to achieve in the situation.

+ **Sample Question**

TOEFL Listening

Why does the woman say this:

- Ⓐ To indicate that nothing is really wrong with the dorms
- Ⓑ To show that she does not know what to talk about
- Ⓒ To try to end the conversation with the man
- Ⓓ To emphasize many things going wrong with the dorms

Script

M: I hear that you were trying to find a room outside the campus. Is it true?

W: Yes, it is. I really hate living in the dorms.

M: Why do you say that?

W: Where do I begin? The cafeteria food tastes really bad most of the time, the people are always very noisy, and my roommate is dirty.

M: It sounds like you're going through quite a lot. I also noticed that your dorms were really small and old.

W: Yes, you guessed it. They are so old that the elevators do not work half of the time. Even when they do, they squeak and shake. Everyone is scared to ride in them. Plus, the dorms are so small that there is no place that I can park my car.

M: Hang in just a bit longer until you find a place outside the campus.

W: Yes, I hope I can move out quickly.

Answer & Explanation

The answer is (D). When the man asks the woman why she hates living in the dorms, she says, "Where do I begin?" and begins to talk about all the dorm's problems.

Building Skills

Understanding Different Purposes

- When a speaker says a specific statement, it can have many **different purposes**. Here are some examples:
  - to request / suggest
  - to apologize / complain / compliment
  - to express surprise / satisfaction / disapproval
  - to emphasize / persuade / warn

Listen carefully and answer the questions.

1. Listen to part of a lecture. Choose why the professor says the following statement. (MP3) 038

   > But I think it was worth it, as I was even more shocked than the rest of you.

   (A) To compliment the students on how well they did on the quiz
   (B) To emphasize the importance of the quiz
   (C) To tell the students to get started with the assignments

2. Listen to part of a lecture. Choose why the professor says the following statement. (MP3) 039

   > We're not going to go into details right now, but the general rule is that ...

   (A) To emphasize the general rule related to tires
   (B) To discuss various factors that determine the type of tires
   (C) To get students to concentrate on the lecture

Listening for the Underlying Meaning

- A single statement can have **different meanings** depending on the circumstances. For example, you may ask "*Do you like movies?*" to get information about the other person, or to suggest going to a movie.

- To figure out what the speaker really means, you must understand the meaning within the **context**.

Listen carefully and answer the questions.

1. Listen to part of a conversation. Choose what the woman means when she says the following statement. (MP3) 040

   > W: I should help Mary with her assignment?

   (A) I don't have any reason to help her.
   (B) I didn't know that I need to help her.
   (C) Mary doesn't need any help from me.

2. Listen to part of a lecture. Choose what the professor means when he says the following statement. (MP3) 041

   > Nevertheless, I wouldn't say that we are anywhere close to being successful in winning the battle against diseases. Far from it.

   (A) The professor does not want to talk about diseases.
   (B) The professor is trying to say there are still many diseases to cure.
   (C) The professor believes that we can overcome all the diseases if we try harder.

Basic Drills

🔊 Listen and choose the correct answer for each question. 🎧 MP3 042-044

1. Why does the woman say this: 🎧

   (A) To ask if he knows how long she was gone
   (B) To find out if the man stole her notes in the library
   (C) To show that she did not expect it to happen
   (D) To describe who has stolen her notes

2. Why does the woman mention helicopters flying in one spot?

   (A) To emphasize the difficulty of controlling helicopters
   (B) To explain how helicopters can fly in one spot
   (C) To show how easy it is to fly a helicopter
   (D) To find out if the students know how it is done

3. Why does the woman say this: 🎧

   (A) To ask the man for advice
   (B) To agree with the man
   (C) To get the man to talk more
   (D) To complain to the man

🔊 **Listen and choose the correct answer for each question.** MP3 045-047

4. Why does the speaker say this: 🎧

   (A) To mention what their jobs require
   (B) To emphasize songwriters' importance in music
   (C) To suggest students become songwriters
   (D) To ask the students which singers they like

5. Why does the woman say this: 🎧

   (A) To ask the man if he knows why
   (B) To mention that she does not know why
   (C) To encourage the man to talk about it
   (D) To disagree with the man

6. Why does the teacher say this: 🎧

   (A) To show that being quiet can be bad
   (B) To indicate that she is embarrassed
   (C) To ask the class a few silly questions
   (D) To encourage the students to keep quiet

Listen and choose the correct answer for each question. MP3 048-050

7. Why does the man say this: 🎧

   (A) To meet with the other runners
   (B) To bring something to the race
   (C) To show his confidence
   (D) To agree with the woman

8. Why does the teacher say this: 🎧

   (A) To ask if the students understand him
   (B) To show that he can understand golf
   (C) To encourage students to talk about golf
   (D) To show that he does not like golf

9. Why does the teacher say this: 🎧

   (A) To indicate that the discussion will be about something else
   (B) To emphasize that she wants to discuss it
   (C) To explain the concepts of stem cell research
   (D) To show that she does not know anything about cloning

Listening Practice 1

🔊 **Listen and choose the correct answer for each question.** (MP3) 051

1 What is the discussion mainly about?

(A) Why people still believe in fortune-telling
(B) How people can get their fortunes told
(C) Who can read other people's fortunes
(D) When we should get our fortunes told

2 Why does the teacher mention crystal balls and palm readings?

(A) To introduce a new topic into the discussion
(B) To compare them with tarot cards and horoscopes
(C) To identify fortune-telling methods that work
(D) To give more examples of fortune-telling methods

Listen again to part of the discussion. Then answer the question.

3 Why does the teacher say this: 🎧

(A) To emphasize that fortune-telling works
(B) To state that no one can prove if fortune-telling is real
(C) To ask the students about the truth of fortune-telling
(D) To find out the truth about fortune-telling

Dictation

🔊 **Listen again and fill in the blanks.** (MP3) 051

T: Does anyone believe in tarot cards _____ _____?

M: Yes, I check my horoscope in the newspapers every day.

W: That's silly. You know it's not true.

M: I know it's not real, but I find myself reading it all the time.

T: Well, who is to say if it's true or not? But _____, like crystal balls and palm readings, _____ _____ _____ as being false.

W: So how come people still believe in fortune-telling?

T: A lot of it has got to do with _____. We often find ourselves with problems in life. It is in our nature to find the reason for such problems. A lot of the problems are really our own fault, but our minds _____ _____ _____ _____. Instead, we want to look for some way _____ _____ our problems on something else. This is where fortune-telling _____ _____. It gives us a way out of taking _____. It's easier to blame something that can't talk back, _____ _____ _____.

M: So it's not very good for humans _____ _____ _____ _____?

T: Yes. All we are doing is finding more excuses, _____ _____ _____ ourselves. Therefore, we keep finding people or things to blame our problems on, even if they _____ _____ _____ _____ with them.

Vocabulary ✏️

☐ **horoscope** a description of someone's future or personality based on his or her birthday ☐ **fortune-telling** predicting future events ☐ **blame** to place responsibility for something bad on someone ☐ **in the long run** in the far future ☐ **have nothing to do with** be unrelated to

Listening Practice 2

Listen and choose the correct answer for each question. (MP3) 052

1. Why is the student seeing the teacher?

   (A) To discuss the final test
   (B) To talk to him about a project
   (C) To discuss her performance in class
   (D) To talk to him about a paper

2. What solution does the teacher provide?

   (A) He wants her to signal him when she wants to participate.
   (B) He wants her to be better prepared for class.
   (C) He wants her to be more aggressive and quicker.
   (D) He wants her to make friends in the class.

Listen again to part of the conversation. Then answer the question.

3. Why does the teacher say this:

   (A) To mention that he knows all her problems
   (B) To indicate that he is not interested in the student's problem
   (C) To encourage the woman to talk about her problem
   (D) To assure the woman that everyone has similar problems

Dictation

Listen again and fill in the blanks. MP3 052

T: Hello, Tina. How are you? It's good to see you. What can I do _____ _____ ?

W: Hello. I'm fine, thank you. I have come _____ _____ something with you. I'm _____ _____ _____ _____ in class. I don't think I'm doing too well.

T: Well, you're right. Your test scores are fine, but you could probably improve your grade in class _____ . Is there something I should know about? If something _____ _____ _____ , it's better _____ _____ _____ _____ .

W: No, it's nothing serious. It's a bit hard to say. I am not _____ _____ , but somehow I _____ _____ _____ _____ well in class.

T: Is it because other students ask too many questions?

W: Yeah ... each time that I want to say something, someone speaks before me, and I feel like I don't ever _____ _____ _____ to speak. I just find myself lost.

T: Hmm ... I see. So you find the guys talk too much and too quickly?

W: Yes. I feel so slow _____ _____ .

T: No, no. You should never feel like that. I sometimes feel that some of them actually _____ the class with their endless questions. I have a suggestion. _____ _____ _____ , just look at me when you want to say something and I will call on you.

W: OK. I'm not sure _____ you will be able to see me.

T: No. I will be looking out for you. I think a lot of people will be happy to hear what you have to say in class too.

- **performance** something done; accomplishment
- **participation** taking part in or joining in
- **dumb** stupid; foolish
- **disrupt** to prevent something from continuing by creating a problem

Listening Practice 3

🔊 **Listen and choose the correct answer for each question.** MP3 053

1. What is the lecture mainly about?

   (A) The power of Spain and Portugal
   (B) Spain's control of the seas
   (C) Spain losing control of the seas to England
   (D) The power of the Spanish Armada

2. What can we infer about Queen Elizabeth?

   (A) She was a gentle ruler.
   (B) She was friendly to others.
   (C) She was a poor ruler.
   (D) She was very ambitious.

Listen again to part of the lecture. Then answer the question.

3. Why does the teacher say this: 🎧

   (A) To start talking about the war between the British and the Spanish
   (B) To explain where else the Spainsh had control
   (C) To indicate the end of the lecture about Spain's control of the seas
   (D) To test if the students know what she is talking about

Dictation

🔊 **Listen again and fill in the blanks.** (MP3) 053

Spain and Portugal came _____ _____ the seas after Columbus _____ America. Basically, Spain and Portugal _____ _____ _____ the world as they wished, and no one could really _____ their control of the seas. But unfortunately, Spain didn't keep its control of the seas for a long time.

There was one country _____ _____ that was set to explore the world _____ _____ _____. _____ Queen Elizabeth I, England came to rule the seas. But first, _____ _____ _____ _____ the strong Spanish _____.

Under King Philip II of Spain, Spain was _____ _____ _____ _____, dominating the Atlantic _____ to the Americas. Elizabeth's response was _____ _____ _____ _____ to attack the Spanish ships and claim their treasures for England. In the 1560s, Spain entered a war with the Netherlands. Elizabeth decided to support the Dutch. Spain responded _____ _____ a huge fleet, known as the Spanish Armada.

The English fleet of 200 boats was manned by less experienced sailors, but their boats were lighter and more _____ than the Spanish ships. The Spanish fleet had a hard time moving, since it was big and heavy. They tried to escape, but unfortunately, they _____ a terrible storm that destroyed _____ _____ _____. The defeat of the Spanish Armada marked the beginning of British power at sea.

Vocabulary ✏️

☐ **dominate** to rule; to control   ☐ **conquer** to get control of a country by fighting   ☐ **overcome** to fight and win against someone or something   ☐ **fleet** a group of ships; the entire naval force of a country   ☐ **mighty** very powerful or big   ☐ **assemble** to put together the parts of something   ☐ **agile** able to move quickly and easily   ☐ **encounter** to meet unexpectedly

iBT Practice

TOEFL Listening

Note-Taking

3. Function

TOEFL Listening | VOLUME | HELP ? | OK ✓ | NEXT ▶ | HIDE TIME 00:10:00

1 What is the lecture mainly about?

(A) Types of skin cancer
(B) Harmful sunlight
(C) Keeping beautiful skin
(D) Curing skin diseases

2 According to the lecture, what are the signs of non-melanoma cancer?

Click in the correct box.

	Yes	No
(A) Open sores		
(B) Shiny bump		
(C) Fair skin moles		
(D) Ink-spilled spots		
(E) Reddish patch		

Listen again to part of the lecture. Then answer the question.

3 Why does the teacher say this: 🎧

(A) To talk more about other forms of cancer
(B) To get the students interested
(C) To check if the students understand
(D) To end the talk about skin cancer

4 According to the lecture, why does skin turn brown when exposed to the sun?

(A) To appear as a sign of skin cancer
(B) To make the skin look more healthy
(C) To protect itself from UV rays
(D) To prevent melanoma

Note-Taking: Abbreviations (1)

When you are listening and trying to take notes at the same time, it can be difficult to write quickly. One way to take quick notes is to write abbreviations of words. An abbreviation is a shortened form of a word, and there are many commonly used abbreviations.
Here are some examples:

Abbreviation	b/c	vs.	i.e.	e.g.	etc.
Meaning	because	versus	that is	for example	et cetera

Listen again and fill in the blanks using keywords. MP3 054

Topic: _____

- reason: _____
- two types of skin cancer
    1. _____
        – UV radiation: causes _____
        – open sores / _____ / raised edge / shiny bump / _____
    2. melnm
        – appearance of _____
        – person with _____ skin
- both can be fatal if _____
- precaution: _____

Word Review

Choose the best word to replace the underlined word.

1. Whenever things don't go as planned, my brother always blames me.
   (A) mocks   (B) compliments   (C) criticizes   (D) punishes

2. The criminal claimed that he had nothing to do with the robbery.
   (A) dealt with   (B) had no time for   (C) was unrelated to   (D) took up

3. The president's speech was disrupted by a reporter asking a question.
   (A) promoted   (B) attended   (C) interrupted   (D) selected

4. The king quickly assembled an army in preparation for war.
   (A) abandoned   (B) assessed   (C) trained   (D) gathered

Choose and write the correct word to complete the sentence.

| overcome | precaution | fatal | in the long run |
| agile | radiation | mighty | conquer |

5. Although our situation is difficult right now, everything will pay off _____.

6. Napoleon tried to _____ all of Europe, and nearly succeeded.

7. In life, there are so many difficulties that you need to _____.

8. The _____ warrior managed to fight off 200 enemies all by himself.

9. The athlete was far more _____ than most people, so he didn't need as much training to improve his speed.

10. Although _____ is used to cure cancer, large amounts of it can cause illness and death.

11. The soldier took a(n) _____ gunshot to the heart and died instantly.

12. Stretching is a(n) _____ you should take before swimming, to avoid drowning.

LINGUAFORUM + iBT + mTOEFL + LISTENING

Part A
Main Idea
Detail

Part B

Function

Attitude

Part C
Organization
Connecting Content
Inference

CHAPTER 4

Attitude

+ Introduction

- Attitude questions ask you about a speaker's attitude, opinion, or level of certainty toward a particular topic.
- To answer these questions, you must listen not just to *what* is said, but also to *how* it is said.
- Some attitude questions replay a specific statement from the listening passage.
- There is usually 0-1 Attitude question for each passage.

+ Recognizing the Questions

- What is the professor's attitude towards X?
- What is the student's opinion of X?
- What can be inferred about the man when he says this: 🎧 (replay)

+ Strategies

1. Pay attention to the speaker's tone of voice. Depending on the tone, intonation, stresses, etc., a single statement can convey many different meanings.
2. Listen to the speaker's vocabulary. The speaker's choice of words gives clues about whether the speaker feels positive or negative, happy or sad, or certain or uncertain about a particular topic.
3. Use the context. In most cases, the speaker does not say directly how he or she feels by saying statements like "*I'm happy about …*" or "*I disagree with you.*" Therefore, you must draw a conclusion from the context.

+ **Sample Question**

MP3 055

TOEFL Listening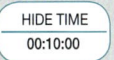

What does the man mean when he says this: 🎧

- (A) He finds it hard to believe that the woman is nearly finished with all her classes.
- (B) He wants to tell her that it is not good to finish quickly.
- (C) He is not sure what she is talking about.
- (D) He is worried that the woman will not complete all her subjects.

Script

W: Did you get called to the professor's room last week?

M: No, I think he only called for you. What did he say to you?

W: He was a bit surprised that I've nearly completed all my subjects already. I just need one more semester to graduate.

M: 🎧 That's really great! But how could that be possible? You've only just completed your second year.

W: I know, I was a bit surprised too. But I took 6 subjects per semester. I didn't want to waste my time.

M: You got to be kidding! I thought we could only take a maximum of 5 every semester.

W: You're right, but I got special permission to take one extra class every semester. It was really hard, but I'm glad that I'm nearly done with college.

Answer & Explanation

The answer is (A). After he hears that she has only one semester left, he shows surprise at first, and then asks her how that could be possible. However, he does not express any doubts or worries about her as in (C) or (D).

Building Skills

Recognizing Tone of Voice

- **Tone of voice** is the way our voice sounds. It includes intonation, stresses on words, the speaker's way of speaking, etc.

- Different tones of voice can indicate different feelings or opinions like surprise, interest, anxiety, concern, like / dislike, certainty / uncertainty, agreement / disagreement, etc.

Listen carefully and answer the questions.

1. Listen to part of a conversation. Choose what the man's attitude is when he says the following statement. **MP3 056**

   > M: They are building a new library. I guess it's best for the school.

   (A) He understands the school's decision.
   (B) He is complaining about the school's decision.
   (C) He is glad about the school building a new library.

2. Listen to part of a lecture. Choose how the speaker feels about cockroaches. **MP3 057**

   > In fact, cockroaches are the best adapted animal in the world.

   (A) He dislikes the shape of their body.
   (B) He is impressed by the adaptability of cockroaches.
   (C) He is concerned about cockroaches remaining on Earth.

Recognizing Degree of Certainty

- A speaker's **degree of certainty** can be expressed with the words he or she says, and the way those words are said.

- There are some **keywords** that give clues about the speaker's degree of certainty:
  - certainty: sure, obviously, definitely, truly, etc.
  - uncertainty: well, rather, doubt, maybe, probably, etc.

 Listen carefully and answer the questions.

1. Listen to part of a lecture. Choose what the man implies about the different ways of typing quickly.
   MP3 058

   > The most important thing you have to do is to find which way is the best for you.

   (A) He cannot find any effective way to improve his typing.
   (B) He is not sure how fast students can type.
   (C) He thinks students should find their own ways to improve their typing skill.

2. Listen to part of a lecture. Choose what the woman's attitude is when she says the following statement. **MP3 059**

   > Well, there can be other things that affect the voice, but let's keep it simple today.

   (A) She is not sure what other things can affect the tone.
   (B) She does not like to talk in a simple way.
   (C) She only wants to talk about vocal cords.

Basic Drills

Listen and choose the correct answer for each question. MP3 060-062

1. What do the two students think about the new school logo?

   (A) They are pleased with it.
   (B) They are confused by it.
   (C) They think it is alright.
   (D) They do not like it.

2. What does the teacher think about Stradivarius and his violins?

   (A) Stradivarius was lucky to use special wood.
   (B) Stradivarius had the skills to make beautiful sounding violins.
   (C) Stradivarius is not popular these days.
   (D) Stradivarius violins are not worth as much as people say they are.

3. What is the teacher's attitude about the Holocaust?

   (A) He thinks that it was a terrible incident.
   (B) He is pleased that the event occurred.
   (C) He does not remember what really happened.
   (D) He wants everyone to forget about the Holocaust.

Listen and choose the correct answer for each question. MP3 063-065

Listen again to part of the conversation. Then answer the question.

4. What does the man mean when he says this: 🎧

   (A) He knows why the woman has a bad back.
   (B) He has the same problem as the woman.
   (C) He is always comfortable in physics class.
   (D) He takes the same physics class as the woman.

5. What is the man's attitude toward the Underground Railroad?

   (A) It did not influence the country's history.
   (B) It only saved a few people from slavery.
   (C) It was a very important part of US history.
   (D) It helped slaves reach the northern states by train.

6. How does the woman feel about India?

   (A) It is a small and boring country.
   (B) It is a dirty place with nothing to see.
   (C) It only has the Ganges River.
   (D) It has many places for people to see.

Listen and choose the correct answer for each question. (MP3) 066–068

7. What is the teacher's attitude toward the book?

   (A) He does not like the book.
   (B) He likes the book very much.
   (C) He is not sure if it's a good book.
   (D) He does not know much about the book.

Listen again to part of the conversation. Then answer the question.

8. What does the man mean when he says this: 🎧

   (A) Staying in the dorms is a good way to make friends.
   (B) Staying in the dorms is not helpful for the students.
   (C) Living off campus is a better idea for students.
   (D) Making friends in the dorms is a waste of time.

Listen again to part of the conversation. Then answer the question.

9. What does the teacher mean when she says this: 🎧

   (A) She blames the woman for confusing her.
   (B) She wants the man to only talk about written forms.
   (C) She admits that the mistake is her fault.
   (D) She wants to talk only about spoken languages.

Listening Practice 1

🔊 **Listen and choose the correct answer for each question.** MP3 069

1 What did the student already study?

Click on 2 answers.

(A) Italian art
(B) British history
(C) French cinema
(D) French literature

2 What does the student need to decide first?

(A) She needs to decide on the reason for studying a particular subject.
(B) She needs to decide on whether it's a good idea to go abroad.
(C) She needs to decide on which country she would like to go to.
(D) She needs to decide on where to live in Italy.

Listen again to part of the conversation. Then answer the question.

3 What does the man mean when he says this: 🎧

(A) He wants to know how long she will be gone.
(B) He wants to know if she has a rough idea.
(C) He is frustrated that the student is being rude.
(D) He is making fun of her going abroad.

Dictation

🔊 **Listen again and fill in the blanks.** (MP3) 069

M: Hello. How may I help you?

W: Hi. I have a few questions about studying abroad. I have been thinking about _____ _____ for a long time but can't _____ _____ _____ _____ about where to go.

M: Well, have you _____ _____ chosen _____ _____, or do you want to travel the world?

W: No ... I want to go to Europe, but I just can't decide which country. I am _____ _____ _____ should go to a country where I don't have any problem with the language, or go to a place where I will have to learn the language.

M: Alright. I am guessing that England is _____ _____ _____ _____. So what are your other choices?

W: I know a little French and _____ Italian. If I chose _____ _____, I would have to take language courses first.

M: What is your major?

W: I am an English major. But I also have _____ _____ _____ on French cinema and one _____ _____ _____. Since I am a literature major, I am _____ _____ _____ _____ to France and studying French literature.

M: That's not a bad idea. I think going to Italy is a great idea too, but I want to suggest you go somewhere that is going to help you with your studies. French literature is very important, and you will _____ if you study it. So, as hard as French is, it might be _____ _____.

W: Yes, thank you. You really have been a great help.

M: Glad to have helped. Take care, and _____ _____ _____ of your decision.

Vocabulary

- **continent** one of the seven divisions of land masses on earth
- **literature** stories, poems, and plays that have artistic value
- **benefit** to get an advantage from

Listening Practice 2

🔊 **Listen and choose the correct answer for each question.** (MP3) 070

1 According to the lecture, what is the role of the holes on the violin?

(A) They make the violin strings vibrate in the body.
(B) They make the violin body look more beautiful.
(C) They strengthen the violin body and stop the vibration.
(D) They prevent the sound from escaping too quickly.

2 According to the lecture, what is important in violins to make them sound beautiful?

Click in the correct box.

	Yes	No
(A) The length of the strings		
(B) The shape of the body		
(C) The thickness of the wood		
(D) The number of holes		

Listen again to part of the lecture. Then answer the question.

3 What does the woman mean when she says this: 🎧

(A) There is only one way to make violins sound beautiful.
(B) It is important to use the same type of wood in making violins.
(C) The strength of the violin is the same with every violin.
(D) The characteristics of wood can change the sound of a violin.

Dictation

🔊 **Listen again and fill in the blanks.** 🎵 070

_____ are popular in classical music, and famous classical _____ _____ have all used violins in their music at one time or another. It is _____ to be one of _____ _____ to play, yet the most beautiful sounding. Players use a bow made of horsehair, and _____ _____ on any of the four strings. Different tones are made by pressing the string to the fingerboard with our fingers. So what makes the violin sound so special?

    The first answer _____ _____ _____ to some. It is _____ _____ _____ of the violin. The two long f-shaped holes on each side of the strings allow sound waves to vibrate _____ _____ _____ just enough. The holes also limit the sound waves from escaping too quickly. _____ _____ _____, the overall shape of the violin body, the size and placement of the holes are all highly important in making sure that violins sound beautiful. _____ violins _____ _____ vibrating the body, getting the correct _____ _____ _____ is very important. If the body is too thick, it will not vibrate properly. On the other hand, if the body is too _____, the sound waves might shake the body too much and cause unwanted noise, not to mention a very weak violin. In addition, different wood has different _____ and different _____ characteristics.

Vocabulary

☐ **composer** someone who writes music ☐ **instrument** an object used to make music ☐ **bow** a long wooden object used to play the violin or cello ☐ **drag** to move something slowly ☐ **string** a thin rope or cord ☐ **fingerboard** the part of a stringed instrument where the players press the string with their fingers

Listening Practice 3

🔊 **Listen and choose the correct answer for each question.** MP3 071

1 What is the lecture mainly about?

(A) Rich countries of the world
(B) Relationship between the US and Japan
(C) World War II and Japan
(D) Business success of the Japanese

2 Why did Americans feel threatened by the Japanese?

(A) They attacked the US by surprise.
(B) They were spying against the US.
(C) They were hard-working people.
(D) They were openly competitive with the US.

3 How does the teacher feel about the way Americans reacted to Japan's success?

(A) She does not show any emotions.
(B) She is not concerned with the way Americans reacted to Japan.
(C) She thinks that Americans have a right to say what they want.
(D) She feels that Americans were wrong to have treated Japanese badly.

Dictation

🔊 **Listen again and fill in the blanks.** MP3 071

Hello, class. Today we are going to talk about _____ _____ _____ _____, Japan. You all know about the big _____ giants. What about Japanese carmakers? Right now, they are world-class, but I can remember a time when Americans were _____ _____ Japanese cars. People _____ _____ to make people buy cars made in the USA. Now, _____ _____ _____. Many Americans _____ Japanese cars.

Japan and the US have always had _____ _____ _____. This is so because Americans _____ _____ by the Japanese long ago. This was mainly due to _____ _____ _____ on Pearl Harbor. During the war, Americans didn't trust Japanese-Americans, fearing that they were spying for Japan.

After World War II, the US became the most powerful country in the world. They had won the war and had become rich through the war. But many things slowed down the US, such as the Vietnam War. Americans wasted a lot of money, _____ _____ _____ in the Vietnam War. In the 1980s, Japan _____ as a major superpower with powerful companies that slowly but surely _____ many industries.

Americans _____ _____ to find out the Japanese _____ for success, and _____ _____ _____ also made fun of them. They _____ _____ as robots who didn't know how to enjoy life. It was _____ of Americans to characterize Japanese _____ _____ _____ _____.

I see that we don't have any more time. We will _____ our discussion next week.

Vocabulary

☐ **awkward** embarrassing; difficult ☐ **due to** because of ☐ **slow down** to cause to proceed more slowly
☐ **emerge** to appear; to become known ☐ **desperate** needing or desiring something very much ☐ **formula** a plan or method used to achieve a result ☐ **ridicule** to make fun of ☐ **racist** having belief that one's own race is better than other races

iBT Practice

TOEFL Listening

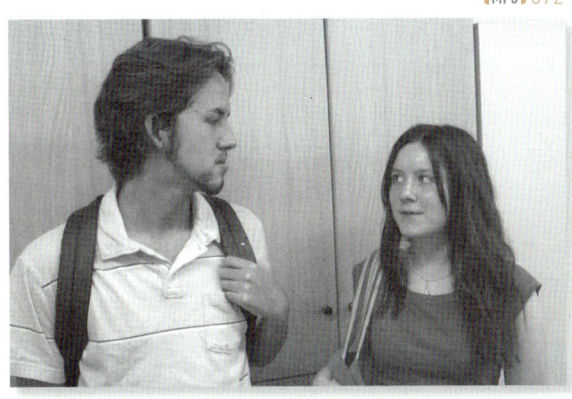

Note-Taking

*i*BT Practice CONTINUED

4. Attitude

TOEFL Listening   VOLUME   HELP   OK   NEXT   HIDE TIME 00:10:00

1 Why does the man talk to the woman?

- Ⓐ To ask her if she knows what urban legends are
- Ⓑ To tell her of a few good urban legends
- Ⓒ To introduce a new type of story to her
- Ⓓ To explain the ways to spread false stories

2 According to the woman, what can cola actually do to human teeth?

- Ⓐ It melts the teeth like acid within one week.
- Ⓑ It makes the teeth turn black in a week.
- Ⓒ It can kill us by acting like acid.
- Ⓓ It cannot do any more harm than normal candy.

Listen again to part of the conversation. Then answer the question.

3 What does the woman mean when she says this: 🎧

- Ⓐ She is too busy to tell him another story.
- Ⓑ She is not sure if she heard the man correctly.
- Ⓒ She does not know the reason why.
- Ⓓ She does not want to tell the man about it.

4 How do most urban legends spread?

- Ⓐ By the newspaper
- Ⓑ By the sewers
- Ⓒ By books
- Ⓓ By the internet

Further Study

Note-Taking: Abbreviations (II)

There are many commonly used abbreviations. However, you can form your own abbreviation for any word. Here are some ways you can use:

– Leave out the vowels.

Abbreviation	ppl.	yr.	cntry.	rsn.	envrmnt.
Meaning	people	year	century	reason	environment

– Write just the beginning of a long word.

Abbreviation	gov.	lang.	pop.	esp.	diff.
Meaning	government	language	population	especially	different

Listen again and fill in the blanks using keywords. MP3 072

Topic : _____
= short and mostly _____ stories

– Purpose : _____
– Examples :
  • _____
  • _____ living in the sewers of NY
– How they spread : through _____

Word Review

Choose the best word to replace the underlined word.

1. People were terrorized by the possibility of a nuclear war.
   (A) annoyed (B) disappointed (C) puzzled (D) scared

2. The hero emerged from the darkness and came to everybody's rescue.
   (A) appeared (B) hid (C) hurried (D) shaped

3. Everyone ridiculed the president after they heard about his embarrassing scandal.
   (A) admired (B) entertained (C) made fun of (D) thanked for

4. Nobody believed the man's story because they knew it was made-up.
   (A) common (B) complex (C) fake (D) natural

Choose and write the correct word to complete the sentence.

| literature | awkward | horrific | runaway |
| apparently | continent | racist | urban |

5. Our neighbors, who are getting divorced, had _____ been unhappy about their marriage for years.

6. The atomic bombing of Hiroshima and Nagasaki is a truly _____ event in history that should never be repeated.

7. The generous family agreed to protect the _____ soldier who had just escaped from war.

8. Asia is the largest _____ in the world, while Australia is the smallest.

9. The author is one of the most important poets in Chinese _____.

10. Some boys feel _____ around girls because they don't know what to do or say.

11. The politician's _____ remarks made him highly unpopular among African Americans.

12. Our family grew tired of _____ life, so we decided to move to the countryside.

Memo

Connecting Information Questions

Connecting Information questions test your understanding of the organization of ideas and the relationship between or among ideas. In this type of question, you will be tested in three ways: with Organization, Connecting Content, and Inference questions.

PART C

LINGUAFORUM + iBT + mTOEFL + LISTENING

Part A
Main Idea
Detail

Part B
Function
Attitude

Part C

Organization

Connecting Content

Inference

CHAPTER 5

Organization

+ Introduction

- Organization questions ask you about how a speaker presents his or her ideas.
- Some Organization questions may ask about why a speaker mentions a certain piece of information.
- These questions are more common for lectures than conversations.
- There is usually 0-1 Organization question for each passage.

+ Recognizing the Questions

- How does the professor talk about/explain/discuss X?
- Why does the professor mention X?
- In what order does the student talk about X?

+ Strategies

1. Recognize how a speaker organizes ideas in order to support the main points. Some typical organization patterns include definition/example, time order, list, comparisons/contrast, cause/effect, etc.
2. Listen for signal words. Signal words like *for example*, *however*, *as a result of*, etc. indicate the organization patterns of the presented information.
3. Recognize why a speaker mentions a certain piece of information. The speaker may be giving an example, changing the topic, or providing an introduction or conclusion. Or he or she may be just starting a digression – side comments unrelated to the main topic.

+ **Sample Question**

MP3 073

TOEFL Listening

How does the professor talk about snakes?

- Ⓐ By explaining how they lost their legs
- Ⓑ By giving examples of snakes' food
- Ⓒ By giving a definition of venomous snakes
- Ⓓ By comparing different ways of catching prey

Script

Snakes are from the lizard family. But snakes lost their legs through a process called evolution. Regardless, snakes still have a rough skin and a long tongue as well as a tail. However, they are different in the ways they catch prey.

Most snakes use their mouth to catch their prey. They use their sharp teeth and bite into the animal. Many snakes have poison called venom, and they inject it into the animal when they bite. The venom will make the animal's heart stop, and the snake can take its time eating it.

Anacondas are a little different. They also have big teeth and sometimes attack with their mouth. However, anacondas are constrictor snakes. They do not have any venom. This means that instead of biting and injecting venom, the anaconda will wrap its thick body around the animal and squeeze. They squeeze the animal so hard that it cannot breathe and dies quickly.

Answer & Explanation

The answer is (D). The professor focuses his lecture mainly on how snakes catch their prey. In addition, he compares the method of capturing prey in most snakes, which are venomous, with that in anacondas, which are nonvenomous.

Building Skills

Understanding Relationships

- **Signal words**, also known as **transitions**, are words which indicate the relationship between ideas, and will help you recognize the organization of ideas.
  - definition/exemplification: in other words, that is, to illustrate/for example, for instance, such as, etc.
  - time order: first, next, finally; before, previously; afterwards, later, etc.
  - list: and, too, in addition, moreover, besides, etc.
  - comparison/contrast: similarly, like, compared to, likewise/but, yet, on the other hand, etc.
  - cause/effect: because, due to, since/as a result, therefore, so, etc.

Listen carefully and answer the questions.

1. Listen to part of a lecture. Choose the correct relationship among the following words in the box. MP3 074

   | soccer shoes |
   | ballet shoes |
   | basketball shoes |

   _____ of different types of shoes
   Main Topic

   (A) Categories
   (B) Examples
   (C) Comparisons

2. Listen to part of a lecture. Match the correct pattern of organization with each sentence. MP3 075

   | definition | exemplification | categorization | comparison |

   Q1. The three groups are called herbivores, carnivores and omnivores. → _____

   Q2. Herbivores are animals that only eat plants. → _____

   Q3. Lions and tigers are well-known carnivores. → _____

Understanding Purpose in Organization

- There are many **different purpose**s why a speaker mentions a certain piece of information. Here are some examples:
    - to give an example
    - to give a more detailed explanation
    - to change a topic
    - to provide an introduction or a conclusion
    - to start a digression

Listen carefully and answer the questions.

1. Listen to part of a conversation. Choose the correct answer for each question.

    Q1. Why does the woman mention *Native Son*? _____

    Q2. Why does the woman mention a story writing competition? _____

    (A) To start the conversation
    (B) To give examples of American classics
    (C) To emphasize the personality of Richard Wright
    (D) To explain how Richard Wright became famous

2. Listen to part of a lecture. Choose why the professor mentions the following statements.

    Q1. *The most famous painting is the head of George Washington.*

    (A) To give background about why Gilbert's life was strange
    (B) To give an example of Gilbert's portrait paintings

    Q2. *Now, Gilbert's life was unusual.*

    (A) To start talking about Gilbert's life
    (B) To explain why he painted people's faces very well

Basic Drills

🔊 **Listen and choose the correct answer for each question.** MP3 078-080

1. How does the woman talk about symbiosis?

   (A) By comparing different animal partnerships
   (B) By giving an example of animal partnership
   (C) By explaining the effects of animal partnerships
   (D) By categorizing different animl partnerships

2. How does the teacher talk about computers?

   (A) He gives examples of keyboards.
   (B) He explains why people used punch cards.
   (C) He lists different kinds of computers.
   (D) He explains the changes in the use of computers.

3. Why does the teacher talk about a graph?

   (A) To test the students about prices
   (B) To introduce a different concept
   (C) To emphasize the importance of companies
   (D) To explain the concept easily

Listen and choose the correct answer for each question. MP3 081-083

4. Why does the woman mention King Tutankhamen?

    (A) To ask the man about the king
    (B) To compare Egyptian kings with English kings
    (C) To give an example of an Egyptian king
    (D) To list all the names of Egyptan kings

5. Why does the teacher mention every child going to school?

    (A) To talk about different school systems
    (B) To emphasize the importance of going to school
    (C) To explain schools in the US
    (D) To describe what students study in school

6. How does the teacher talk about solar power?

    (A) By talking about the pros and cons of solar power
    (B) By giving examples of machines that use solar power
    (C) By comparing solar cells to batteries
    (D) By giving instructions on how to use solar cells

Listen and choose the correct answer for each question. MP3 084-086

7. How does the man explain how speakers make noise?

   (A) By categorizing different electric signals
   (B) By giving examples of electric signals
   (C) By explaining it in order of chronology
   (D) By comparing it with magnets

8. How does the teacher talk about spiders?

   (A) By giving examples of the water spider's food
   (B) By comparing the water spider to other spiders
   (C) By explaining why some spiders have to live under water
   (D) By explaining how spiders live under water

9. Why does the teacher mention privacy?

   (A) To compare blogging with writing diaries
   (B) To start talking about using the internet
   (C) To point out the problem of blogging
   (D) To emphasize the importance of blogging

Listening Practice 1

🔊 **Listen and choose the correct answer for each question.** (MP3) 087

1. What is the man's problem?

   (A) He does not like lockers on the lower floor.
   (B) He does not have a locker to use.
   (C) He needs a locker on the lower floor.
   (D) He got hurt by opening the lockers.

2. What does the woman offer to do for the man?

   (A) She will change classes to the ground floor.
   (B) She will change lockers with the man.
   (C) She will go and talk to the school.
   (D) She will help the man go up the stairs.

3. Why does the man mention hurting his legs?

   (A) To ask for the woman's help
   (B) To warn the woman to be careful
   (C) To explain the problem that he has
   (D) To compare his locker with the woman's

Dictation

Listen again and fill in the blanks. (MP3) 087

M: Did you get a locker _____ _____?

W: Yes, I did. I got _____ _____ _____.

M: Me, too. Which floor is your locker on?

W: It is _____ _____ _____ _____. Why do you ask?

M: I _____ _____ _____ _____ about two months ago, but I got a locker on the 5th floor.

W: So _____ _____ _____?

M: All my classes this semester are _____ _____ _____ _____. It'll be a problem, because I _____ my legs last month. I can't walk up the stairs _____ _____ _____.

W: Oh, that's _____. Did you complain to the school?

M: Of course I did, but they said there was nothing that they could do. All the lockers are full. I'll have to _____ _____ _____ _____ semester.

W: Oh, that is terrible. Oh, _____ _____ _____ _____. I have many classes on the 4th floor. Do you want to change lockers?

M: Wow, that's a great idea! Are you alright with that?

W: Sure, I _____ _____ it at all. Let's go and do it now _____ we have time.

M: Thanks so much. You're _____ _____!

Vocabulary

☐ **ground floor** the first floor of a building ☐ **I don't mind** It's okay with me; I don't care ☐ **not at all** certainly not; absolutely not

Listening Practice 2

Listen and choose the correct answer for each question. MP3 088

1 What is the talk mainly about?

(A) Ways to spread pollen and seeds
(B) Using plants to share pollen and seeds
(C) Helping animals share nectar
(D) The role of insects and animals

2 How does the teacher talk about pollen and seeds?

(A) She compares the two together.
(B) She emphasizes what happens after anmials move them.
(C) She explains how insects and animals help spread them.
(D) She describes why plants need to share them.

3 According to the lecture, how can plants share pollen or seeds?

Click on 2 answers.

(A) By using insects to carry the pollen for them
(B) By sharing seeds using their roots in the ground
(C) By having hooks on seeds that attach to the fur of animals
(D) By using their nectar to attract furry animals

Dictation

🔊 **Listen again and fill in the blanks.** (MP3) 088

_____ _____ _____ in this world have children, or what are called _____. Plants also have offspring, but _____ animals, do not have mobility. _____ means the ability to move around. Plants have roots that _____ _____ deep in the ground. But the plants still need _____ _____ their pollen or get their seeds _____ _____. So instead of moving around, plants use _____ _____ _____ to help them.

Some plants use bees to help them share with other plants. They _____ _____ and other insects by sharing sweet _____ called nectar. When the bees sit on the flower to get the nectar, the pollen sticks on the bees' legs. The bees then look for another flower for nectar. Some pollen will _____ _____, and new pollen will _____ _____ _____. This is why most bees have yellow legs.

Some fruit plants rely on big furry animals _____ _____ _____ _____. They have seeds that have little hooks. They attach _____ _____ _____ of animals when they pass by the plant. Later, the animal will shake the seed off. _____ _____, the seed will have traveled very far.

Vocabulary ✏️

☐ **offspring** a person's child or an animal's young   ☐ **bury** to put in the ground and cover with dirt   ☐ **pollen** a fine powder produced by flowers   ☐ **seed** the small, hard part of a plant that can grow into a new plant   ☐ **furry** covered with hair   ☐ **hook** a curved piece of a material that is used to catch or hold things

Listening Practice 3

🔊 **Listen and choose the correct answer for each question.** (MP3) 089

1 Why does the man talk to the woman?

(A) To tell the woman about cows having four stomachs

(B) To discuss what kinds of food cows eat

(C) To ask if cows really have four stomachs

(D) To inform the woman about what cows eat

2 According to the conversation, why do some animals need so many stomachs?

(A) To digest the meat they eat

(B) To keep the food in their stomachs

(C) To waste time eating their food

(D) To absorb as much energy as possible from plants

3 How does the speaker talk about cow stomachs?

(A) By giving examples of cow foods

(B) By giving reasons why they need multiple stomachs

(C) By listing the bad points of having multiple stomachs

(D) By comparing them to her stomach

Dictation

Listen again and fill in the blanks. MP3 089

M: My science teacher told us that cows have four stomachs. _____ _____ _____? I can't believe it.

W: Of course. A lot of animals that only eat vegetables have multiple stomachs.

M: _____ _____? What other animals have so many stomachs?

W: Well, animals in the cow family all have four stomachs. _____ _____ _____ _____ both have many stomachs. _____ _____ have many stomachs.

M: Why do they need to have so many stomachs?

W: Plants and grass have _____ _____ _____. They need different stomachs _____ _____ as much energy as they can when they _____ _____.

M: This all _____ _____. But are they _____ _____ animals with many stomachs?

W: Oh, I remember _____ animal. Camels also have many stomachs. They need them to digest _____ food.

M: Thorny food? What do you mean?

W: They eat sticks and dry branches. Their stomachs can digest them easily.

M: It sounds like animals _____ a lot of time just eating a meal. They must get so tired.

W: Oh, I'm sure that the animals _____ _____ _____ _____ that way.

Vocabulary

- **multiple** many
- **buffalo** a large animal similar to a cow that has curved horns
- **absorb** to soak up; to take in
- **digest** turning food you have eaten into substances that your body needs
- **thorny** having many sharp points

iBT Practice

TOEFL Listening

 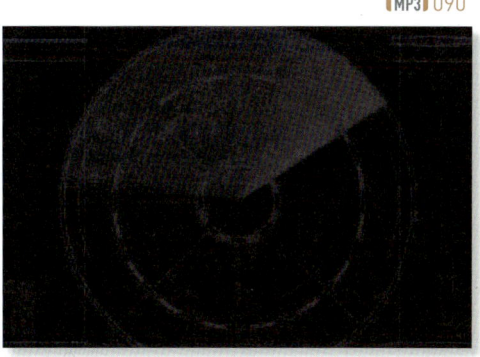

Note-Taking

iBT Practice CONTINUED

1. According to the lecture, why did the Germans fly back from Britain?

   A) Their radar was not working.
   B) They were not ready to fight.
   C) The British knew they were coming.
   D) Hitler ordered them to come back.

2. What are some of the uses of radar?

   Click on 2 answers.

	Yes	No
A) Bouncing signals		
B) Tracking airplanes in the sky		
C) Listening to the radio		
D) Checking the speed of cars on the road		

3. How does the teacher introduce radars?

   A) By talking about Germany during World War II
   B) By explaining what radars are
   C) By comparing Germany to Britain
   D) By giving examples of different radars

4. Why does the teacher mention radar systems in airports?

   A) To give an example of a true radar system
   B) To show that radars are used in many places
   C) To contrast them with true radar systems
   D) To categorize different radar systems

Note-Taking: Abbreviations (III)

Prepositions are words that show the relationship between a noun and another part of the sentence. Because they connect information together, you should pay attention to them when taking notes. You can make your own abbreviations, or use the following commonly used forms:

Abbreviation	b.f.	fr.	w/	w/o	w/in
Meaning	before	from	with	without	within

Listen again and fill in the blanks using keywords. MP3 090

Topic: Radar

* Two-part system = _____ + _____

  1. transmitter
     – send _____ into the sky
     → _____ objects → fly back to a receiver
  2. _____ = very big dish to receive _____

* Use of radar
  • planes
  • _____ : check cars – radar guns
  • _____ : study space – _____
  • airports : only have _____, transmitters are on _____

5. Organization 101

Word Review

Choose the best word to replace the underlined word.

1. The policemen needed more time to determine who the criminal was.
   (A) decide   (B) permit   (C) persuade   (D) protect

2. Plants have the amazing ability to convert sunlight into food.
   (A) change   (B) concentrate   (C) hold   (D) squeeze

3. I don't mind you borrowing my things, as long as you ask me about it first.
   (A) I'm okay with   (B) I'm angry with   (C) I agree with   (D) I'm against

4. Darker colors absorb light better than lighter colors do.
   (A) cover   (B) emit   (C) reflect   (D) take in

Choose and write the correct word to complete the sentence.

| multiple | digest | object | solar |
| normal | supply | commercial | offspring |

5. A basic principle of economics is that price is determined by _____ and demand.

6. Although _____ energy is good for the environment, it is much more expensive than most other forms of energy.

7. Most animals are very protective about their _____, especially after they have just given birth to them.

8. Nobody thought that the actress would win anything, so everybody was very surprised when she won _____ awards.

9. After you've eaten a meal, you must give yourself plenty of time to _____ the food before exercising.

10. My new cell phone is nothing special; just a(n) _____ phone with very basic functions.

11. The toothpick is a(n) _____ that is used to pick food out of your teeth.

12. The movie was interrupted by so many _____ messages that people began to get angry.

LINGUAFORUM + iBT + mTOEFL + LISTENING

Part A
Main Idea
Detail

Part B
Function
Attitude

Part C +

Organization

Connecting Content

Inference

CHAPTER 6

Connecting Content

+ Introduction

- Connecting Content questions ask you about the relationship between different pieces of information in a lecture or conversation.
- You will be asked to organize information from the passage by filling in a chart or table.
- There are three types of Connecting Content questions: determining whether a certain detail is Yes(true) or No(false), classifying items in categories, and placing events or steps in order.
- There is usually 0-1 Connecting content question for each passage.

+ Recognizing the Questions

- Indicate whether or not each of the following is true. Click in the correct box for each phrase.
- Match each of the following with the correct features. Click in the correct box for each phrase.
- Put the following events in the correct order. Drag each phrase to the space where it belongs.

+ Strategies

1. Connecting Content questions are most likely to appear when a speaker mentions two or more concepts, and then describes them. Identify key categories and take notes on the characteristics of each category.
2. If a speaker discusses events or steps in a process, keep track of the order correctly. Recognize the main steps and take notes on what happens at each step.
3. Try to guess which type of Connecting Content questions you may be asked. It will make note-taking easier, as you will know what details to focus your notes on.

+ **Sample Question**

TOEFL Listening

In the conversation, the man and the woman discuss Jupiter. Indicate whether each of the following is related to Jupiter.

Click in the correct box for each phrase.

	Yes	No
(A) It is the largest planet in the solar system.		
(B) It is big enough to fit 9 planets of the solar system inside.		
(C) It has 63 moons.		
(D) Scientists think it is full of solid rock surfaces.		

Script

M: Jane, you study astronomy, don't you?
W: Yes, I do. Why do you ask?
M: I have to write about planets, and I was hoping you could help me.
W: Sure. What do you need to know?
M: Anything about planets will do. I went to the school library, but it didn't help me.
W: How about Jupiter? It's the largest planet in our solar system. It is so large that we can fit the remaining 8 planets of our solar system inside, including Earth.
M: Wow, I had no idea it was that big. Is there anything else interesting about Jupiter?
W: It has 63 moons. Oh, Jupiter is one of the gas giants.
M: Why do they call it that?
W: Scientists think that it is full of gas, and no solid rock surfaces. That's why the color's always changing as well.
M: Alright, I think I got more than I need. Thanks for the ideas!

Answer & Explanation

The answer is Yes for (A) and (C), and No for (B) and (D). The woman says that Jupiter is big enough to fit 8 planets of the solar system inside, not 9. She also says that scientists think Jupiter is full of gas, not solid rock surfaces.

Building Skills

Connecting Content in Comparison

- **Categorizing questions** usually come from parts that give comparisons and contrasts or classify information. Identify key categories first and take notes on the characteristics of each category.

- Differentiating between when you might be asked a **yes/no question** or a **categorizing question** is tricky. Here is a useful tip to help you guess.
  - yes/no question: the speaker mentions several details about *one* topic.
  - categorizing question: the speaker mentions several details about *two* or *more* topics.

Listen carefully and answer the questions.

1. Listen to part of a conversation. Write the reasons why the man should buy each type of computer. (MP3) 092

Notebook	Desktop

2. Listen to part of a conversation. Write **K** if it applies to kickboxing or **B** if it applies to boxing.
   (MP3) 093

   (A) Can use hands only. _____
   (B) Can use hands, legs, and knees. _____
   (C) Can use elbows. _____

Connecting Content in **Process**

- **Ordering questions** are usually asked when the speaker describes events or steps in order. Listen for these signal words: first, second, third; It begins with …, and after that …, then …, finally …, etc.

- The order in which the speaker gives information does not always match the actual order. Here are some words that can mix up the order: before that …, we'll talk about this first …, we'll take about that later…, etc.

Listen carefully and answer the questions.

1. Listen to part of a conversation. Put the directions to the main building in order. (MP3) 094

   (A) Walk down the road to the junction
   (B) Walk up the hill
   (C) Walk 10 minutes from the hill
   (D) Turn right at the junction

   (　　) → (　　) → (　　) → (　　)

2. Listen to part of a lecture, and put the following in the correct order. (MP3) 095

   (A) Send pictures to other machines
   (B) The only way to get in contact with people
   (C) Type messages out automatically

   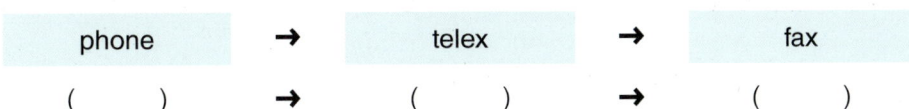

Basic Drills

 Listen and choose the correct answer for each question. MP3 096-098

1. In the conversation, the woman is talking about which classes she is going to drop. Indicate whether or not each of the following is true about the woman.

   Click in the correct box for each phrase.

	Yes	No
(A) She wants to drop math.		
(B) She thinks science is too difficult.		
(C) She misunderstood some of the school's rules.		
(D) She will drop English, math and science.		

2. In the lecture, the teacher explains the steps in which we get petroleum. Put the following steps in the correct order.

   Drag each sentence to the space where it belongs.

1	
2	
3	
4	

   (A) Pump crude oil from the ground.
   (B) Boil the oil slowly.
   (C) Collect the gas.
   (D) Cool gas and turn it into liquid.

3. In the lecture, the teacher talks about different types of animals. Indicate whether each of the following is a cold-blooded or warm-blooded animal.

   Click in the correct box for each phrase.

	Warm-Blooded	Cold-Blooded
(A) Maintain their body temperature most of the time		
(B) Do not keep their body temperature constant		
(C) Need to sit in the sun to keep warm		
(D) Include snakes and lizards		

Listen and choose the correct answer for each question. MP3 099-101

4. In the conversation, the man discusses different majors he might choose. Indicate whether each of the following is related to computer systems or business IT.

   Click in the correct box for each phrase.

	Computer Systems	Business IT
(A) Computer networks		
(B) Management		
(C) Different hardware		
(D) Accounting		

5. In the lecture, the teacher explains how to be healthy. Indicate whether or not each of the following is a way to be healthy.

   Click in the correct box for each phrase.

	Yes	No
(A) Eat well-being food you've studied		
(B) Make a sudden change in your daily life		
(C) Start exercising slowly		
(D) Lose weight very fast		

6. In the lecture, the teacher talks about the Amazon River. Indicate whether or not each of the following is a feature of the Amazon River.

   Click in the correct box for each sentence.

	Yes	No
(A) People don't need the waters of the Amazon.		
(B) It is the second longest river in the world.		
(C) It has recently suffered from floods.		
(D) It contains the largest amount of water.		

Listen and choose the correct answer for each question. MP3 102–104

7. In the discussion, the teacher talks about different pens. Put the following events in the correct order.

   Drag each phrase to the space where it belongs.

1	
2	
3	
4	

   (A) People used pens with a metal ball tip.
   (B) Cavemen dipped branches in ink.
   (C) People used fountain pens.
   (D) People used quills.

8. In the lecture, the teacher talks about how colors, shapes, and sounds affect us. Indicate whether or not each of the following is a feature of fast food restaurants.

   Click in the correct box for each sentence.

	Yes	No
(A) Use dark colors to make people hungry		
(B) Use rounded tables to make people uncomfortable		
(C) Play upbeat music to get people excited		
(D) Try to make people eat fast		

9. In the lecture, the teacher talks about seahorses. Indicate whether each of the following is related to male seahorses or other male animals.

   Click in the correct box for each phrase.

	Sea-horses	Other animals
(A) Sleep while mothers take care of their babies		
(B) Always stay around their babies		
(C) Don't eat while taking care of babies		
(D) Hide their babies if there is danger		

Listening Practice 1

🔊 **Listen and choose the correct answer for each question.** (MP3) 105

1 What is the lecture mainly about?

(A) The work of James Randi
(B) The life of Uri Geller
(C) The existence of mind power
(D) Famous magicians

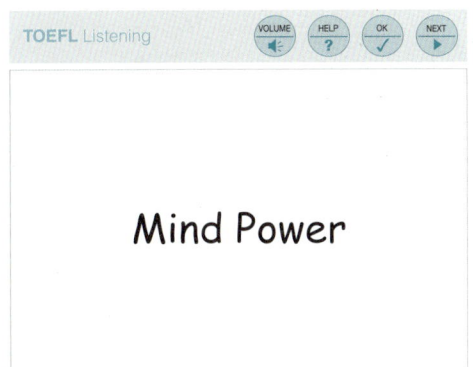

2 Why does the professor mention James Randi?

(A) To give another example of a person with mind powers
(B) To contrast with Uri Geller
(C) To support Uri Geller's work
(D) To prove that mind powers exist

3 In the lecture, the professor discusses Uri Geller and James Randi. Indicate whether each of the following is related to Uri Geller or James Randi.

Click in the correct box for each phrase.

	Uri Geller	James Randi
(A) Claimed to have supernatural power		
(B) Was a famous magician		
(C) Believed mind power is not real		
(D) Bent spoons and fixed watches		

6. Connecting Content 111

Dictation

🔊 **Listen again and fill in the blanks.** (MP3) 105

There are many people _____ _____ _____ that claim to have certain powers of the mind. Sometimes they insist that they can do _____ things, like bending spoons simply by using their mind or _____ _____ _____ in the air. But it is unclear if special mind powers really _____.

Uri Geller is one of the most famous people that claim to have supernatural powers. He _____ _____ his power on television, and the whole world quickly heard about him. He bent spoons _____ _____ _____ on television to show _____ _____ of his mind power. After watching his show, most people thought that he really had great mind powers. He soon _____ _____ _____ to show off his powers and tell people about the power of the mind. _____, there were some people that did not believe in his powers.

James Randi was _____ _____ _____. Unlike Uri, James tried to show everyone that there is no such thing as mind power. He came on television many times to tell everyone that mind power is not _____. He claimed on television that he would give $1 million to anyone _____ _____ _____ that they have supernatural powers. He first _____ _____ in the 1970s, but nobody has won the money. Randi and Uri continue to argue with each other and try to prove each other _____.

Vocabulary ✏️

☐ **insist** to say very firmly   ☐ **bend** to change shape and become curved   ☐ **float** to rest on water without sinking
☐ **exist** to be real   ☐ **show off** to display proudly   ☐ **offer** to propose; to provide

Listening Practice 2

🔊 **Listen and choose the correct answer for each question.** (MP3) 106

1 What is the discussion mainly about?

(A) The meaning of different oaths
(B) Methods of healing people
(C) Doctors taking the Hippocratic Oath
(D) The story of Hippocrates

2 According to the discussion, who was Hippocrates?

(A) He was a famous Greek veterinarian.
(B) He was the father of modern medicine.
(C) He performed surgery on sick people.
(D) He healed animals in his hospital.

3 In the discussion, the teacher mentions the Hippocratic Oath. Indicate whether or not each of the following applies to the Hippocratic Oath.

Click in the correct box for each phrase.

	Yes	No
(A) Doctors take the oath before they become doctors.		
(B) All doctors take the oath.		
(C) It has changed little by little but general meaning is the same.		
(D) It is valid for all living things, including humans.		

6. Connecting Content 113

Dictation

Listen again and fill in the blanks. (MP3) 106

T: Modern doctors _____ _____ _____ _____ of studies and testing. When they are finished, they take something called the Hippocratic _____. Hippocrates made the oath for doctors _____ _____ before they became doctors.

W: Who's Hippocrates?

T: Hippocrates was a famous Greek _____. Many call him the father of modern medicine. He taught many people about helping sick people get better.

M: So why must doctors take the oath?

T: The oath basically states that doctors should do everything to help sick people, and make them _____.

M: I think that's a great oath. Do doctors still take the Hippocratic Oath?

T: Of course they do. It changes _____ _____ _____ as the years go by, but the overall meaning is still the same. However, not all doctors take the oath.

W: Really? What kinds of doctors do not take the oath?

T: Veterinarians, for example. They only treat and heal pets or animals. So they do not need to take the oath. Apparently, the oath is only _____ _____ _____.

W: That's strange. Pets also need the love and care of doctors. I heard that pet medicine and human medicine are the same.

T: Well, the oath is really _____ _____. When a person becomes _____ _____ _____ _____, they will _____ help others in the best way that they can.

□ **oath** a formal promise   □ **bit by bit** little by little; gradually   □ **valid** effective; available   □ **formality** something that is done but does not have real meaning or importance

Listening Practice 3

🔊 **Listen and choose the correct answer for each question.** 🎧 107

1 What is the conversation mainly about?

(A) Ways to cross the English Channel
(B) Functions of air skirts
(C) Floating cars on water
(D) The characteristics of hovercrafts

Listen again to part of the conversation. Then answer the question.

2 What does the man mean when he says this: 🎧

(A) He doesn't understand the woman's joke.
(B) He can't believe the woman doesn't know.
(C) He thinks the woman is being funny.
(D) He wants the woman to explain.

3 In the conversation, the man and woman talk about different qualities of hovercrafts. Indicate whether or not each of the following is related to a hovercraft.

Click in the correct box for each phrase.

	Yes	No
(A) It runs on wheels on land.		
(B) It turns and stops slowly.		
(C) It travels floating above the surface.		
(D) It can travel only on land and water.		

Dictation

🔊 **Listen again and fill in the blanks.** (MP3) 107

M: Do you know of any vehicle that can _____ _____ _____, water and land?

W: I don't think that there's _____ _____ that can use all three _____. It can't be a boat, plane, or a car.

M: You're right. It's _____ _____ _____ _____. But there is something called a hovercraft that can really travel on all three.

W: What's a hovercraft?

M: Hovercrafts are vehicles that use airpower _____ _____ just above the surface. They have very powerful fans that blow air _____ _____ _____. It looks like a car, but it doesn't have _____.

W: What does it have _____?

M: It has something called an air skirt. It keeps the air underneath the hovercraft. When running, the hovercraft is sitting _____ _____ _____ of air.

W: So what is that _____ _____?

M: _____ _____ _____? It means that it can go on water or land _____ _____ _____.

W: That is amazing, _____ _____ _____. But why don't we see a lot of hovercrafts around?

M: There are a few reasons. Hovercrafts turn and stop very _____, I mean very slowly. They are also very _____ _____ _____ a lot. Still, they are good for some things. Until the Channel Tunnel was built in Europe, big hovercrafts _____ _____ _____ many people across the English Channel.

☐ **vehicle** a machine used for traveling ☐ **surface** the top layer of something ☐ **vibrate** to move back and forth very rapidly; to shake

iBT Practice

TOEFL Listening

Placebo Effect

Note-Taking

TOEFL Listening

1 What is the discussion mainly about?

- A Testing animals
- B Testing medicine
- C Fake medicine
- D The placebo effect

2 Why do companies use fake medicine?

- A Testing on mice is not safe.
- B Real medicine is expensive.
- C Some patients do not like medicine.
- D They want to test for the placebo effect.

3 What is the teacher's attitude towards testing medicine on humans?

- A He thinks it is not safe at all.
- B He thinks it is cruel and unfair.
- C He thinks it is simple but ineffective.
- D He thinks it takes a lot of time and money.

4 In the discussion, the teacher explains how medicine is tested. Put the following steps in the correct order.

Drag each phrase to the space where it belongs.

1	
2	
3	
4	

- A Give some people real medicine, and the rest fake pills.
- B Choose about 100 people.
- C See if the medicine is effective.
- D Test the medicine on animals

Further Study

Note-Taking: Using Symbols (I)

Another way to take quick notes is to use symbols. Using symbols not only saves time, but also makes your notes easier to read. Here are some examples you could use:

Symbol	Meaning	Symbol	Meaning
↑	increase	↔	in contrast with
↓	decrease	/	or
→	lead to, cause	&	and
←	come from, because of	@	at

e.g. Smoking can cause cancer. ⇨ smoking → cancer
Black is in contrast with white. ⇨ black ↔ white

Listen again and fill in the blanks using keywords. (MP3) 108

Topic: Medicine Testing

- first, animals → then, humans
  - some danger but _____
- * Testing Process on humans

- choose 100 → ⎡ half, real medicine
              ⎣   vs.   ⎤ → results
                half, _____

- reasons for fake medicine
  - psych. problem, "_____"
- _____ medicine
  - people took real medicine > fake medicine
- simple process, but _____

Word Review

Choose the best word to replace the underlined word.

1. I think I am going to drop my history class to make time for my new job.
   (A) attend   (B) cancel   (C) fail   (D) register for

2. Whenever something goes missing, everybody suspects I was the one who lost it.
   (A) agrees   (B) confirms   (C) denies   (D) supposes

3. The old man insisted that he could run a marathon because he exercised daily.
   (A) claimed   (B) distrusted   (C) predicted   (D) warned

4. Do not be alarmed if the plane vibrates. It's perfectly normal.
   (A) crashes   (B) freezes   (C) releases   (D) shakes

Choose and write the correct word to complete the sentence.

| valid | float | formality | show off |
| bend | surface | oath | fake |

5. I had to _____ my body to get through the tiny door.

6. Did you know your body will _____ on the moon because there is almost no gravity there?

7. He doesn't have a lot of friends because he likes to _____ too much.

8. Before the lawyer could present his case, he had to take a(n) _____ promising he'd only say the truth.

9. This coupon is only _____ for one more day, so you better hurry if you want to use it.

10. Interviews at this company are merely a(n) _____ because the jobs always end up going to friends or family of the CEO.

11. You cannot know how deep the water is by just looking at its _____.

12. The teenagers were caught trying to use _____ ID to buy alcohol.

LINGUAFORUM + iBT + mTOEFL + LISTENING

Part A
Main Idea
Detail

Part B
Function
Attitude

Part C +

Organization

Connecting Content

Inference

CHAPTER 7

Inference

+ Introduction

- Inference questions ask about information that is implied in the passage.
- These questions ask you to draw conclusions or make predictions based on the information you have heard.
- Some inference questions may replay a specific statement from the listening passage.
- There is usually 0-1 Inference question for each passage.

+ Recognizing the Questions

- What can be inferred about the woman?
- What does the professor imply about X?
- What will the student probably do next?
- What will the professor most likely discuss next?

+ Strategies

1. Do not use your personal knowledge. Your answers should be based on facts or details that are mentioned in the passage, and nothing else.
2. Draw conclusions from synthesized details. The answer to Inference questions is not often based on a single detail. Therefore, you need to synthesize pieces of information to form a conclusion.
3. Pay attention to the speaker's last remarks. If you are asked a question about what is most likely to happen next, the speaker's last remarks will contain useful information.

+ Sample Question

TOEFL Listening

What will the man probably do?

- Ⓐ Apply to other schools
- Ⓑ Take the TOEFL test
- Ⓒ Ask the teacher about the letter
- Ⓓ Register for biology classes

Script

W: Are you excited about starting college in the fall? The weather is going to be beautiful, and lots of people will be choosing which college they want to go to.

M: Yes, but I never thought that I would need to prepare so many things.

W: Is that so? Have you sent in your application to the colleges already?

M: Well, I've taken the TOEFL test. Most colleges want that. I've sent the test results to the colleges, as well as my application essay.

W: So what else do you have to do now? Or are you waiting for an answer?

M: I'm not finished yet. I'm supposed to send in three letters from my teachers. I've gotten two back, but I haven't heard from my old biology teacher from last semester.

W: Why don't you visit his office? I'm sure he just forgot.

M: Yes, I am planning to do that.

Answer & Explanation

The answer is (C). The man's last remark – "I am planning to do that." – shows that he is probably going to visit the teacher and ask about the letter.

Building Skills

Making Inferences

- **Making inferences** means using information in the text to guess other things about the text.

- You must make inferences based on information that is presented in the passage, not your personal knowledge.

- Some incorrect answers may make sense but will be based on information that is not mentioned in the passage.

Listen carefully and answer the questions.

1. Listen to part of a lecture. Write T(True) if the following sentence is inferred from the lecture, and F(False) if it is not. (MP3) 110

   Q1. Shaolin originates from China. _____
   Q2. Shaolin is only practiced by a group of monks. _____
   Q3. Shaolin was not known in the western world before. _____

2. Listen to part of a conversation. Choose the most logical inference based on the following statement. (MP3) 111

   Q1. M: I only know that it has the faces of four US presidents.

   (A) The man did not know how big the faces really were.
   (B) The man knows a lot about Mt. Rushmore.

   Q2. W: The nose of Abraham Lincoln is about 2 meters. That is taller than you.

   (A) The man has a larger nose than that of Abraham Lincoln.
   (B) The man's height is less than 2 meters.

Gathering Information

- The answer to Inference questions is often based on a number of pieces of information from the passage, rather than on a single detail.

- In gathering information, the key is to identify the facts. After you have gathered all the facts, synthesize them to draw a logical conclusion or predict an outcome.

- Questions like *"What facts lead to the conclusion?"* will help you make inferences and draw logical conclusions.

Listen carefully and answer the questions.

1. The following is a list of the major details from the conversation. Make a prediction about what the man will probably do next. (MP3) 112

   - They can borrow 5 books from the library.
   - The woman needs to borrow 2 more books to finish her assignment.
   - The man wants to help. He can borrow 4 more books from the library.

   (A) Borrow books from the library to lend the woman
   (B) Complain to the library staff about the rules
   (C) Complete the assignment for the woman

2. Listen to part of a lecture. Choose 3 details that are necessary to make the following inference. (MP3) 113

   > Most birds' nests are not as hard as swallows'.

   (A) Most birds' nests are made of leaves and branches.
   (B) Swallows use their saliva to build their nest.
   (C) The saliva hardens like cement.
   (D) Nest hunters have to climb very high.
   (E) Swallows' nests are rare and expensive.

Basic Drills

 Listen and choose the correct answer for each question. MP3 114–116

1. What is inferred about hydrogen?

   (A) It is not as cheap as petroleum.
   (B) It is hard to separate it from water.
   (C) It is more popular than petroleum.
   (D) It causes a lot of air pollution.

2. What will the man probably do?

   (A) He will meet his music club members on the weekend.
   (B) He will ask the music club to go on the field trip.
   (C) He will take the girl to the music club meeting.
   (D) He will cancel the music club meeting.

3. What will the man probably do?

   (A) He will not help the woman.
   (B) He will not take the test.
   (C) He will lend a book to the woman.
   (D) He will help the woman study.

Listen and choose the correct answer for each question. MP3 117–119

4. What does the woman imply about the bike?

   (A) She rides the bike only on weekends.
   (B) She needs the bike for her classes.
   (C) She does not use the bike anymore.
   (D) She keeps the bike in her room.

Listen again to part of the talk. Then answer the question.

5. What does the man imply?

   (A) It is the only reason for the bags.
   (B) There are no good reasons to talk about.
   (C) There are other reasons for airtight bags.
   (D) There are problems with airtight bags.

6. What is probably true about the chemicals?

   (A) They are bad for the animals.
   (B) They give less allergies than animal scents.
   (C) They do not smell very good.
   (D) They are being replaced by animal scents.

Listen and choose the correct answer for each question. MP3 120-122

7. What will the man probably do?

   (A) He will not trust the university website.
   (B) He will go to the bookstore to buy more books.
   (C) He will try buying things on the internet.
   (D) He will not take the woman's advice.

8. What does the man imply about SUVs?

   (A) Their large size creates safety problems.
   (B) They are not a popular type of car on the roads compared to normal cars.
   (C) They can avoid a lot of accidents with smaller cars.
   (D) They are a danger only to other SUVs on the road.

9. What does the teacher imply about the book?

   (A) It is a very boring book.
   (B) It is not a very good book.
   (C) It is not very interesting.
   (D) It is very educational.

Listening Practice 1

🔊 **Listen and choose the correct answer for each question.** (MP3) 123

1 Why does the man go to see the woman?

(A) To tell the woman about the coast guard
(B) To discuss different emergency rescue services
(C) To complain about his essay on police officers
(D) To get help from the woman about his essay

2 What will the man probably do?

(A) He will ask his teacher about the essay.
(B) He will write about the coast guard.
(C) He will look for coast guards on the beach.
(D) He will write about something else.

3 In the conversation, the woman mentions the functions of coast guards. Indicate whether each of the following is a function of the coast guard.

Click in the correct box for each phrase.

	Yes	No
(A) Patrolling the seas		
(B) Training swimmers		
(C) Working with police officers		
(D) Rescuing people in the water		

Dictation

🔊 **Listen again and fill in the blanks.** (MP3) 123

M: I have to write a long essay _____ _____ _____ rescue service. It can't be about fire, rescue, police or the ambulance. I _____ _____ _____ _____ than those. Can you help me out?

W: Sure. _____ _____ _____ ... Well, there's the coast guard. I'm sure that you would have a lot to write about.

M: What can I _____ _____ _____? I don't know anything about them, _____ that their uniform is red and white.

W: There are so many things you can write about. They have the same power and work as police officers on the streets do. They catch bad people, _____ _____ that there's no trouble, _____ _____ _____. The big difference is that they patrol the sea.

M: Is that all? Then there's not much difference _____ police officers on the street _____ on the sea.

W: No, coast guards are also like lifeguards on beaches and swimming pools. They train very hard _____ _____ people in the water. They must always be healthy, and even learn to swim in the sea _____ dangerous storms.

M: Wow, they are more interesting than I thought. How wrong I was. I think I'll write about them after I _____ _____ _____ about them in the library. Thanks for helping me out.

- **emergency** an unexpected and dangerous situation which happens suddenly   □ **rescue** to save from danger
- **patrol** to move around a place in order to keep it safe   □ **lifeguard** someone whose job is to rescue drowning people at swimming pools or beaches

Listening Practice 2

🔊 **Listen and choose the correct answer for each question.** (MP3) 124

1. According to the lecture, what were the advantages of Zeppelins?

   Click on 2 answers.

   (A) Hydrogen in the tubes
   (B) Cheap to operate
   (C) Quiet and stable when flying
   (D) Ability to carry more things than planes

2. What does the man imply about the result of the *Hindenburg* accident?

   (A) It supported the usefulness of airships.
   (B) It identified the problems and people improved airships.
   (C) It marked the ending of airships being used as transportation.
   (D) It influenced the birth of airships for advertisements.

3. Why does the professor mention Germans using the Zeppelins as spy planes and carrying bombs?

   (A) To emphasize the importance of Zeppelins
   (B) To indicate the dangers of Zeppelins
   (C) To contrast other planes with Zeppelins
   (D) To describe the shape of Zeppelins

Dictation

Listen again and fill in the blanks. MP3 124

The early 1900s saw a big advancement in air travel. Soon after the Wright brothers performed their first flight, people _____ _____ new ways to fly. Many tried to make flying aircraft, but an airship called the Zeppelin was the most popular aircraft during the early years of flight.

The Zeppelin was like a floating balloon. It had a very large tube at the top, _____ _____ _____. Hydrogen was used because it was _____ _____ _____ _____. So like helium balloons, the Zeppelin floated _____. Small propellers were used to change direction of the airship.

The benefits of Zeppelins seemed _____. The passenger compartment was below the tube, and although it was very slow, it was very quiet and stable. Planes during that time were very expensive. _____ _____ _____ _____, people could travel in Zeppelins for a very cheap price. However, the Zeppelins could not carry as much _____ as other planes. Regardless, during both World Wars, the Germans used the Zeppelins as spy planes and to carry _____.

_____, the Zeppelins had a sad and quick ending. A very large Zeppelin, called the *Hindenburg*, _____ and burned very quickly, _____ _____ the dangerous hydrogen in the big tubes. The accident happened _____ _____ _____ to the US, and it killed hundreds of people. It was the last Zeppelin to carry many people _____ _____. There are still a handful of airships _____ _____, but only for advertisements.

- **advancement** improvement; progress   □ **hydrogen** a colorless gas that is the lightest of all gases
- **compartment** a separate room for a particular purpose   □ **stable** unlikely to move or shake   □ **regardless** despite everything
- **at once** at the same time

Listening Practice 3

Listen and choose the correct answer for each question.  MP3 125

1 Why does the woman go to see the man?

(A) To interview the man for a newspaper
(B) To ask about becoming a reporter
(C) To discuss the school newspaper
(D) To ask about the methods of writing

2 What will the woman probably do?

(A) She will not become a reporter.
(B) She will quit her studies to take the test.
(C) She will meet with the editor-in-chief.
(D) She will interview the man for the newspaper.

3 How does the man talk about the tests?

(A) By identifying her problem and offering her a job
(B) By comparing the test with other tests in school
(C) By stating the tests in the order that she needs to take them
(D) By explaining the questions that come up on the tests

Dictation

Listen again and fill in the blanks. MP3 125

W: Hey, Derek. I _____ _____ _____ _____ about a few things.

M: Sure. How can I help?

W: I remember that you _____ _____ _____ for the school newspaper for some time. Was it good working there?

M: Yes, it was _____ _____ _____ _____ _____. It's a pity I had to quit because of my studies, because I would still love to do it.

W: Good. I asked you because I'm thinking of getting into the school newspaper myself.

M: That's great. I really _____ _____ to try it.

W: Yes, but as you know, I'm a first year student, and I don't know _____ _____ _____ _____ _____.

M: I didn't think about that. I was a second year student, so I can't say if it's possible or not. You'll have to ask the editor-in-chief about it first. But _____, I don't see why first year students can't become reporters.

W: I'm glad _____ _____ _____ it, thanks. Oh, could I ask you another question?

M: Of course you can. What else would you like to know?

W: Must I sit through a test before I can work there? I want _____ _____ _____ _____ anything that I might have to do.

M: Yes, the editors will test your writing skills. When you pass that, then you will _____ _____ _____ _____. That's all I can remember. Then, if your results are good enough, you'll be hired as a junior reporter. I suggest that you go and meet with the editor-in-chief.

W: Thanks a lot. I think I'll do that _____ _____.

Vocabulary

☐ **qualified** having the required knowledge, skill, or experience   ☐ **editor-in-chief** the editor at a magazine or newspaper who decides what will be printed in it

iBT Practice

TOEFL Listening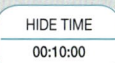

Note-Taking

*i*BT Practice CONTINUED

TOEFL Listening

1 What is the teacher talking about?

- Ⓐ The life and work of Napoleon
- Ⓑ Modern French history
- Ⓒ Great leaders of the world
- Ⓓ The mistakes of Napoleon

2 What changed Napoleon's life?

- Ⓐ The French Revolution
- Ⓑ The war against Corsica
- Ⓒ The French invasion of Corsica
- Ⓓ Conquering Egypt

3 What did Napoleon achieve other than his victories in war?

Click on 2 answers.

- Ⓐ He increased the wealth of France.
- Ⓑ He established the Napoleonic Code.
- Ⓒ He made the French language and culture popular.
- Ⓓ He ordered French scholars to study Egyptian hieroglyphics.

4 Why does the teacher mention Egypt?

- Ⓐ To contrast Egyptian armies with European armies
- Ⓑ To give an example of Napoleon's other achievements
- Ⓒ To list all the countries Napoleon invaded
- Ⓓ To emphasize the importance of culture

Note-Taking: Using Symbols (II)

There are some math symbols you can use while taking notes. Here are some examples:

Symbol	Meaning	Symbol	Meaning
>	greater than	+ (pro)	benefits, advantages
<	less than	− (con)	drawbacks, disadvantages
=	equal to, is	×	times
≠	not equal to, is not	∴	therefore

e.g. Our class has less than 40 students. ⇨ class < 40

Living alone gives you privacy but also loneliness. ⇨ Living alone: + privacy,
− loneliness

Listen again and fill in the blanks using keywords. MP3 126

Napoleon: great soldier, _____, fierce leader

− He was not _____, and not _____ either
− Historical event: _____
  ∴ He got _____ from the govt.
− Napoleon's achievement: • Egyptian research
  • _____

Word Review

Choose the best word to replace the underlined word.

1. If you are ever in danger, don't worry. I'll <u>rescue</u> you.
   (A) encourage   (B) locate   (C) save   (D) warn

2. This chair keeps shaking. Maybe you could make it more <u>stable</u> with a repair.
   (A) broken   (B) complex   (C) soft   (D) firm

3. The worker begged for another chance to <u>demonstrate</u> his skills.
   (A) improve   (B) learn   (C) practice   (D) prove

4. As school president, I try to <u>participate in</u> as many school debates as possible.
   (A) break off   (B) conduct   (C) join in   (D) prepare

Choose and write the correct word to complete the sentence.

| advancement | manage | emergency | constant |
| patrol | qualified | sensitive | regardless |

5. The artist was very _____ to criticism; one bad remark would put him into a deep depression.

6. You should only call the ambulance when you have a(n) _____.

7. The police _____ our neighborhood every night, so there is nothing to worry about.

8. The doctor came very close to finding a cure for cancer thanks to a big _____ in his research.

9. Although everybody tried to stop us, we went through with our plans _____.

10. The company asked me to gain more experience before applying for the position because I wasn't _____ enough.

11. Even though I have a lot of work to do, I think I'll _____ to finish it in time.

12. I'm tired of your _____ complaining. Don't you ever stop?

Memo

Actual Test
1-3

Listening Section Directions

This section measures your ability to understand conversations and lectures in English.
In this part, you will listen to 1 conversation and 2 lectures. You will hear each conversation or lecture only one time.

After each conversation or lecture, you will answer questions about it. The questions typically ask about the main idea and supporting details. Some questions ask about a speaker's purpose or attitude. Answer the questions based on what is stated or implied by the speakers.

You may take notes while you listen. You may use your notes to help you answer the questions. Your notes will not be scored.

If you need to change the volume while you listen, click on the **Volume** icon at the top of the screen.

In some questions, you will see this icon: This means that you will hear, but not see, part of the question.

Some of the questions have special directions. These directions appear in a gray box on the screen.

Most questions are worth 1 point. If a question is worth more than 1 point, it will have special directions that indicate how many points you can receive.

You must answer each question. After you answer, click **Next**. Then, click on **OK** to confirm your answer and go on to the next question. After you click on **OK**, you cannot return to previous questions.

A clock at the top of the screen will show you how much time is remaining. The clock will not count down while you are listening. The clock will count down only while you are answering the questions.

Actual Test 1

TOEFL Listening

1 Why does the man talk to the woman?

- A To know what he should do in computer labs
- B To ask about how he can learn computers
- C To ask about the lab assistant's contact number
- D To tell her why he wants to study computers

2 According to the conversation, why might the man know the lab assistant?

- A The lab assistant is a student in the school.
- B The lab assistant is the woman's friend.
- C The lab assistant does not know about computers.
- D The lab assistant is the woman's father.

Listen again to part of the conversation. Then answer the question.

3 What does the woman imply when she says this:

- A Complete strangers are better teachers than assistants.
- B Assistants and strangers are not good teachers.
- C Complete strangers might not be good teachers.
- D Nobody can really teach beginners well.

4 Why does the woman mention a book?

- A To suggest another way to help the man
- B To try to sell it to the man
- C To ask him to get it for her in the library
- D To stop helping the man

5 What will the man probably do?

- A He will learn computers from a complete stranger.
- B He will take classes on computing for beginners.
- C He will buy a new computer for himself.
- D He will visit the bookstore and look for the book.

Actual Test 1

6 What is the discussion mainly about?

- A) The dangers of whales staying still
- B) The instincts of whales
- C) Whales in colder waters
- D) Whales saving energy

7 Why does the teacher mention small animals living in warmer waters?

- A) To help support the theory of whales saving energy
- B) To ask if the students know what animals live in warmer waters
- C) To describe the life of small animals in warmer waters
- D) To compare eating habits of small animals in cold and warm waters

8 According to the theory, why do whales move to warmer waters?

- A) They are too cold in colder waters and die.
- B) They want to find more food in the warmer waters.
- C) They feel like swimming around for fun.
- D) They like the taste of food in warmer waters.

Listen again to part of the discussion. Then answer the question.

9 What does the teacher imply when he says this:

- A) The whales have a small map of the ocean in their heads.
- B) The whales are not very good at remembering the ocean.
- C) The whales have no problem finding their way in the ocean.
- D) The whales share a map of the ocean with each other.

10 What is the teacher's attitude about the theory of whales saving energy by swimming to warmer waters?

- A) He does not believe it.
- B) He does not know much about it.
- C) He believes that there is some truth to it.
- D) He does not have any opinion on it.

Listen again to part of the discussion. Then answer the question.

11 What does the man mean when he says this:

- A) He believes that the theory is valid.
- B) He does not understand the theory well.
- C) He believes that whales do not swim.
- D) He does not agree with the theory.

Actual Test 1

12 What is the talk mainly about?

- A) The effects of greenhouses
- B) The causes of global warming
- C) Tall buildings in large cities
- D) Saving gas for heat

13 According to the teacher, what will happen if the world's icebergs melt?

- A) The world will get hotter by 0.6 degrees Celsius.
- B) There will be no more gases in the air.
- C) There will be more greenhouses.
- D) The whole world will be flooded.

14 According to the talk, what is the problem with tall buildings?

- A) They trap heat in the windows.
- B) They have shiny windows that reflect heat.
- C) They act like roofs in greenhouses.
- D) They pollute the environment and produce gases.

15 What absorbs heat in our atmosphere?

- A) Tall buildings
- B) Plastic roofs
- C) Gas particles
- D) Plants on the ground

16 Why does the teacher mention gases acting like a plastic roof?

- A) To describe what we need to prevent global warming
- B) To contrast plastic roofs with metal roofs
- C) To talk about different materials used on roofs
- D) To illustrate what the gases are doing to the atmosphere

17 What is the teacher's attitude towards global warming?

- A) He does not think much of it.
- B) He is very worried about it.
- C) He does not know about it.
- D) He is excited about it.

Actual Test 2

1 What does the man need from the bookstore?

- Ⓐ He needs a book for his English class.
- Ⓑ He wants to put up a note on the bulletin board.
- Ⓒ He wants to know the way to get to the cafeteria.
- Ⓓ He needs to get notes for his class.

2 According to the woman, what is a better way to get to the cafeteria?

- Ⓐ Turn right, take the lift and walk to the end
- Ⓑ Turn left, walk to the end and take the lift to B1
- Ⓒ Take the lift and turn left at the stairs
- Ⓓ Turn left and take the lift upstairs

3 In the conversation, they are talking about ways to find a book. Indicate whether each of the following is the librarian's recommendation.

Click in the correct box for each phrase.

	Yes	No
Ⓐ Get the professor to request a copy of the book		
Ⓑ Go to the cafeteria and ask someone for the book		
Ⓒ Go to the cafeteria to post a note on the bulletin board		
Ⓓ Go and request a copy of the book by himself		

4 What will the man probably do?

- Ⓐ He will eat in the cafeteria.
- Ⓑ He will check another bookstore.
- Ⓒ He will look for his professor.
- Ⓓ He will go to the cafeteria.

Listen again to part of the conversation. Then answer the question.

5 What does the woman mean when she says this: 🎧

- Ⓐ Students do not usually buy textbooks this late in the semester.
- Ⓑ Students always joke about buying a book during this time.
- Ⓒ Students do not use the book until later in the semester.
- Ⓓ Students lose their books on the subway all the time.

Actual Test 2

6 What is the talk mainly about?

- A Companies in the news
- B Different cultures
- C Ethical issues in journalism
- D Mass communication

7 What is a large part of the problem with journalists and ethics?

- A Journalists always try to write good reviews.
- B Journalists are influenced by culture or corrupted by companies.
- C Companies are corrupted by journalists.
- D Companies teach us about things in life.

8 According to the speaker, what is the major role of journalists?

- A They must deliver the news as unbiased as possible.
- B They should reshape the news to what most people like.
- C They must favor certain companies for business.
- D They should put their personal opinion in the news.

9 Why does the teacher mention television, magazines and newspapers?

- A To ask the students if they know about mass communication
- B To report on the companies that do not use them
- C To identify which media do not have ethical problems
- D To give the students a few examples of mass media

Listen again to part of the lecture. Then answer the question.

10 Why does the teacher say this:

- A To identify what they receive from companies
- B To imply that some fault lies with the companies
- C To give examples of whom else the companies corrupt
- D To describe the wrongdoings of journalists

Listen again to part of the lecture. Then answer the question.

11 Why does the teacher say this:

- A To start talking about the cause of the problem
- B To ask the class about the problem
- C To end the talk about journalists
- D To emphasize the jobs of journalists

Actual Test 2

12 What is the discussion mainly about?

- A) The idea of efficiency
- B) Old and new bicycles
- C) Riding bicycles safely
- D) Lowering efficiency

13 What is the benefit of using larger wheels on bicycles?

- A) We can ride safely without falling off the bicycle.
- B) We can make more pedals and wheels.
- C) We can travel longer distances with one circle of the pedals.
- D) We can make pedaling much easier than with smaller wheeled bicycles.

14 According to the discussion, what was wrong with classic high-wheeled bicycles?

- A) They were too efficient for people to ride around on.
- B) They were too easy to pedal.
- C) They had too many gears that didn't work.
- D) They were too high, and people fell off too easily.

15 What does the teacher imply about gears?

- A) They do not help bicycle riders much.
- B) They make bicycles look more modern.
- C) They affect the efficiency of bicycles.
- D) They stop people from falling off their bikes.

16 What does the teacher imply about high-wheeled bicycles?

- A) People increased efficiency without thinking about safety.
- B) They were more concerned about the rider's safety.
- C) The pedals were easier to pedal with larger wheels.
- D) High-wheeled bicycles could only travel long distances.

Listen again to part of the discussion. Then answer the question.

17 Why does the teacher say this:

- A) To explain more about the shape of the high-wheeled bicycles
- B) To mention a disadvantage of high-wheeled bicycles
- C) To contrast high-wheeled bicycles with modern bicycles
- D) To identify the most efficient bicycles we have today

Actual Test 3

TOEFL Listening

1 What is the student discussing with the professor?

- Ⓐ How he can improve his final grade
- Ⓑ Whether he can change the grade on his exam
- Ⓒ If he can change the course assignment
- Ⓓ Whether he can make up for one of his assignments

2 What does the student want to do about the course assignment?

- Ⓐ He wants to take an exam instead of writing short papers.
- Ⓑ He wants to write a long paper instead of the short assignments
- Ⓒ He wants to ask if he can do something other than take exams.
- Ⓓ He wants to know if he can do a presentation instead of writing papers.

Listen to part of the conversation. Then answer the question.

3 Why does the man say this:

- Ⓐ He wants to borrow something from the professor.
- Ⓑ He wants to know the time.
- Ⓒ He wants to see if the professor is free to talk.
- Ⓓ He doesn't understand what the professor said.

4 Why did the professor assign short papers?

- Ⓐ She didn't want to read long papers.
- Ⓑ She thought it might be less work for the students.
- Ⓒ She wanted the students to write more.
- Ⓓ She wanted the students to become more involved in the course.

5 What will the student probably do?

- Ⓐ He will take the teacher's course.
- Ⓑ He will drop the course.
- Ⓒ He will only take a few exams.
- Ⓓ He will remind the teacher in class.

Actual Test 3

6 What is the discussion mainly about?

- Ⓐ The discovery of DNA
- Ⓑ Writing scientific books
- Ⓒ The theory of evolution
- Ⓓ Living with apes

7 Why doesn't the woman agree with the man?

Click on 2 answers.

- Ⓐ DNA facts prove that we evolved from apes.
- Ⓑ Darwin did not have scientific evidence to prove his findings.
- Ⓒ There are still many types of monkeys and apes in the world.
- Ⓓ Animals are designed to adapt to different environments.

Listen to part of the conversation. Then answer the question.

8 What can be inferred about Darwin's theory of evolution?

- Ⓐ Very few people are interested in finding out the truth about it.
- Ⓑ Darwin is the only person who could have scientifically proven that it's true.
- Ⓒ Modern science can neither prove nor disprove its validity.
- Ⓓ Nobody was interested in Darwin's other theories.

9 How does the woman support her views about evolution?

- Ⓐ She shows the man some information regarding evolution.
- Ⓑ She gives reasons why Darwin's theory could be wrong.
- Ⓒ She compares Darwin's theory to those proven by DNA.
- Ⓓ She lists the types of monkeys and apes around the world.

10 In the discussion, the professor and the students are talking about evolution. Indicate whether each of the following is related to Darwin's theory of evolution.

Click in the correct box for each phrase.

	Yes	No
Ⓐ DNA testing shows that humans evolved from apes.		
Ⓑ Darwin supported all his views with scientific proof.		
Ⓒ DNA testing proved some of Darwin's theories.		
Ⓓ Nowadays, many people believe in Darwin's theory.		

11 What is the teacher's attitude towards Darwin's theory of evolution?

- Ⓐ He is not sure if it's true or false.
- Ⓑ He thinks it should be accepted as a scientific fact.
- Ⓒ He believes it to be a valid concept.
- Ⓓ He doesn't think it's correct.

Actual Test 3

12 What is the talk mainly about?

- Ⓐ The cost of software programs
- Ⓑ The size of software companies
- Ⓒ Users of different software programs
- Ⓓ Different types of software programs

13 According to the lecture, who are the makers of freeware programs?

- Ⓐ Companies that want to make a lot of money
- Ⓑ Companies that want to show their demo programs
- Ⓒ Programmers that make programs for fun or to showcase their talent
- Ⓓ Private users who want to make a little money

14 According to the lecture, what is the purpose of making commercial ware programs?

- Ⓐ To make well-known programs
- Ⓑ To make funny programs
- Ⓒ To make money
- Ⓓ To let users test their programs

15 Why does the teacher mention downloading programs from the internet?

- Ⓐ To talk about different software types
- Ⓑ To ask what the students think about stealing
- Ⓒ To list the programs she downloads from the internet
- Ⓓ To explain how to download programs from the internet

Listen again to part of the lecture. Then answer the question.

16 What can be inferred about commercial wares?

- Ⓐ Few people use them because they are so complicated.
- Ⓑ They are very beneficial to programmers.
- Ⓒ Once you study them, they are actually very simple.
- Ⓓ Many people already know the functions of commercial ware programs.

17 In the lecture, the professor is talking about software programs. Indicate whether each of the following is related to freeware, shareware, or commercial ware.

Click in the correct box for each phrase.

	Freeware	Shareware	Commercial Ware
Ⓐ Usually very big and complicated			
Ⓑ Don't need to pay anything to use			
Ⓒ Usually very small and simple			
Ⓓ Can use for free, but should pay if you like it.			

Orientation

I. TOEFL *i*BT / Next Generation TOEFL
II. 점수 환산 기준

I. TOEFL *i*BT / Next Generation TOEFL

2005년 9월을 기점으로 1998년 미국에서부터 시행된 TOEFL CBT은 인터넷을 기반으로 하는 TOEFL *i*BT 체제로 바뀌었다. 일부에서는 새롭게 시행되는 토플에 한국인들이 특히 강한 문법이 없어지고 한국인들이 상대적으로 약한 Speaking이 추가되어 이제 토플로 고득점을 획득하기는 어려울 것이라 생각하는 경우가 있는 것 같다. 하지만 새로운 토플을 면밀히 분석하여 그에 맞는 공부 방법으로 철저히 대비한다면 iBT에서도 고득점을 얻는 것이 충분히 가능하다.

1 TOEFL이란?

TOEFL(Test of English as a Foreign Language)은 영어가 모국어가 아닌 사람(EFL학습자 또는 non-native speakers of English)이 미국, 캐나다 등 영어 사용권 국가의 대학이나 대학원에 입학할 경우 치러야 하는 영어 사용 능력 검정시험이다. TOEFL시험은 미국 New Jersey주의 Princeton에 본부를 둔 ETS(Educational Testing Service)의 주관으로 전세계적으로 시행되고 있으며 5,000여 대학이나 교육기관에서 공인시험으로 인정하고 있다.

* What is ETS?

ETS는 Educational Testing Service의 약자다. ETS는 1947년에 설립된 미국 북동부의 New Jersey에 위치한 국가공인 시험 전문 비영리기관(Nonprofit Institution)이다. ETS는 TOEFL 등 영어에 대한 시험뿐만 아니라 미국의 고등학교, 대학교, 대학원 입학에 관련된 영어, 수학, 논리, 전공에 대한 시험을 주관한다. ETS에서 주관하는 대표적인 시험으로는 SAT(미국 대학 입학 능력 평가), GRE(미국 대학원 입학 능력 평가), GMAT(미국 경영대학원 입학 능력 평가), LSAT(미국 법대 입학 능력 평가) 등이 있다. 합격 또는 불합격에 대한 판정은 하지 않으며 단지 해당 시험 분야에 대한 능력만을 평가한다.

2 TOEFL *i*BT란?

2006년부터 전세계적으로 새롭게 시행되고 있는 인터넷 기반의 새로운 토플 시험을 Next Generation TOEFL(차세대 토플) 또는 TOEFL *i*BT(Internet-based Test)라고 한다.

* TOEFL *i*BT는 2005년부터 순차적으로 전세계적으로 시행되었다.
  2005년 9월 – 미국에서 시행
  2005년 10월 – 캐나다, 독일, 프랑스, 이탈리아 등 4개국에서 시행
  2006년 – 한국을 포함, 전세계적으로 시행 (한국에서는 2006년 9월 시행)

* TOEFL *i*BT는 인터넷을 기반으로 ETS에서 지정한 날짜(주로 금요일과 토요일)에 연중 30~40회 정도 시행이 되며, 시험장소가 대폭 확대되어 가까운 곳에서 편리하게 시험을 볼 수 있다.

* TOEFL *i*BT의 시험 등록은 인터넷, 메일, 전화 등 다양한 매체를 통해 가능하며, 비용은 $140~$170이다.

3. TOEFL iBT의 주요 변화

- **문법(Structure)이 없어지고 Speaking이 추가**

  새로운 토플에서는 기존의 structure 평가영역이 사라지고 실제 의사소통 기능을 갖는 통합형 평가 방식 위주의 speaking이 보강되었다.

  * 이는 문법이나 영어구조에 대한 학습은 중요하지 않고 speaking이 더 중요하다는 의미는 아니다. 우리와 같이 제한된 시간에만 영어에 노출되어 있는 EFL환경에서는 문법과 어휘 등 언어구조에 대한 학습이 필수적이라는 인식에는 이견이 없다. 따라서 새로운 토플체제하에서도 문법학습은 여전히 중요하다고 할 수 있다.

- **통합형 문제(Integrated Tasks)의 도입**

  영어를 사용하는 실제 환경의 구현을 위해 [읽고+듣고+쓰기]와 같은 실제 의사소통 기능을 갖는 통합형 평가 방식(Integrated-Skills Approach)의 문제가 출제된다. 새롭게 도입된 통합형 문제 유형은 다음과 같다.

  Read / Listen / Speak
  Listen / Speak
  Read / Listen / Write

- **Core Academic Skills Assessment 강화**

  기존의 영어시험이 제시된 영어문장의 이해도를 주로 평가하는 것이라면 새로운 토플은 note taking, paraphrasing, synthesizing, summarizing 등과 같은 영어로 수업을 진행하는데 필요한 실질적인 능력(Core Academic Skills)을 요구하고 있다.

- **Reading과 Listening의 난이도는 현재의 CBT와 같은 수준**

  외형상 새로운 토플에 많은 변화가 있기는 하지만 Reading과 Listening은 대부분 기존에 익숙한 CBT 문제 유형을 그대로 사용하고 있다. 또한 새로운 토플에 등장하는 문장의 구조나 어휘범위, 토픽범위, Writing Topics 등이 기존의 CBT와 동일한 수준이다.

4　TOEFL iBT의 각 영역별 개요

	Reading (독해)	Listening (청해)	Speaking (말하기)	Writing (작문)
구성	• 총 지문 수: 3-5개 • 총 문제 수: 36-70개 • 각 지문 당 문제 수: 12-14개 • 각 지문 당 단락 수: 4-8개 • 각 지문 당 어휘 수: 약 700 단어	• Conversation: 2-3개 • Lecture: 4-6개(Interactive Lecture 2-3개; Academic Lecture 2-3개) • Conversation은 2-3분 정도 (400-500 단어의 길이), Lecture는 4-5분 정도 (600-800 단어의 길이) • 2-3개의 Conversation (각 5문제씩)과 4-6개의 Lecture(각 6문제씩)에서 총 34-51문제 출제	• Independent Speaking (개별 말하기): 2문제 • Integrated Speaking (통합형 말하기 시험): 4문제; (읽고 듣고 말하기): 2문제 • Integrated Speaking의 독해 지문은 75-100 단어 수준으로 45초의 읽기 시간이 주어진다. • Integrated Speaking의 듣기 지문은 150-280 단어 수준으로 1-2분 정도의 길이다. • 총 6문제 출제	• Integrated Writing (통합형 작문): 1문제(20분 동안 150-225 단어 정도 작성) 　- Integrated Writing의 독해 지문은 230-300 단어 수준으로 3분의 읽기시간이 주어진다. 　- Integrated Writing의 듣기 지문은 230-300 단어 수준으로 2분 정도의 길이다. • Independent Writing (개별 작문): 1문제(30분 동안 최소한 300 단어 이상 작성) • 총 2문제 출제
시간	총 60-100분 (각 지문당 20분씩)	대략 60-90분 정도 (듣는 시간을 제외하고 실제 문제를 푸는데 걸리는 시간은 20-30분)	대략 20분.	대략 50분 (Integrated Writing: 20분; Independent Writing: 30분)
문제 유형	(1) Vocabulary Questions (2) Reference Questions (3) Sentence Simplification Questions (4) Factual Information Questions (5) Negative Fact Questions (6) Inference Questions (7) Rhetorical Purpose Questions (8) Insert Text Questions (9) Prose Summary Questions (10) Classifying, Categorizing, and Organizing Information Questions	(1) Main Idea Questions (2) Supporting Detail Questions (3) Organization Questions (4) Organization-Rhetorical Connection Questions (5) Content-Identifying Relationship Questions (6) Content-Linking Questions (7) Stance / Attitude Questions (8) Function-Purpose Questions	(1) Independent Speaking Personal Preference (2) Independent Speaking Paired Choice (3) Reading / Listening / Speaking Campus Situation Topic (4) Reading / Listening / Speaking Academic Course Topic (5) Listening / Speaking Campus Situation Topic (6) Listening / Speaking Academic Course Topic	(1) Reading / Listening / Writing Academic Course Topic (2) Independent Writing based on Experience & Knowledge
특징	• Glossary(어휘사전) 제공: 단어를 클릭하면 해당 단어의 설명이 나타난다. • Review(복습) 기능: 체크한 답과 그렇지 않은 답의 상태를 알 수 있어 그냥 지나간 문제를 확인할 수 있다. • 각 지문의 제목이 제시된다. • 문제는 보통 지문의 순서대로 주어지며, 문제가 왼쪽에, 지문이 오른쪽에 제시된다.	• Note Taking(받아적기) 가능: 듣는 동안에 요점을 종이에 쓸 수 있다. • 강의의 핵심 구문을 모니터 상에 제시한다. • 들은 내용을 그대로 다시 들려주고 푸는 Replay Item을 도입했다.	• Note Taking을 이용해 효율적으로 Speaking Task의 답변을 준비할 수 있다. • Independent Speaking은 일상 생활의 경험에 관한 질문 등 매우 익숙한 토픽에 대한 질문이다. • Integrated Speaking은 읽고 들은 내용을 바탕으로 Speaking Task가 주어진다. • 각 문제당 15-30초 정도의 답변 준비 시간이 주어지고 실제 답변 시간은 45초 또는 60초다.	• Note Taking을 이용해 효율적으로 Writing Task의 답변을 준비할 수 있다. • Independent Writing의 주제는 기존의 CBT TOEFL의 185 Writing Topics와 거의 동일하다. • Integrated Writing은 읽고 들은 내용을 바탕으로 Writing Task가 주어진다.

5. TOEFL *i*BT의 점수체계

● **Next Generation TOEFL Scores**

Four skill scores

Reading: 0 – 30
Listening: 0 – 30
Speaking: 0 – 30
Writing: 0 – 30

Total score: 0 – 120

* 각 영역별(Reading, Listening, Speaking, and Writing)로 0-30의 scale로 할당되며 total 120 scale이 만점이다. 또한 성적 통지표에는 4개의 영역 점수(four skill scores)와 더불어 total score난이 별도로 표기된다.

* Score Report는 테스트 후 15일 이후에 온라인에서 확인하거나 우편으로 받아볼 수 있다.

● **각 영역별 배점체계**

	Reading (독해)	**Listening** (청해)	**Speaking** (말하기)	**Writing** (작문)
구 성	● 보통 문제당 1점의 원점수가 주어진다. ● Prose Summary Questions나 Classifying, Categorizing, and Organizing Information Questions 문제 유형은 부분 점수가 부여되는 Partial-Credit Item으로 0-4점 사이의 원점수가 부여된다. ● 모든 원점수를 합하여 30점 만점으로 환산한다.	● 보통 문제당 1점의 원점수가 주어진다. ● 일부 Supporting Detail Questions 문제의 경우 2점의 원점수가 주어질 수 있다. 이 경우, 해당 문제에 점수기준이 명시되어 있다. ● 모든 원점수를 합하여 30점 만점으로 환산한다.	● Scoring Rubrics를 바탕으로 각 문제당 0-4점 사이의 원점수가 주어진다. ● 6명의 human raters에 의해 채점된다. ● 모든 원점수를 합하여 30점 만점으로 환산한다.	● Scoring Rubrics를 바탕으로 각 문제당 0-5점 사이의 원점수가 주어진다. ● 2명의 human raters에 의해 채점된다. ● 모든 원점수를 합하여 30점 만점으로 환산한다.
문제 수	36-70	34-51	6	2
환산 점수	0-30	0-30	0-30	0-30

* 한국인의 토플 평균 점수는 200-210점(CBT기준)으로 추산된다. 이는 링구아 토플시리즈의 i-TOEFL단계에 해당하는 수준으로 약 5,000-6,000단어 정도의 어휘력을 갖는 것으로 추정하며, 이를 링구아 토플 중급학습자로 분류한다.

* 보통 미국 대학에서 요구하는 토플 점수는 213점(CBT기준)으로 TOEFL *i*BT 80점에 해당하는 점수이다.

II. 점수 환산 기준

TOEFL Total Score Comparison

Internet-based Total	Computer-based Total	Paper-based Total
120	300	677
120	297	673
119	293	670
118	290	667
117	287	660–663
116	283	657
114–115	280	650–653
113	277	647
111–112	273	640–643
110	270	637
109	267	630–633
106–108	263	623–627
105	260	617–620
103–104	257	613
101–102	253	607–610
100	250	600–603
98–99	247	597
96–97	243	590–593
94–95	240	587
92–93	237	580–583
90–91	233	577
88–89	230	570–573
86–87	227	567
84–85	223	563
83	220	557–560
81–82	217	553
79–80	213	550
77–78	210	547
76	207	540–543
74–75	203	537
72–73	200	533
71	197	527–530
69–70	193	523
68	190	520
66–67	187	517
65	183	513
64	180	507–510
62–63	177	503
61	173	500
59–60	170	497
58	167	493
57	163	487–490
56	160	483
54–55	157	480
53	153	477
52	150	470–473
51	147	467
49–50	143	463
48	140	460
47	137	457
45–46	133	450–453
44	130	447
43	127	443
41–42	123	437–440
40	120	433
39	117	430
38	113	423–427
36–37	110	420
35	107	417
34	103	410–413
33	100	407
32	97	400–403
30–31	93	397
29	90	390–393
28	87	387
26–27	83	380–383
25	80	377
24	77	370–373
23	73	363–367
22	70	357–360
21	67	353
19–20	63	347–350
18	60	340–343
17	57	333–337
16	53	330
15	50	323–327
14	47	317–320
13	43	313
12	40	310
11	37	310
9	33	310
8	30	310
7	27	310
6	23	310
5	20	310
4	17	310
3	13	310
2	10	310
1	7	310
0	3	310
0	0	310

Range Comparison

Internet-based Total	Computer-based Total	Paper-based Total
111–120	273–300	640–677
96–110	243–270	590–637
79–95	213–240	550–587
65–78	183–210	513–547
53–64	153–180	477–510
41–52	123–150	437–473
30–40	93–120	397–433
19–29	63–90	347–393
9–18	33–60	310–343
0–8	0–30	310

TOEFL Score Comparison for Listening

Internet-based Total	Computer-based Total	Paper-based Total
30	30	67–68
30	29	66
29	28	65
28	27	63–64
27	26	62
26	25	60–61
25	24	59
23	23	58
22	22	56–57
21	21	55
19	20	54
18	19	53
17	18	52
16	17	51
15	16	50
14	15	49
13	14	48
12	13	47
11	12	46
10	11	45
9	10	44
7	9	42–43
6	8	41
5	7	40
4	6	38–39
2	5	36–37
1	4	34–35
1	3	32–33
0	2	31
0	1	31
0	0	31

Range Comparison for Listening

Internet-based Total	Computer-based Total	Paper-based Total
29–30	28–30	65–68
26–28	25–27	60–64
22–25	22–24	56–59
18–21	19–21	53–55
15–17	16–18	50–52
12–14	13–15	47–49
9–11	10–12	44–46
5–7	7–9	40–43
1–4	4–6	34–39
0–1	0–3	31–33

Memo

최신 경향을
가장 확실하게 반영한
토플 중급 입문자를 위한
완벽 대비서

링구아포럼

iBT b+ plus TOEFL 시리즈

① b+ TOEFL 시리즈에서만 제공하는 TOEFL 최신 경향!
② iBT TOEFL **70점 대로 도약**하기 위한 **최상**의 **전략 제시**!

* 무료 iBT TEST 1회 제공
* Actual Test 1회 추가 제공

www.linguaforum.com

Scripts & Answer Key

MP3파일 제공 http://test.linguaforum.com

LinguaForum

Scripts & Answer Key

LinguaForum

Part A

1 Main Idea

Sample Question   p.11

친구들끼리 잡담을 하고 일을 함께 하는 것은 일반적이다. 그러나 가끔, 흡연이나 절도와 같은 나쁜 일을 함께 하기도 한다. 집단 내의 또래들이 물리적인 압력은 아니지만 정신적인 압박을 가해서, 어쩔 수 없이 일탈행동을 하게되는 경우가 있다. 이와같은 압박을 동료간의 사회적 압력이라고 한다.

대부분의 동료간의 사회적 압력은 리더의 잘못된 생각에서부터 시작된다. 집단에는 언제나 리더가 있기 마련인데, 리더의 잘못된 생각을 나머지 구성원들이 따르게 된다. 집단의 나머지 구성원들은 리더의 제안을 거절하기가 부담스럽고, 점점 더 많은 구성원들이 리더의 제안을 따라가고 나머지 구성원들도 똑같이 따른다. 모든 사람이 그것이 잘못된 것임을 알지만, 집단에서 소외되는 느낌을 원치 않기 때문이다.

동료들간의 사회적 압력에 따르는 것은 현명하지 못하다. 만약 잘못된 것이라면, 친구들은 다른 한 사람의 말을 듣고 따를 필요가 없다. 진실된 친구는 서로를 이해하며, 다른 친구들이 잘못된 일을 하는 것을 막아 준다.

Building Skills   p.12

Listening for Keywords

1. Keywords : public transportation, popular, subway trains
   Main idea : Subway trains are the most popular transportation.
2. English, teachers

1. Many people ride on public transportation. Some choose to ride in buses, while others use taxis. The most popular are subway trains. These long trains run underground, carrying a lot of passengers. It is a great way to travel, because subway trains are always on time, and stop in many popular places. They are also one of the cheapest ways to travel. There's really no reason why a person should use anything else!

   많은 사람들은 대중교통을 이용한다. 어떤 사람들은 버스를 타고, 다른 사람들은 택시를 탄다. 가장 인기 있는 것은 지하철이다. 지하철은 많은 승객을 태우고, 지하로 운행한다. 지하철은 항상 제 시간에 다니고, 사람들이 많이 찾는 곳 여러 군데에 정차하기 때문에 이동하기에 좋은 수단이다. 또한 가장 저렴한 교통 수단 중 하나다. 사실, 사람이 다른 것을 이용해야 할 이유가 없다.

2. W: Who is your teacher in English class?
   M: I got Miss Roberts. She's a great teacher. She likes to teach us by using games. How about you?
   W: Mr. Jackson is our English teacher. He's such a funny teacher. He jokes a lot when he teaches us English. I think he's better than our old teacher.
   M: Oh, tell me about it. He was a terrible teacher.

   W: 영어 수업 선생님이 누구셔?
   M: 우리는 로버츠 선생님이셔. 그분은 좋은 선생님이야. 우리한테 게임하면서 가르쳐 주는 걸 좋아하셔. 너희는?
   W: 우리 영어 선생님은 잭슨 선생님이셔. 그분은 정말 재미있는 선생님이야. 영어 가르쳐 주시면서 농담도 많이 하시지. 내 생각에는 지난번 선생님보다 나은 것 같아.
   M: 어, 맞다니까. 정말 지독한 선생님이었어.

Listening to the Introductory Section

1. (C)   2. (B)

1. Learning a new language can be very difficult, but we still need to learn it if we want to live overseas. Some people might attend classes, or even find friends that speak the language. Here are some ways to make it easier to learn a new language.

   새로운 언어를 배우는 것은 매우 어렵겠지만, 외국에 나가서 살려면 외국어는 배워야 한다. 어떤 사람들은 학원에 다니거나, 그 외국어를 사용하는 친구를 사귀기도 한다. 외국어를 좀 더 쉽게 배울 수 있는 방법에는 다음과 같은 것들이 있다.

2. Let's discuss why the human body gets addicted to caffeine. Caffeine is found in drinks such as coffee, tea and cola. The chemical is very poisonous to the human body. Yet why do so many people drink coffee or cola? The reason is simple. Caffeine is very addictive.

   왜 사람의 몸이 카페인에 중독되는 것인지 논의해 보자. 카페인은 커피, 차와 콜라 같은 음료 속에 들어있다. 이 화학물질은 사람 몸에 정말 유해하다. 그런데 왜 많은 사람들이 커피나 콜라를 마시는 걸까? 이유는 간단하다. 카페인은 중독성이 있기 때문이다.

Basic Drills   p.14

1. (B)	2. (A)	3. (D)	4. (C)	5. (D)
6. (B)	7. (C)	8. (C)	9. (A)	

1.
M: I sure hope it doesn't rain tomorrow.
W: Why is that? Do you have something planned for tomorrow?
M: Yes, our football team is going to play against another school.
W: I thought people play football even in the rain.
M: I guess so, but it's very tough to play in the rain. The lucky team wins.
W: Wow, I didn't know that. Why does the lucky team win?
M: It's very hard to see in the rain. We also fall easily.

M: 내일은 정말 비가 안 왔으면 좋겠어.
W: 왜 그러는데? 내일 무슨 약속이라도 있어?
M: 응, 우리 학교 축구 팀이 다른 학교랑 경기를 하거든.
W: 나는 사람들이 비가 와도 미식축구를 하는 줄 알았는데.
M: 그러기는 하지만, 그런데 비 속에서 경기하는 건 너무 힘들어. 운 좋은 팀이 이기지.
W: 와, 그건 몰랐네. 왜 운 좋은 팀이 이기는 거야?
M: 비 속에서는 잘 안 보이잖아. 잘 넘어지기도 하고.

•• 해설 ••
핵심어는 미식축구와 비이다. 비가 오면 경기에 지장이 있어서 날씨 얘기가 나왔지만 날씨가 핵심이 아니기 때문에 (A)는 답이 될 수 없다. (C), (D)는 지엽적인 설명일 뿐이다.

tough 힘든, 어려운

2. Class, we're going to talk about how cavemen used to hunt for food. Most people think that cavemen threw stones or spears by themselves. However, scientists have found that cavemen hunted in groups. In fact, cavemen were very smart. Many of them were trained to hunt for big animals. Some would stand in front of the animals and distract them, while other people in the group attacked from the side or the back. The cavemen were very good hunters.

여러분, 동굴에 살던 원시인들이 어떻게 먹잇감을 사냥했는지에 대해서 얘기해 봅시다. 많은 사람들이 원시인들은 각자 돌이나 창을 던졌을 거라고 생각하죠. 그런데, 과학자들이 원시인들은 집단으로 사냥을 했다는 것을 알아냈어요. 사실, 동굴 원시인들은 아주 영리했어요. 그 중의 많은 사람들이 큰 동물을 사냥하도록 훈련받았습니다. 몇몇 사람들이 동물의 정면에서 주의를 딴 데로 돌리는 동안 나머지는 측면이나 후면에서 공격을 했습니다. 동굴 원시인들은 정말 대단한 사냥꾼이었어요.

•• 해설 ••
강의 도입부에 선생님이 "… we're going to talk about how cavemen used to hunt for food."라고 배울 주제를 명확하게 언급했다.

hunt 사냥하다   distract 주의를 딴 데로 돌리다

3. People used to write on a rough and hard paper called parchment. It turned yellow when left outside for a long time. In fact, parchment is not really paper. It is dried skin of a sheep or a goat. This is why the color turns yellow after a long time. People do not use parchment to write anymore, but still use the leather in musical instruments.

사람들은 양피지라고 불리는 거칠고 딱딱한 종이 위에 글씨를 써 왔다. 그것은 오랫동안 밖에 놔둘 경우 노랗게 변했다. 사실, 양피지는 종이가 아니다. 그것은 양이나 염소 가죽을 말린 것이다. 이것이 오래 두게 되면 노랗게 변하는 이유이다. 사람들은 더 이상 양피지를 글씨 쓰는 데에 사용하지는 않지만, 그 가죽을 아직도 악기의 제작에 사용한다.

•• 해설 ••
종이의 유래가 되는 양피지(parchment)를 소재로, 이것의 재료, 색깔, 용도 등을 설명하고 있다.

rough 거친   parchment 양피지

4.
M: Hey, Melanie. Have you seen Jack?
W: No, I haven't seen him all day. Do you need to see him?
M: He promised to help me move to another house, but he's already an hour late.
W: Yes, I heard that he does that a lot.
M: It's the third time that he broke his promise.
W: Don't worry. I'm sure he will show up sooner or later.
M: I really hope so. I can't move all this by myself.

M: 멜라니, 안녕. 너 혹시 잭 봤어?
W: 아니, 하루 종일 못 봤어. 걔를 만나야 돼?
M: 나 이사하는 거 도와준다고 했는데, 벌써 한 시간이나 늦네.
W: 맞아, 나도 걔가 자주 약속시간에 늦는다고 들었어.
M: 약속 어긴 게 벌써 세 번째야.
W: 걱정 마. 언젠가는 나타나겠지.
M: 정말 그러길 바란다. 나 혼자서는 이사 못하거든.

•• 해설 ••
핵심 질문은 첫마디의 "Have you seen Jack?"이다. 이어서 잭을 찾는 이유를 설명한다. 멜라니에게 대신 잭을 찾아달라고 하지도 않았고, 대신 이사하는 것을 도와달라는 것도 아니므로 (A), (B)는 답이 아니다.

5. Humans have invented millions of things since the

beginning of man. Of all those inventions, the most important of all is the wheel. The wheel turns the whole world around. Everywhere we look, we can see all types of wheels. Literally, all the inventions of the world have needed the help of the wheel. Without the wheel, we would be lost in a square world.

　　사람들은 인류의 기원 이래로 수백만 가지의 것들을 발명해냈다. 그 모든 발명품 중에서 가장 중요한 발명품은 바퀴이다. 바퀴는 전 세계를 바꿔놓았다. 어디를 보던 간에, 우리는 갖가지 종류의 바퀴를 찾을 수 있다. 말 그대로, 세상의 모든 발명품들은 바퀴의 도움을 필요로 했다. 바퀴가 없었더라면, 우리는 네모난 세상에서 헤맸을 것이다.

•• 해 설 ••

바퀴(wheel)가 핵심어이다. "the most important of all"이라고 소개하며 중요한 이유를 말하고 있다. 어떤 발명품 중에서도 바퀴가 가장 중요하다는 것을 설명하기 위해서 인간이 많은 것을 발견했다고 언급한 것이므로 (A)는 답이 될 수 없다. (B)의 바퀴의 종류 역시 구체적으로 말하고 있지 않다.

literally 말 그대로

6. W: What do you want to eat for dinner later?
   M: I'm not sure. How about some Italian food?
   W: No, we just had pizza. I don't think I want any more Italian food today.
   M: Alright, we can have some Asian food.
   W: That sounds good. Let's get some fried noodles.
   M: I was talking about some noodle soup.
   W: Sure, I'm sure the restaurant has both fried noodles and noodle soup.

   W: 이따가 저녁 때 뭘 먹고 싶어?
   M: 아직 모르겠는데. 이탈리아 음식은 어때?
   W: 싫어. 방금 피자 먹었잖아. 오늘은 이탈리아 음식은 그만 먹고 싶어.
   M: 알았어. 아시아 음식도 괜찮은데.
   W: 그게 좋겠다. 볶음국수를 먹자.
   M: 나는 탕면을 얘기한 건데.
   W: 괜찮아. 식당에 볶음국수하고 탕면 다 있을 거야.

•• 해 설 ••

저녁으로 무엇을 먹으러 갈 것인지에 대해 의견을 모으고 있다.

7. 　　Health is becoming an important topic in our everyday lives. The things we eat and do can affect our health. How can we become healthy? Just eating right and exercising may not be enough. We also need to care for our mind. A healthy body is of no use if we do not have a healthy mind.

   　　건강은 우리의 일상생활에서 중요한 주제가 되고 있다. 우리의 음식과 생활습관은 건강에 영향을 줄 수 있다. 우리는 어떻게 건강해질 수 있을까? 그저 제대로 먹고 운동하는 것만으로는 충분하지 않을 수 있다. 우리는 마음 또한 잘 다스려야 한다. 건전한 정신없이, 건강한 몸은 아무 소용이 없다.

•• 해 설 ••

"How can we become healthy?"가 주제문이다. 제대로 먹고 운동하는 것만으로는 충분히 건강해질 수 없다고 했으므로 (A), (B)는 답이 될 수 없다. 육체적 건강 뿐만 아니라 정신적 건강도 돌볼 필요가 있다고 했으므로 (D)도 답이 아니다.

8. W: Have you chosen your classes already?
   M: Yes, I have. How about you?
   W: No, not yet. I have to talk to Mr. Adams about it.
   M: Why? Didn't you read the booklet we got last week?
   W: Yes, I did, but it does not have enough information. I want to know more about some classes.
   M: I see what you mean. Well, good luck trying to find him. I heard he's a very busy man.

   W: 너 신청할 과목들은 골랐니?
   M: 어 골랐어. 너는?
   W: 아니. 아직. 애덤스 선생님하고 그것에 대해서 좀 이야기를 해 봐야겠어.
   M: 왜? 지난 주에 받은 소책자 안 읽어봤어?
   W: 아니. 읽어봤는데. 거기 나와 있는 정보가 충분하지가 않아서. 몇 과목들에 대해서 좀 더 알고 싶거든.
   M: 무슨 뜻인지 알겠다. 그럼. 선생님 꼭 찾길 바래. 그 분 꽤나 바쁘시다더라.

•• 해 설 ••

여자는 남자에게 과목을 이미 선택했는지 묻고 자신은 아직 과목을 정하지 못했다고 이야기한다. 남자에게 애덤스 선생임을 찾아달라는 요구는 없었으므로 (A)는 답이 아니다. 또한, 소책자는 여자에게도 있으므로 (D)도 답이 아니다.

booklet 소책자

9. 　　Coming back to carnivorous animals, I mentioned that these animals only eat meat. We have to understand that these animals have a killer instinct. This is why most make very bad pets at home, as it takes a skilled and trained professional to handle wild animals. A carnivorous animal can even attack its owner if it is hungry, because they like the taste of blood. It is best to leave wild animals in the wild, where they feel at home.

다시 육식동물로 돌아와서, 나는 이 동물들이 고기만을 먹는다고 언급했다. 이런 동물들에게는 살생본능이 있다는 것을 이해해야 한다. 이것이 바로 그들을 집에서 애완용으로 기르기 어려운 이유이다. 야생동물을 다루는 데는 능숙하고 훈련된 전문가가 필요하기 때문이다. 육식동물은 피의 맛을 좋아하기 때문에, 배가 고플 때면 주인까지도 공격할 수 있다. 야생동물은 스스로 편하게 생활할 수 있는 야생에 남겨 두는 것이 최선이다.

•• 해 설 ••

"We have to understand that these animals have a killer instinct."라고 말했다. 육식동물의 이러한 본능 때문에 집에서 애완용으로 기르기에는 위험하다고 했다.

carnivorous 육식동물   instinct 본능

Listening Practice 1 p.17

1. (C)   2. (B)   3. (B)

W: You look very tired. Didn't you sleep?
M: No, I only slept for three hours last night.
W: What did you do?
M: Well, it's my neighbor upstairs. He turns up his music so loud every night. I know it's a school dorm, but it's still too loud. It's like he has a party every night.
W: Oh, did you tell him to turn it down? He should be quiet after midnight. That's part of the dorm rules.
M: Yes, I told him to be quiet, but he didn't listen to me. He says that he will be quiet, but he turns up the music 10 minutes later.
W: I think you should talk to the RAs. They will solve your problem.
M: What is an RA?
W: An RA is a resident assistant. RAs are actually students, too. They are responsible for everyone in the dorm. They have to make sure that everyone is comfortable.
M: Oh, why didn't I know about this RA? I will talk to the RA when I go back to my room tonight. I really need to have some sleep.
W: Don't worry. I'm sure the RA will work something out.

W: 너 피곤해 보이는데. 잠 안 잤어?
M: 응. 어젯밤에 세 시간 밖에 못 잤어.
W: 뭘 했는데?
M: 글쎄, 우리 위층 애 때문이야. 걔가 맨날 밤마다 음악을 너무 크게 튼단 말이야. 학교 기숙사인건 알지만, 그래도 너무 시끄러워. 걔는 맨날 파티하는 것 같다니까.
W: 아, 소리 좀 줄이라고 얘기는 했어? 자정 지나면 조용해야 하는데. 기숙사 규칙 중 하나잖아.
M: 응. 조용히 하라고 얘기 했지. 그런데 내 말은 듣지를 않아. 조용히 한다고 하고선, 10분 이따가 다시 음악을 크게 튼다니까.
W: 그럼 조교한테 얘기해야겠네. 그 사람들이 문제를 해결해 줄 거야.
M: 조교라니?
W: 기숙사 조교 말이야. 기숙사 조교들도 마찬가지로 학생들이야. 그 사람들이 전 기숙생들을 책임지지. 그 사람들은 모두가 편안할 수 있도록 해줘야 해.
M: 아, 내가 왜 기숙사 조교를 몰랐지? 오늘 밤에 내 방에 가면 기숙사 조교한테 얘기해야겠다. 나한테는 정말 잠이 필요해.
W: 걱정지마. 기숙사 조교가 분명히 어떻게 해결해 줄 거야.

•• 해 설 ••

1. 남자는 윗층 방이 너무 시끄러워서 잠을 잘 자지 못한 것이 불만이다. 여자는 그 해결 방안으로 기숙사 조교(RA)에게 말해보라고 권한다.

2. "What is an RA?"라고 묻는 남자의 질문에 대한 여자의 대답을 주의하여 듣자. "They have to make sure that everyone is comfortable."라고 말하고 있다.

3. "I will talk to the RA when I go back to my room tonight. I really need to have some sleep."이라고 남자가 마지막에 말하고 있다. (C)는 이미 남자가 해봤지만 소용이 없었다.

dorm (dormitory) 기숙사   resident 거주자
assistant 조수, 조교

Listening Practice 2 p.19

1. (C)   2. (B)   3. (D)

Many people visit supermarkets. Supermarkets have so many things that it is hard to keep track of everything. This is why supermarkets use a lot of modern technology. They use technology to make shopping quicker and easier.

Barcodes are on every product in the supermarket. The barcode system shortens cashier lines because fewer mistakes are made. The cashier scans barcodes through a scanner. The scanner reads the code and adds the total amount. When all the items are scanned, the computer displays the total price.

Although barcodes have been very popular, there is a new technology overtaking barcodes. The system is called RFID. Instead of barcodes, every item in the supermarket will have very small microchips. Large microchip scanners in the checkout lanes detect the microchips on the items inside the shopping carts. This allows shoppers to walk through the cashier without scanning each item. This can save a lot of time. There are already large supermarkets in Germany that have this system.

많은 사람들은 슈퍼마켓에 간다. 슈퍼마켓에는 아주 많은 것들이 있어서 모든 것을 전부 다 알고 있기는 어렵다. 이것이 슈퍼마켓에서 최신 기술을 사용하는 이유다. 쇼핑을 빠르고 쉽게 만들기 위해서 그들은 기술을 사용한다. 바코드는 슈퍼마켓의 모든 제품에 붙어 있다. 바코드 시스템은 실수를 적게 내도록 함으로써 계산대 대기 줄을 줄여 준다. 계산원은 스캐너로 바코드를 스캔한다. 스캐너가 코드를 읽고 더해서 총액을 계산해 낸다. 모든 상품이 스캔되면, 컴퓨터가 총액을 보여준다.

바코드가 매우 널리 사용되고 있지만, 바코드를 앞지르고 있는 새로운 기술이 있다. 그것은 RFID 시스템이다. 바코드 대신에, 슈퍼마켓의 모든 제품은 아주 작은 마이크로칩을 가지게 될 것이다. 계산대 통로에 설치되는 커다란 스캐너가, 쇼핑 카트에 담겨 있는 상품들에 부착된 마이크로칩을 감지한다. 이는 구매자가 각각의 개별 상품을 스캔하지 않고 계산대를 통과할 수 있게 한다. 이것은 시간을 많이 아낄 수 있다. 독일의 대형 슈퍼마켓에는 이미 이런 시스템을 가진 곳도 있다.

•• 해 설 ••

1. 슈퍼마켓의 최신 기술들에 대해 말하고 있다. 예전에는 바코드를 사용했었으나 이를 대체할 더 편리해진 RFID가 등장했다고 한다.

2. "a new technology overtaking barcodes"로 RFID가 소개되어 있다.

3. 스캐너를 통해 바코드가 읽혀져 가격이 합산되고 나면, 컴퓨터가 최종가격을 보여준다는 사실을 통해 바코드가 컴퓨터로 스캔된다는 (D)가 답이다.

keep track of ~에 대해 계속 알고 있다
overtake 앞지르다, 추월하다   checkout 계산대   lane 통로
detect 감지하다

Listening Practice 3   p.21

1. (C)   2. (D)   3. (B), (D)

T: Today, we are going to discuss fossils. Does anyone know what fossils are?
M: They are dinosaur bones in the ground.
T: Close, but not really. Fossils are old parts of prints of bones or plants. Fossils give us information about the Earth's history.
M: Can soft parts of animals become fossils?
T: Not usually. They are usually made by very hard things, like bones and shells. However, whole insects have been preserved in stones. Mammoths have been found frozen in ice. Mammoths are large elephants that lived during the stone age.
M: Oh, when I visited the Grand Canyon, the guide said that there were a lot of fossils there. Is this true?
T: Yes. There are many layers of fossils in the Grand Canyon. Each layer is older than the layer above it.
W: So, can fossils tell us anything else besides how old an animal or plant is?
T: Yes, we can learn other things from fossils: the development of animals and plants, as well as the age of each layer.
M: And I think fossils tell us information about the weather in that area.
T: Right! We can also find out information about minerals and fuels. Well, that's all for today's class.

T: 오늘은, 화석에 대해서 토론해 볼 거예요. 화석이 뭔지 아는 사람?
M: 땅 속에 묻힌 공룡 뼈요.
T: 비슷한데, 정답은 아니에요. 화석은 뼈나 식물의 오래된 흔적의 일부입니다. 화석은 우리에게 지구의 역사에 대한 정보를 주죠.
M: 동물의 부드러운 부분도 화석이 될 수 있습니까?
T: 보통은 아닙니다. 일반적으로 매우 딱딱한 것들, 예를 들면 뼈나 껍질로부터 만들어지는 겁니다. 그렇지만, 곤충은 통째로 돌 속에 보존돼 왔어요. 맘모스는 얼음 속에서 얼어 붙은 채로 발견되기도 했고요. 맘모스는 석기 시대에 살았던 거대한 코끼리들이죠.
M: 아, 제가 그랜드 캐년에 갔을 때, 안내원이 거기에 화석이 아주 많다고 했어요. 정말이에요?
T: 그래요. 그랜드 캐년에는 화석층이 많이 있죠. 각 층은 상층부보다 더 오래된 거예요.
W: 그러면, 화석으로 동물이나 식물이 얼마나 오래되었는지 말고도 알 수 있는 것이 있어요?
T: 그렇죠. 화석으로 동물과 식물의 진화나, 각 층의 나이와 같이 다른 것들도 알 수 있습니다.
M: 제 생각에는 화석이 그 지역의 날씨에 대한 정보도 알려 준다고 생각합니다.
T: 맞아요! 또 광물이나 연료에 대한 정보도 알 수 있어요. 자, 오늘 수업은 여기까지 합시다.

•• 해 설 ••

1. 도입부에 선생님이 "we are going to discuss fossils."라고 오늘 배울 것에 대해 말했기 때문에 주제는 화석(fossil)이다. 그 중에서도 화석이 무엇인지, 그리고 화석을 통해서 얻을 수 있는 정보가 무엇인지가 주로 다루어졌다.

2. "Mammoths are large elephants that lived during the stone age."라고 분명히 말했다.

3. "We can learn other things from fossils: the development of

animals and plants." "We can also find out information about minerals and fuels."을 통해 알 수 있다.

fossil 화석   shell 껍질   preserved 보존된   layer 층

iBT Practice   p.23

1. (D)   2. (B)   3. (A)   4. (D)

T: Let's talk about the Great Depression today. Has anyone heard of the Great Depression?
W: Wasn't it during the early 1900s, when America went through a lot of problems?
M: I thought the whole world was affected, not just America.
T: Yes, it was not just America, but the whole world. The depression followed just after the Big Boom in the US. The economy was going so well that people were scared it would drop. So in the end, they began to sell everything, and prices dropped very quickly.
M: Wow, I didn't know that it was that bad.
T: They didn't name it the Great Depression for nothing. Many people were out of jobs, and the value of money was getting lower and lower every day.
W: So what did people do for a living?
T: Most people traveled around the country to find more jobs. That was when the phrase "go west" was popular. People thought that there were more jobs in the western states, such as California.
M: Were there really that many jobs in California?
T: Well, there were jobs, picking cotton and oranges, but too many people came. Most people starved to death, looking for jobs. The ones who survived the Great Depression had gone through so much that we cannot possibly imagine it today.

T: 오늘은 대공황에 대해서 이야기해 봅시다. 대공황이라는 말을 들은 적이 있는 사람?
W: 1900년대 초, 미국이 많은 문제를 겪을 때 아닌가요?
M: 저는 미국뿐만 아니라, 세계가 영향을 받았던 걸로 알고 있는데요.
T: 맞습니다. 미국만이 아니라, 전세계가 영향을 받았습니다. 대공황은 미국의 큰 호황 직후에 일어났습니다. 경제가 매우 잘 돌아가고 있었기 때문에, 사람들은 곧 침체될 것이라는 두려움을 느꼈어요. 그래서 결국엔, 사람들이 모든 것을 팔기 시작했고, 그러자 가격이 급격하게 떨어졌죠.
M: 와, 그렇게 심각했는지 몰랐어요.
T: 대공황이라고 불리는 데는 충분한 이유가 있었어요. 많은 사람들이 실직했고, 화폐가치는 하루가 다르게 낮아졌거든요.
W: 그러면 사람들은 무엇을 해서 먹고 살았어요?
T: 대부분의 사람들이 일자리를 찾기 위해 전국을 돌아다녔습니다. 그 때가 바로 '서부로 가라'라는 말이 유행했던 때죠. 사람들은 캘리포니아 같은 서부의 주에는 일자리가 더 많을 거라고 생각했어요.
M: 캘리포니아에 정말 일자리가 많았어요?
T: 글쎄, 목화나 오렌지 따기 같은 일자리는 있었지만, 사람들이 너무 많이 몰려들었죠. 대부분의 사람들이 일자리를 찾다가 굶어 죽었습니다. 대공황을 살아남은 사람들은 우리가 오늘날 상상하지도 못할 만큼 정말 많은 것들을 겪은 것이죠.

•• 해설 ••

1. "Let's talk about the Great Depression today."라고 선생님이 처음에 언급했다. 대공황이 중심소재이다.

2. 사람들은 서부에 일자리가 더 많을 것이라고 생각했기 때문에 서부로 옮겨갔다.

3. "The depression followed just after the Big Boom in the US."를 통해 Big Boom이 대공황 바로 이전이었음을 알 수 있다.

4. 선생님이 대공황에 대해 설명하며 "... they began to sell everything, and prices dropped very quickly"라고 말한 것을 통해 정답이 (D)임을 알 수 있다.

Great Depression 대공황   go through ~을 겪다
affected 영향을 받은   boom 붐, 호황   drop 떨어지다
not for nothing 충분한 이유가 있는   starve to death 굶어 죽다
survive 살아 남다

Further Study   p.25
Topic : Great Depression
- Actual state – during the early 1900s
  – whole world was affected including the US
  – just after the Big Boom in the US
  – no jobs & money value ↓
- Reaction – people went west to find jobs
  e.g. California: most starved to death because too many people came

Word Review p.26

1. (C)   2. (C)   3. (B)   4. (B)
5. fossils   6. rough
7. literally   8. instinct
9. resident   10. assistant
11. layer   12. for nothing

Part A
2
Detail

Sample Question p.29

W: 우리 과학수업 어떤 것 같아?
M: 괜찮은 것 같은데, 가끔은 꽤 지루할 때도 있어.
W: 나도 동감이야. 정말 지루할 때도 있어. 수업이 재미있을 수 있다고 생각 안 하니?
M: 맞아. 내가 듣기로는 선배 학년 수업은 실험실도 쓸 수 있고, 다른 재미있는 실험도 할 수 있다더라.
W: 그래, 지난주에 그들이 알에 대해서 실험 했다는 것이 기억난다. 정말 재미있을 것 같았어. 내일은 물에 대한 실험을 한다고 하더라.
M: 그건 불공평해. 우리는 교실에만 앉아서 읽기만 하잖아.
W: 네가 맞아. 선생님께 그것에 대해서 말씀 드리자. 우리가 왜 실험실을 사용할 수 없는지 모르겠다니까.
M: 그래, 선생님이 말씀하신 내용을 눈으로 직접 확인 한다면 우리 성적도 오를 게 확실해.

Building Skills p.30

Focusing on the Important Details

1. Q1. O   2. Q1. T
   Q2. X   Q2. F
   Q3. X   Q3. F
               Q4. F

1. T: The US has 50 states. Which do you think is the biggest?
   W: Isn't it Texas? I read it in a book, I think. Wait, I remember that it was another state.
   T: You're right. Alaska is the largest state in the US. It is large enough to stretch from the east coast to the west coast. It's a huge state.

   M: 미국에는 50개의 주가 있지. 어디가 가장 크다고 생각해?
   W: 텍사스 아니야? 책에서 그렇게 읽은 것 같은데. 잠깐, 다른 주였던 것 같기도 하고.
   M: 그래, 맞아. 알라스카가 미국에서 제일 큰 주야. 동해안부터 서해안까지 이를 수 있을 만큼 충분히 크지. 거대한 주야.

2. There are many birds in this world, but the

hummingbird is the smallest. They are less than 5 centimeters long. They beat their wings the fastest. They are so fast that we can't see their wings moving with our naked eye. The hummingbird needs to do this so that it can hover in front of flowers while it sucks nectar.

> 세상에는 많은 새들이 있지만, 가장 작은 것은 벌새다. 그들의 길이는 5센티미터도 안 된다. 그들의 날갯짓은 가장 빠르다. 너무 빨라서 우리는 그 날개가 움직이는 것을 육안으로는 볼 수가 없다. 벌새들은 꿀을 빠는 동안 꽃 앞에 날고 있기 위해서 날개를 빨리 움직여야만 한다.

Recognizing Rephrased Details

1. (B)
2. Q1. T
   Q2. T
   Q3. F
   Q4. F

1. W: Many people know the White House, but few know why it was named the White House.
   M: That's easy. It's white.
   W: Well, you're only half correct. The British set fire to it during a war in 1812.
   M: That's terrible. Did the whole house burn?
   W: No. Only some parts burned. People used white paint to hide the black marks.
   M: Oh, so that's why people call it the White House.

   W: 많은 사람들이 백악관은 아는데, 왜 그 이름이 백악관인지 아는 사람은 별로 없어.
   M: 쉽잖아. 하얀색이니까 그렇지.
   W: 글쎄. 반은 맞았어. 영국군이 1812년 전쟁 때 불을 질렀어.
   M: 그거 심한데. 그래서 완전히 타버렸어?
   W: 아니. 일부만 탔지. 사람들이 검은 흔적을 가리려고 흰 페인트를 썼어.
   M: 아, 그래서 사람들이 백악관이라고 부르는 거구나.

2. People like to measure things. So, it is natural for people to think of ways to measure something. Even earthquakes can be measured. They are measured by the Richter scale. It is named after the inventor, Dr. Richter. The scale goes up in numbers. An earthquake of 2 is very weak. However, earthquakes at 6 or 7 on the Richter scale can be very dangerous.

   > 사람들은 여러가지를 측정하길 좋아한다. 따라서, 사람들이 어떤 것을 측정하는 방법을 생각해 내는 것은 당연하다. 지진조차도 측정될 수 있다. 지진은 리히터 규모로 측정된다. 그것은 발명자인 리히터 박사의 이름을 딴 것이다. 그 규모 단위는 숫자로 되어 있다. 규모 2의 지진은 매우 약하다. 그러나, 리히터 규모 6이나 7의 지진은 매우 위험할 수 있다.

Basic Drills p.32

1. (C)	2. (A)	3. (C)	4. (B)	5. (D)
6. (C)	7. (D)	8. (B)	9. (A), (C)	

1. W: There's a new opera opening tonight. Do you want to go and watch it?
   M: I'm not too keen on that idea. I prefer watching comedies or family movies.
   W: Really? I didn't know that. I thought you liked action or horror movies. Well, let's go to the movies, then. I don't mind watching anything.
   M: Thanks for understanding. I'll pay for the tickets.

   W: 오늘밤에 새 오페라가 시작된다는데. 가서 안 볼래?
   M: 그다지 가고 싶지는 않은데. 나는 코미디나 가족 영화 보는 걸 더 좋아해.
   W: 정말? 몰랐네. 나는 네가 액션이나 공포영화를 좋아한다고 생각했는데. 그래. 그럼 영화를 보러 가자. 나는 아무거나 봐도 괜찮아.
   M: 이해해줘서 고마워. 표는 내가 살게.

   •• 해설 ••
   "I prefer watching comedies or family movies."라고 남자가 말했다. (A), (B)는 여자가 착각한 내용이다.

   keen (on) 간절히 ~하고 싶은, ~을 열망하는

2. When we talk of killer whales, we think of them as friendly animals in the sea. But there are two big wrong ideas about killer whales. First, killer whales are not whales. They belong in the dolphin family. Second, killer whales can be friendly, but they are very dangerous when hunting. They catch and kill penguins and seals for food.

   > 범고래라고 하면, 우리는 바닷속의 친근한 동물로 생각한다. 그러나 범고래에 대한 두가지 잘못된 통설이 있다. 첫째, 범고래들은 실제로 고래가 아니다. 그들은 돌고래과에 속한다. 둘째, 범고래들은 친근할 수도 있지만, 사냥을 할 때에는 매우 위험하다. 그들은 먹이로 펭귄이나 바다표범을 잡아 먹는다.

   •• 해설 ••
   범고래(killer whale)에 대한 잘못된 통설 중 하나가 이것이 고래(whale)에 속한다는 것인데, 사실은 돌고래과(dolphin family)에 속한다고 말했다.

3. T: Does anyone have a lucky number?
   W: I do. I always like the number 7. A lot of people in

movies also choose 7.
M: I like number 1. I always like being first in things. I don't like losing.
T: Well, in math, there is no such thing. Let's look at the numbers on a die. There are 6 numbers on it. When we roll it, each number has an equal chance. For example, number 4 has a 1 in 6 chance.

T: 행운의 숫자가 있는 사람?
W: 저요. 저는 언제나 숫자 7이 좋아요. 영화에서도 많은 사람들이 7을 고르잖아요.
M: 저는 숫자 1을 좋아해요. 저는 뭐든지 일등이 되는 게 좋아요. 지는 건 싫어요.
T: 자, 수학에는, 그런 것이 없습니다. 주사위의 숫자들을 봅시다. 여섯 숫자가 쓰여 있죠. 주사위를 굴리면, 각각의 숫자는 모두 똑같은 확률을 가집니다. 예를 들어, 숫자 4는 6분의 1의 확률을 가지죠.

•• 해설 ••

"I like number 1. I always like being first in things."라고 남자가 말했다.

4. Life was very dangerous in the 19th century US army. But it was not because of fighting with enemies, or because of bombs. It was because of many diseases. People in the army studied a lot to find out how to stop them. They soon found out that they were because of flies. They were carrying diseases and sitting on the food. The army put up screens on the windows, so that the flies could not come in. Finally, the soldiers started getting healthier.

19세기 미군의 삶은 매우 위험했다. 그런데 그것은 적과의 전투나 폭탄 때문이 아니었다. 그것은 여러 질병 때문이었다. 군대에서 사람들은 어떻게 이를 막을 수 있는지에 대해서 매우 많이 연구했다. 그들은 질병의 원인이 파리에 있다는 것을 알아냈다. 그것들이 질병을 옮기고 다니며 음식 위에 앉기도 했다. 파리가 들어오지 못하게 하기 위해 군은 창문에 방충망을 설치했다. 결국, 군인들은 건강해지기 시작했다.

•• 해설 ••

19세기 미군의 삶이 위험했던 이유는 적과의 전투나 폭탄 때문이 아니라 질병 때문이었다고 도입부에 언급했다. 이 질병은 파리가 옮긴다는 것을 알아냈다.

screen 방충망

5. W: When do we have to sign up for a room in the hostel?
M: You didn't do it yet? Today is the last day!
W: What? It can't be. I only got the e-mail last week.
M: Oh, you're mistaken. We got an e-mail exactly one month ago.
W: You mean that we had one month to sign up?
M: That's correct. If I were you, I'd hurry and sign up. I heard that most people signed up in the first 3 days.

W: 호스텔 방을 언제 예약해야 되지?
M: 아직도 안 했어? 오늘이 마지막 날인데!
W: 뭐라고? 그럴 리가 없어. 지난주에야 이메일을 받았단 말이야.
M: 아, 네가 잘못 생각한 거야. 우리는 정확히 한 달 전에 이메일 받았어.
W: 예약할 수 있는 기간이 한 달이나 있었다고?
M: 그래 맞아. 내가 너였다면 얼른 예약하겠다. 사람들 대부분이 첫 3일 안에 예약했다고 들었어.

•• 해설 ••

문제에서 묻는 바를 잘 파악하여 답하자. 등록 안내 이메일은 한 달 전에 보내졌으므로 한 달간의 등록기간이 있었다. 그러나 여자는 마지막 날까지도 아직 등록하지 못한 상태이다.

6. T: What kind of hobbies do you have?
W: I like playing basketball. I'm 180 centimeters tall, and I think I'm pretty good at the game.
M: I like to stay at home. I make miniature car models.
T: That's interesting. How many car models do you have at home?
M: I have 60 models at home. I try to buy at least one every month.
W: That is a lot of cars. When did you start making miniature cars?
M: I think I started when I was 13. My dad bought one for my birthday. I couldn't stop making them ever since.

T: 여러분들은 어떤 취미를 가졌죠?
W: 저는 농구를 좋아합니다. 저는 키가 180센티미터고, 농구를 꽤 잘한다고 생각합니다.
M: 저는 집에 있는 걸 좋아합니다. 저는 소형 모형 자동차를 만들어요.
T: 재미있는걸. 집에 소형 모형 자동차가 몇 개나 있니?
M: 집에 60개 있어요. 매달 최소한 하나씩은 사려고 하죠.
W: 자동차 정말 많네. 언제부터 소형 모형 자동차를 만들기 시작한 거야?
M: 아마 13살 때부터였던 것 같아. 우리 아버지가 제 생일 때 하나 사다 주셨어요. 그 이후로 계속 만들게 되었어요.

•• 해설 ••

집에 소형 모형 자동차가 몇 개 있느냐는 선생님의 질문에 60개 있다고 남자가 대답했다.

7. Classic American stories showed birds as a positive image. Owls stood for wisdom, and eagles stood for

courage. There were other animals that had different images. For instance, pigs meant laziness and greed. Rats stood for dirtiness, and bats stood for evil. There are also some animals that stood for both good and bad things. For instance, many think of sharks as being bad. But some Native American stories show sharks as being brave and noble.

전통적인 미국 이야기에서 새들은 긍정적인 이미지로 보여졌다. 올빼미는 지혜를, 독수리는 용기를 상징했다. 다른 이미지를 가지는 그 밖의 다른 동물들도 있었다. 예를 들어, 돼지는 태만과 탐욕을 의미했다. 쥐는 더러움을, 박쥐는 악을 상징했다. 좋은 것과 나쁜 것을 동시에 상징하던 동물도 몇 있었다. 예를 들어, 많은 사람들은 상어를 나쁘게 생각한다. 그러나 일부의 북미 원주민들의 원주민들의 이야기에는 상어가 용맹스럽고 고결한 것으로 나타난다.

•• 해 설 ••

화자의 분류 기준을 파악하고 각각의 예에서 말하고 있는 동물들의 이미지를 연상해보자. "bats stood for evil"로 언급되었다.

greed 탐욕   noble 고결한

8. T: I want to remind everyone to be careful at school. Some people have been robbed.
W: What? That's unbelievable! When did that happen?
M: I got my MP3 player stolen in the library too.
T: Did you report it to the librarian?
M: Yes, I did, but I don't think there's anything that they can do about it.
W: Wow, I guess I shouldn't fall asleep in the library anymore. I mostly go to the library to take short naps between classes.
T: That's a good idea. Thieves steal things when their owners are sleeping. I hope they get caught.

T: 여러분 모두 학교에서 조심하라고 일러주고 싶어요. 일부 학생들이 도둑을 맞았어요.
W: 뭐라구요? 믿겨지지가 않아요! 언제 그랬는데요?
M: 저도 도서관에서 MP3 플레이어를 도난 당했어요.
T: 사서한테 얘기 했니?
M: 예, 얘기는 했는데, 사서도 별다른 뾰족한 수가 없는 것 같아요.
W: 와, 이제 도서관에서 잠들면 안되겠네요. 저는 도서관에 주로 공강 시간에 잠깐씩 낮잠 자러 가거든요.
T: 좋은 생각이에요. 도둑들은 주인이 자고 있을 때 물건을 훔쳐가죠. 그들이 잡혔으면 좋겠군요.

•• 해 설 ••

"I shouldn't fall asleep in the library anymore. I mostly go to the library to take short naps between classes."라고 여자가 말한 것으로 보아 그녀는 종종 도서관에서 잠을 잔 것을 알 수 있다.

rob 도둑질하다

9. M: I heard from Daria that you are not going to graduate school. Is that true?
W: I'm afraid so.
M: What happened?
W: Well, I really wanted to get a scholarship. But I didn't make it, and the university just announced a rise in prices.
M: You have got to be kidding.
W: No. They said that school fees will rise by 20%. I can't afford it anymore.
M: Wow, 20% is a large amount. I guess you'll get a job instead, then.
W: I'm afraid so. It's not like I can sit around and do nothing.

M: 다리아한테서 너 대학원에 안 갈 거라고 들었는데. 그거 정말이야?
W: 그럴 것 같아.
M: 무슨 일 있었어?
W: 글쎄. 정말 장학금을 받고 싶었어. 그런데 못 받았고, 최근에 대학에서 등록금 인상도 공고했어.
M: 농담이지?
W: 아니. 등록금을 20% 인상한대. 나는 이제 그만큼이나 낼 여유가 없어.
M: 와, 20%면 정말 큰데. 그러면 대신 취직을 해야겠다.
W: 그래야 할 것 같아. 그냥 빈둥거리면서 아무것도 안 할 수는 없으니까.

•• 해 설 ••

문제의 원인은 여자가 장학금을 받지 못했고, 인상된 등록금을 낼 형편이 못 된다는 데 있다. 아무것도 하지 않고 있을 수는 없으니 취직을 하려는 것이지, 취직하기 위해 대학원을 포기하는 것은 아니다.

graduate school 대학원

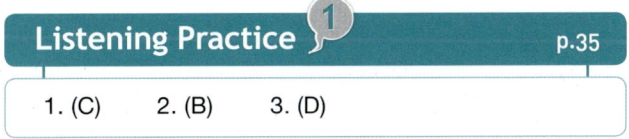

Listening Practice 1   p.35

1. (C)   2. (B)   3. (D)

W: You look worried. Is everything alright?
M: No. I have a really big problem.
W: Oh, tell me what is wrong.
M: Well, you know that I'm a scholarship student, right?

W: Yes, I know you are.
M: I'm supposed to have a B average every semester, or my scholarship gets canceled. That would be a big problem for me.
W: Wow, that's tough. So what is the problem?
M: I had biology class in the morning. I was supposed to hand in an important assignment, but I overslept. When I finally woke up and ran to class, the professor wasn't there. If I don't hand in this assignment, the best I can do in this class is a C.
W: Why didn't you go to his office? I'm sure he would have been there.
M: I did, but he left for a vacation as soon as the class was over. He probably took everyone's assignment too. Oh, I don't know what to do.
W: You can talk to him when he comes back. I'm sure he will understand that it was an honest mistake. You can't just slip the assignment under his door while he is away.
M: Yes, I guess not. I really should have run faster.
W: No, I think you should have woken up earlier.

W: 너 걱정스러워 보인다. 괜찮아?
M: 아니. 정말 큰 문제가 생겼어.
W: 오, 무슨 문제인지 얘기해봐.
M: 글쎄. 너 내가 장학생이라는 거 알지?
W: 응, 알아.
M: 매 학기 마다 평균 B 이상을 받아야 되거든, 아니면 장학금이 취소돼. 그렇게 되면 난 큰일 나는 거지.
W: 와, 그거 어렵겠다. 그런데 뭐가 문제야?
M: 아침에 생물학 수업이 있었거든. 중요한 숙제를 제출했어야 했는데 늦잠을 잤어. 결국에는 깨서 강의실까지 뛰어갔는데, 교수님이 안 계시더라고. 이 강의에서는 이 숙제를 안 내면, 제일 잘 받아봤자 C란 말이야.
W: 교수님 연구실로 찾아가지 그랬어? 거기 계셨을 텐데.
M: 갔었어. 그런데 교수님이 수업 끝나자 마자 휴가를 떠나셨데. 아마 학생들 숙제도 가지고 가셨을 거야. 아, 이제 나는 어떻게 해야 될지 모르겠다.
W: 교수님께서 돌아오시면 얘기드릴 수 있잖아. 일부러 그런 게 아니니까 교수님께서 이해해 주실 거야. 교수님이 안 계시는 동안 연구실 문 아래로 숙제를 그냥 밀어 넣을 수는 없잖아.
M: 그래, 그렇지. 더 빨리 뛰어갈걸 그랬어.
W: 아니. 더 일찍 일어났어야지.

•• 해 설 ••

1. 남자가 장학금을 받으려면 평균 B학점을 받아야 하는데 생물학 수업에 과제를 제출하지 못했고, 그러면 B를 받을 수 없으므로 염려하고 있다. 남자가 원하는 것은 교수님과 연락하여 과제를 성공적으로 제출하려는 것이지 교수님과 장학금 자체에 대해서 얘기하려는 것이 아니므로 답은 (A)가 아닌 (C)이다.

2. 늦잠을 자서 수업을 놓쳤다고 했다. 그러므로 제때 일어나지 못했다는 (B)가 답이다. 한 번 늦잠 잔 것으로 그 사람 자체가 게으르다고 말하기에는 무리가 있으므로 (A)는 답으로 보기 어렵다. 마지막 부분에 남자가 '더 빨리 뛸걸 그랬다'고 하자 여자가 '더 일찍 일어났어야지'라고 한 것을 보아 (C)도 수업을 놓친 직접적인 이유가 아니다.

3. 여자가 "You can talk to him when he comes back."이라고 남자에게 말했다. 그러므로 휴가 후 교수님이 돌아오시면 남자는 교수님과 얘기할 것이다. "You can't just slip the assignment under his door while he is away."라는 여자의 말에 남자가 수긍했으므로 (A)는 답이 아니다. (B)의 전화 얘기는 언급되어 있지 않다.

scholarship 장학금   hand in 제출하다   slip 살짝 밀어 넣다

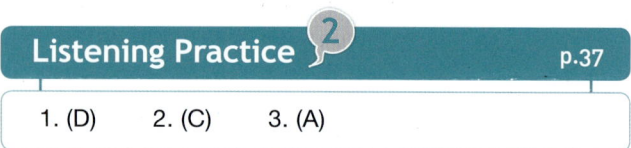

Listening Practice 2   p.37

1. (D)   2. (C)   3. (A)

The gold rush in California of 1849 is the most famous gold rush of North America. Over 80,000 people, called the 49ers because of the year 1849, rushed to Northern California to make easy money. The football team from San Francisco is called the 49ers, after the miners. A lot of people died on their way to California. Even when they did reach California, most of the gold spots were taken, and there was little land to get gold from.

But there were other gold rushes, mostly in the western regions of North America. They were not as dangerous or hard as the Californian gold rush. The Klondike gold rush of 1896 is a fine example.

Klondike is a small town next to Alaska, and is part of Canada. A Native American named Skookum Jim Mason first discovered gold. Unfortunately, at that time, the white people did not like Native Americans. So a friend of Mason, called George Carmack, registered the land under his name. They began to find a lot of gold in the area and built a small place to live.

Soon, more people started hearing about this gold. The new gold miners to Klondike were prepared. They made sure that they had enough food and warm clothes. In fact, they were so prepared that the gold rush was very organized, and people rarely got hurt. Klondike still has a gold mining company, but the gold rush is over.

1849년 캘리포니아의 골드러시는 북아메리카에서 가장 유명한 골드러시이다. 1849년이었기 때문에 포티나이너(49er)라고 불린 8만 명이 넘는 사람들이 쉽게 돈을 벌기 위해 캘리포니아 북부로 몰려들었다. 샌프란시스코의 풋볼 팀은 광부들을 따라 포티나이너스(49ers)라고 불렸다. 많은 사람들이 캘리포니아로 향하는 길에 죽었다. 그들이 캘리포니아에 도착했을 때, 이미 대부분의 금광이 점유되어 있었고, 황금을 얻을 수 있는 땅은 별로 많지 않았다. 그런데, 주로 북아메리카의 서부 지역에는 또 다른 골드러시도 있었다. 그것들은 캘리포니아 골드러시만큼 위험하거나 어렵지는 않았다. 1896년의 클론다이크 골드러시는 좋은 예이다.

클론다이크는 알래스카 옆에 위치한 작은 마을로, 캐나다의 일부다. 스쿠쿰 짐 메이슨이라는 이름의 아메리카 원주민이 처음으로 황금을 발견했다. 불행하게도, 그 당시에, 백인들은 아메리카 원주민을 좋아하지 않았다. 그래서 메이슨의 친구인 조지 카멕은 그의 이름으로 토지를 등록했다. 그들은 그곳에서 많은 양의 황금을 찾기 시작했고 살기 위해서 작은 집도 만들었다.

곧, 더 많은 사람들이 이 황금에 대해서 듣기 시작했다. 그때, 클론다이크로 향하는 새 황금 채굴꾼들은 준비가 되어 있었다. 그들은 충분한 식량과 따뜻한 옷을 갖고 있는지를 확인했다. 사실, 그들이 그렇게 준비되어 있었기 때문에, 골드러시는 매우 조직적이었고, 사람들은 거의 다치지 않았다. 클론다이크에는 아직도 황금 채굴 회사가 있지만, 골드러시는 끝났다.

•• 해 설 ••

1. 북아메리카의 골드러시에 관한 글이다. 캘리포니아 골드러시와 클론다이크 골드러시가 예로 나왔으므로 그 중 하나만 나온 (A)는 답이 아니다. (B)와 (C) 역시 부분적인 설명이다.

2. 1849년 캘리포니아로 금을 캐러 간 사람들을 처음으로 49ers라고 불렀고, 이후에 샌프란시스코의 풋볼팀이 49ers로 불리게 되었다.

3. "Klondike is a small town next to Alaska, and is part of Canada. A Native American named Skookum Jim Mason first discovered gold."라고 했다.

rush 돌진; 돌진하다, 서두르다   miner 광부   spot (특정한) 곳
region 지역   register 등록하다

Listening Practice 3   p.39

1. (D)   2. Yes: (B), (C) / No: (A), (D)   3. (B)

W: What are you planning for your summer holiday?
M: I'm planning on getting a part-time job in the school.
W: Really? What sort of job are you looking for?
M: I was thinking about working in the library as an assistant.
W: Hmm, that job may not be for you.
M: Why do you say that?
W: You are an active person and like music. The library will be too quiet for you. You can't even use the internet or listen to music in there.
M: I guess you're right. What else do you think I can try?
W: I heard that the school team coach is looking for an assistant. He's always very busy with a lot of work.
M: What kind of job do you think an assistant must do? I don't want to just wipe baseball bats and helmets.
W: Now you're just being silly. I heard that the assistant needs to manage a lot of equipment. The assistant also plans the sports activities for the whole semester. It's a big job, but it can also be a lot of fun!
M: Hey, that does sound like a lot of fun! I wonder why I didn't think of that. Thanks a lot. I'll look for him right now.
W: You'd better hurry and find him fast. Quite a few students want to work with him.
M: Don't worry, I know the coach very well. I'll talk to him as soon as I see him, and take that job. I really want that job now.

W: 여름 방학 때 뭐 할 계획이야?
M: 학교에서 아르바이트 할까 생각 중이야.
W: 정말? 어떤 아르바이트를 하려고?
M: 도서관에서 조교로 일하는 걸 생각 중이었어.
W: 음. 그 일은 너랑 안 맞는 것 같은데.
M: 왜 그런데?
W: 너는 활동적인 사람이고 음악을 좋아하잖아. 도서관은 너한테 너무 조용할 거야. 인터넷을 하거나 음악을 들을 수도 없을걸.
M: 네가 맞는 것 같아. 그럼 뭘 해야 하지?
W: 학교 팀 감독이 조수를 찾고 있다고 들었어. 그분은 일 때문에 항상 바쁘시더라.
M: 조수가 해야 되는 일이 뭔지 아니? 나는 야구 방망이랑 헬멧이나 닦기는 싫은데.
W: 이런 바보같이. 내가 듣기로는 조수가 여러 장비를 관리해야 한다더라. 또 전체 학기 동안의 운동 활동 계획도 세워야 되고. 큰 일이긴 하지만, 매우 재미있을 수도 있지!
M: 야, 그거 정말 재미있겠다! 왜 그 생각을 못 했을까. 고마워. 지금 가서 그분을 만나봐야겠다.
W: 될 수 있으면 빨리 가서 찾아뵙는 게 좋을걸. 꽤 많은 학생들이 그분하고 일하려고 하거든.
M: 걱정마, 나는 감독님을 아주 잘 알아. 뵙자마자 말씀 드리고 내가 그 일자리를 차지해야지. 정말 당장 그 일자리를 갖고 싶어.

•• 해 설 ••

1. 두 사람은 아르바이트(part-time job)에 대해 이야기하고 있다. 처음에는

남자가 도서관에서 조교로 일하려고 했지만 여자의 제안을 받아들여 학교 팀 감독의 조수로 생각을 바꾼다.

2. "... the assistant needs to manage a lot of equipment. The assistant also plans the sports activities ..."를 통해 학교 팀 감독의 조수가 하는 일을 알 수 있다. 노래를 듣거나 인터넷을 사용하는 문제는 도서관 조교가 할 수 없는 것으로 언급된 것이므로 정답과 무관하다.

3. 도서관 조교가 남자에게 맞지 않을 것이라고 말하는 여자에게 남자가 그 이유를 묻자. 여자는 이렇게 대답한다. "You are an active person and like music. The library will be too quiet for you."

wipe 닦다   equipment 장비   quite a few 상당수

iBT Practice   p.41

1. (C)   2. (A)   3. (B)   4. (D)

Hello, class. Today we are going to talk about April Fools' Day which takes place on the first day of April. It is a fun holiday because people try to fool or trick others. So when did this holiday originate and why?

No one knows exactly the true origins of this holiday, and we have many theories. Let me offer the ones that are most popular. The holiday seems to go back to ancient times in which people reserved one day just to have fun. People released a lot of stress by making fun of others. So we can see that the ancient people set the model for a holiday in which people could have fun as we do in April Fools' Day.

During the Middle Ages, a number of celebrations developed. The most important of these was the Feast of Fool's. On this day, people made fun of the church. The church, of course, did its best to stop this holiday, but it continued on until the sixteenth century.

The most widespread theory about the origin of April Fools' Day was when the Gregorian calendar began to be used. In 1582, France became the first country to switch from the Julian to the Gregorian calendar. This switch meant that the beginning of the year was moved from the end of March to January 1st. People made fun of those that still used the older calendars. The old calendar's New Year was between March 25th and April 1st. Thus, April Fools' Day was born.

여러분, 안녕하세요. 오늘은 4월의 첫 날인 만우절에 대해서 이야기할 겁니다. 이 날은 모든 사람이 서로와 장난치거나 속이려고 하는 재미있는 명절이죠. 그렇다면 이 명절은 언제부터, 왜 유래되었을까요?

아무도 이 명절의 진짜 기원을 모르지만, 여러 가지 설이 있습니다. 가장 널리 알려진 설을 소개할게요. 이 명절은 사람들이 즐기기 위해서 하루를 따로 지정해 두던 고대에서부터 유래된 것으로 보입니다. 사람들은 서로를 놀리면서 많은 스트레스를 풀었습니다. 즉, 고대의 사람들이 오늘날 우리가 만우절에 그러듯이 재미있게 즐길 수 있는 명절의 원형을 만들었다는 것을 알 수 있습니다.

중세에, 여러 가지의 기념일이 생겨났습니다. 이들 중의 가장 중요한 것은 바보제였습니다. 이 날에, 사람들은 교회를 비웃었습니다. 교회에서는 물론 이 명절을 중단시키려고 최선을 다했지만, 16세기까지 이 명절은 지속되었습니다.

만우절의 기원에 대해서 가장 널리 알려진 설은 그레고리력이 사용되기 시작한 때입니다. 1582년에 프랑스는 율리우스력에서 그레고리력으로 전환한 첫 번째 나라가 되었습니다. 이 전환은 한 해의 시작이 3월 말에서 1월 1일로 바뀌었음을 의미했죠. 사람들은 예전 달력을 여전히 사용하는 사람들을 놀렸습니다. 예전 달력의 새해는 3월 25일에서 4월 1일 사이에 있었습니다. 그렇게, 만우절이 생겨난 것입니다.

•• 해 설 ••

1. 만우절의 유래를 보여주는 여러 가지 이론들을 소개하고 있다. "So when did this holiday originate and why?"를 보아 (A)는 그 중 한 가지만 가리키므로 답이 될 수 없다. (B)역시 만우절의 기원 중 고대 명절만 제시되었기 때문에 답이 아니다. 전체를 포괄하는 단어는 만우절의 기원 (origin)이다.

2. 도입부에 "It is a fun holiday because people try to fool or trick others."라고 만우절을 소개하고 있다.

3. "The church, of course, did its best to stop this holiday ..."라고 했으므로 만우절을 없애려고 노력했다는 (B)가 정답이다. 교회는 만우절을 다른 종류의 명절로 바꾸려고 한 것이 아니라 아예 없애려고 했으므로 (D)는 답이 될 수 없다.

4. 새로운 달력으로의 전환은 새해가 3월말에서 1월 1일로의 바꿈을 의미한다는 강의내용을 통해 사람들이 왜 그레고리력 달력을 사용하는 사람들을 놀렸는지 알 수 있다.

April Fools' Day 만우절   take place 개최되다, 일어나다
fool 장난치다   trick 속이다, 속임수를 쓰다   originate 유래하다
ancient 고대의   reserve 따로 잡아(남겨) 두다   release 풀어 주다
make fun of ~을 놀리다(비웃다)   widespread 널리 퍼진
switch from A to B A를 B로 전환하다

Further Study p.43

The Origin of April Fools' Day

Theory 1   Theory 2   Theory 3

- Theory 1 : ancient times
  – reserved one day to have fun
- Theory 2 : Middle Ages
  – "Feast of Fools" : made fun of the church
- Theory 3 : in 1582
  – Gregorian calendar reform
  – the beginning of the year was moved : between March 25th and April 1st → January 1st

Word Review p.44

1. (B)   2. (B)   3. (D)   4. (A)
5. greed
6. scholarship
7. rush
8. regions
9. equipment
10. quite a few
11. ancient
12. widespread

Part B + 3

Function

Sample Question p.49

M: 네가 학교 밖에서 살 방을 찾고 있다고 들었는데. 정말이야?
W: 응, 그래. 기숙사에서 살기는 너무 싫어.
M: 어째서?
W: 어디서부터 말해야 할 지 모르겠어. 카페테리아 음식은 거의 항상 맛이 없지, 사람들은 언제나 시끄럽고, 내 룸메이트는 지저분하다고.
M: 이만저만 불편한게 아니겠다. 내가 보기에 너희 기숙사는 정말 작고 오래된 것 같던데.
W: 응, 맞아. 얼마나 오래됐는지 엘리베이터는 두 번 중에 한 번은 고장이라니까. 작동이 되더라도 삐걱거리고 흔들려. 다들 무서워서 타지도 못해. 게다가, 기숙사는 너무 작아서 내 차를 주차할 데도 없어.
M: 학교 밖에서 살 데를 찾기 전까지만 조금 더 버텨봐.
W: 그래, 빨리 이사 나갈 수 있으면 좋겠다.

Building Skills p.50

Understanding Different purposes

1. (C)   2. (A)

1.   Many are shocked that I gave the class a surprise test quiz the other day. But I think it was worth it, as I was even more shocked than the rest of you. It showed that many of you have not even touched my year-end assignments, and it worries me. The length of the assignment cannot be finished within a week. Please go back today and start your assignments. You cannot pass this course without completing that assignment. I believe this is fair warning, since it is still early in the semester.

지난 번 내가 깜짝 퀴즈를 보게 하는 바람에 많은 학생들이 놀랐다. 그러나 퀴즈 덕분에 내가 받은 충격이 여러분이 받은 충격보다 더 큰 만큼, 가치가 있었다고 생각한다. 여러분 중의 많은 사람이 내가 준 연말 숙제는 건드리지도 않았다는 게 나타났고, 나는 그게 걱정이 된다. 그 숙제의 분량은 일주일 내에 끝낼 수 있는 게 아니다. 오늘 돌아가면 꼭 숙제를 시작하기 바란다. 그 숙제를 내지 못하면 이 과목을 통과할 수가 없다. 아직 학기 초니까, 이 정도면 타당한 경고라고 생각된다.

Scripts & Answer Key   A15

2. Coming back to tire technology, there are virtually hundreds of different tires for different uses. The different types are usually determined by what surface the tire is designed to be used on, as well as what sort of car and what speed. As such, different materials can give the tires very different characteristics. We're not going to go into details right now, but the general rule is that the faster the tire wears out, the more grip it has. Finding the right balance is the key to a good tire.

타이어 기술로 돌아와서, 여러 가지의 다른 용도를 위한 거의 수백 가지의 타이어들이 존재한다. 그 다른 종류들은 보통 타이어가 어떤 표면에서 사용될 지와 자동차의 종류 및 속도에 따라서 결정된다. 그것에 있어서, 서로 다른 원료는 타이어에 매우 다른 특성을 부여할 수 있다. 지금은 자세하게 들어가지는 않겠지만, 일반적인 원칙은 타이어가 더 빨리 닳을수록 그립(노면에서 미끄러지지 않는 힘)은 더 세다는 것이다. 적당한 균형을 찾는 것이 좋은 타이어의 열쇠이다.

Listening for the Underlying Meaning

1. (A)   2. (B)

1. M: I'm surprised to see you here. Shouldn't you be helping Mary with her assignments?
   W: I should help Mary with her assignment? Why don't you help her?
   M: Calm down. I didn't mean it that way. I thought you were tutoring her after classes.
   W: Oh, I'm sorry. I'm a bit sensitive these days. I've got so much work to do. That's why I turned Mary down when she asked for my help last week.

   M: 여기서 만나다니 놀랍군. 메리 숙제 도와주고 있어야 되는 거 아니야?
   W: 메리 숙제를 도와줘야 된다고? 네가 도와주지 그래?
   M: 진정해. 그런 뜻이 아니었어. 나는 네가 방과 후에 메리한테 과외 가르쳐 준다고 알았지.
   W: 아, 미안해. 요즘 좀 예민해서. 할 일이 너무 많아. 지난 주에 메리가 숙제 도와달라고 했을 때 거절한 것도 그 때문이야.

2. Science and medicine have improved so much over the last hundred years. We have discovered many new ways to heal patients. Technology also allows us to do things that were unimaginable just 20 years ago. Nevertheless, I wouldn't say that we are anywhere close to being successful in winning the battle against diseases. Far from it. There are only a handful of diseases that we have been successful at defeating. Smallpox is such an example, but this was only possible after introducing another form of pox into it.

지난 백 년간 과학과 의학은 매우 많이 발전했다. 우리는 환자를 치료하기 위한 여러 가지의 새로운 방법을 발견해냈다. 기술은 우리가 20년 전만 해도 상상하지 못했던 일들도 할 수 있도록 만들었다. 그러나, 나는 질병과의 전쟁에서의 승리에 가까이 왔다고는 말하지 않겠다. 아직 멀었다. 우리가 이겨내는 데 성공한 질병은 단지 소수에 불과하다. 천연두가 그런 예이지만, 이것은 다른 종류인 우두를 접종한 뒤에야 가능했다.

Basic Drills
p.52

1. (C)   2. (A)   3. (B)   4. (B)   5. (D)
6. (A)   7. (C)   8. (D)   9. (A)

1. W: I got my notes stolen in the library.
   M: Oh, I'm sorry to hear about that. Where did they get stolen?
   W: In the library. I put my bag and notes on the table, and then I went to get a few books.
   M: Then what happened?
   W: When I came back, they were gone. 🎧 I didn't think I was gone that long.
   M: So that means it's someone from this school. Who else would have stolen only your notes?
   W: Yes, I think that's obvious too.

   W: 도서관에서 필기를 도난 당했어.
   M: 오, 그거 정말 안됐다. 어디서 도난 당했는데?
   W: 도서관 안에서. 책상에다가 내 가방하고 필기를 올려 두고, 책 몇 권을 가지러 갔었어.
   M: 그래서 어떻게 됐는데?
   W: 돌아왔을 때는, 없어졌더라고. 내가 자리를 오래 비우지도 않은 것 같은데.
   M: 그렇다면 그건 학교 사람이겠네. 아니면 누가 네 필기만 훔쳤겠어?
   W: 그래, 나도 그건 분명한 것 같아.

•• 해 설 ••

여자가 자리를 비운 시간이 짧았기 때문에 누가 필기를 훔쳐갈 것이라고는 생각하지 못했다는 의미이다. (A)처럼 얼마나 오랫동안 자리를 비웠는지를 물어보려거나 (B)와 같이 혹시 남자가 훔쳐갔는지 알아보려는 것은 아니다. 지금 누가 훔쳐갔는지 알지 못하기 때문에 (D)역시 답이 될 수 없다.

2. Airplanes have so many buttons and lights in the cockpit. Pilots have to practice a long time to fly the plane. It might seem like it is very hard to control. But helicopters are, in fact, much harder to control. The pilot has to use his legs and hands all the time. He cannot rest until the helicopter has landed. Even flying

in one spot in helicopters takes a lot of skill. It truly is very difficult to control a helicopter.

항공기의 조종석에는 매우 많은 단추와 불빛이 있다. 조종사들은 항공기를 조종하기 위해 오랫동안 훈련해야 한다. 항공기는 조종이 매우 어려워 보일 수도 있겠지만, 헬리콥터가 사실 조종하기 더 어렵다. 조종사는 그의 팔과 손을 항상 사용해야만 한다. 그는 헬리콥터가 착륙할 때까지 쉴 수가 없다. 헬리콥터로 한 곳에서 비행하는 경우에도 많은 기술을 필요로 한다. 헬리콥터를 조종하는 것은 정말 매우 어렵다.

•• 해 설 ••

헬리콥터를 조종하는 것이 얼마나 힘든가에 대한 내용이다. 헬리콥터로 한 장소에서 비행하는 것도 많은 기술을 요한다는 문장은 위의 주제(헬리콥터를 조종하는 것은 어렵다)를 잘 강조한다.

cockpit 조종석

3. M: Where are you going with all those empty boxes? Are you moving out?
W: No, I need to clean up my room.
M: But that's a lot of boxes. Are you spring cleaning?
W: Not really, but my parents are coming to visit my dorm soon.
M: Now you're in trouble. How are you going to clean up so quickly?
W: 🎧 Tell me about it. I haven't cleaned my room in two months.
M: I guess you can't do it all by yourself. Let me go and help you out.
W: That would be great. Thank you so much.

M: 그 빈 상자들 갖고서 어디 가는 거야? 이사 가니?
W: 아니. 내 방 정리를 해야 돼서.
M: 근데. 상자가 엄청 많은데. 대청소 하는 건가?
W: 그렇진 않고. 곧 부모님이 기숙사에 오신다고 해서.
M: 너 정말 큰일이다. 그렇게 빨리 어떻게 청소하려고?
W: 그러게 말이야. 두 달 동안 방 청소를 안 했는데.
M: 너 혼자서는 못할 것 같은데. 내가 가서 도와줄게.
W: 그럼 진짜 좋지. 정말로 고맙다.

•• 해 설 ••

"Tell me about it."은 문자 그대로 그것에 대해 말해 달라는 의미로 쓰일 때에도 있지만 종종 동의할 때 맞장구 치는 의미로 쓰이기도 하므로 '그러게 말이야' 정도로 해석한다. 본 대화에서는 더 말해달라는 뜻이 아니라 맞장구치는 의미로 쓰였다.

spring cleaning 대청소   tell me about it 무슨 말인지 잘 안다

4. Singers are popular among many people. They sing all types of songs for people to listen to. But many singers do not write their own music. Instead, there are people called songwriters. They write the songs for singers to sing. 🎧 Perhaps they should have as many fans as the singers do. Without them, many singers would not have anything to sing about.

가수들은 많은 사람들에게 인기가 있다. 그들은 사람들이 들을 수 있도록 모든 종류의 노래를 부른다. 그러나 많은 가수들은 그들의 음악을 직접 작곡하지 않는다. 대신. 작곡가라고 불리는 사람들이 있다. 그들이 가수들이 부를 노래를 쓴다. 사실 그들에게도 또한 가수들만큼 많은 팬들이 있어야 할 것이다. 그들이 없었다면. 많은 가수들은 노래 부를 것이 없었을 것이다.

•• 해 설 ••

가수 못지않게 음악 작곡가가 중요하다는 것이 요지이다. '아마 작곡가가 가수만큼이나 팬이 많을 것'이라는 문장은 요지를 뒷받침하는 역할을 한다.

5. W: When do you think that they will paint the school again? It looks so old and dirty.
M: I heard that they painted it just 5 years ago. It hasn't been very long. People say that the rain keeps getting the buildings dirty.
W: 🎧 I don't know about that. There are two more schools next to ours. Their schools always look new and clean.
M: I guess you're right. There must be some other reason, then. Maybe our school does not clean the buildings often.

W: 학교 페인트 칠은 언제 다시 할 것 같니? 오래되고 지저분해 보이는데.
M: 내가 듣기로는 겨우 5년 전에 페인트 칠했다는데. 별로 오래되지는 않았어. 사람들이 그러는데. 비가 건물을 계속 지저분하게 한대.
W: 그건 잘 모르겠고. 우리 학교 옆에 다른 학교 두 개가 있잖아. 그 학교들은 항상 새 것 같고 깨끗하던데.
M: 그러고 보니. 그렇네. 그럼. 뭔가 다른 이유가 있겠지. 아마 우리 학교는 자주 건물 청소를 안 하나 봐.

•• 해 설 ••

여자는 학교 건물이 오래되고 더러워 보이는 이유가 페인트 칠을 한지 오래되어서라고 보고 있는 반면, 남자는 페인트 칠한 지 그리 오래 되지 않았다며 비 때문인 것 같다고 한다. 여자는 남자의 의견에 동의하지 않기 때문에 완곡한 표현으로 '그건 잘 모르겠고'라고 말한 것이다.

6. When students study in class, they must realize that they must be active to really learn. Most students do not raise their hands and ask the teacher questions. They are either too shy to talk in front of other people,

or they feel that their question is silly. 🎧 This is really a shame, because there is no such thing as a silly question in discussions. In fact, many other people in the class might want to know the same thing, too.

학생들이 수업 시간에 공부할 때, 실제로 배우기 위해서는 적극적이어야 한다는 것을 기억해야 한다. 대부분의 학생들이 손을 들고 선생님에게 질문을 하지 않는다. 그들은 다른 사람들 앞에서 이야기하는 것을 수줍어하거나, 질문이 바보 같다고 생각한다. 이것은 정말로 부끄러운 것인데, 왜냐하면 토론에 있어서 어리석은 질문이라는 건 없기 때문이다. 사실, 학급의 다른 많은 사람들도 같은 것에 대해서 알고 싶어할 수가 있다.

•• 해 설 ••
학생이 배우기 위해서는 적극적이어야 하고 손들거나 질문하는 것을 주저하지 말아야 한다는 내용이다. "This is really a shame, ..."에서 This가 가리키는 것은 자신의 질문이 멍청하다고 느끼는 것인데 이렇게 생각하는 것 자체가 정말 부끄러운 것이라는 말이다. 즉, 질문하지 않고 그냥 가만히 있는 것을 지양해야 한다는 의미로 쓰였다.

silly 어리석은, 바보 같은   shame 애석한(딱한/아쉬운) 일

7. W: Are you ready for the big race tomorrow?
    M: Oh, yeah. I think I am the quickest runner in the school.
    W: Are you sure about that? I heard that there were a few quick runners in the other classes. Other people from their class say that their runners are the quickest.
    M: 🎧 Tell them to bring them on. I will beat all of them.
    W: Wow, you're really confident. Alright, I'll see you tomorrow. I hope that you really win.

    W: 내일 중요한 경기에 대해서 준비 됐어?
    M: 응. 그럼. 내 생각에는 내가 학교에서 제일 빨리 달리는 것 같아.
    W: 확실해? 내가 듣기로는 다른 반에도 빨리 달리는 애들이 몇 명 있다던데. 걔네 반 다른 아이들은 자기네 선수가 제일 빠르다고 하더라.
    M: 데려오라고 해. 내가 다 이겨줄 테니까.
    W: 우와. 너 정말 자신 있구나. 좋아. 내일 보자. 꼭 이기길 바래.

•• 해 설 ••
"Tell them to bring them on."을 '그들을 데려오라고 걔네들한테 말해.'로 해석해서는 곤란하다. 이 말은 정말 데리고 오라는 뜻이 아니라 그 정도로 자신이 있다는 뜻이다. 영어 뿐만 아니라 국어에서도 이런 식의 표현은 쓰이므로 이해하기 쉬울 것이다. 예를 들어, '나보다 행복한 사람 나와보라고 해.'라고 했을 때 정말 나오라는 뜻이 아니라 그 정도로 자기가 행복하다는 것을 자신있게 나타낼 때 하는 말임을 떠올려보자.

confident 자신감 있는

8. Going back to the sport of golf, many people play this silly sport. A person basically hits a small ball with a metal stick. Then they walk and find the ball. They try to hit the ball into a small hole with a flag in it. 🎧 I can't really see the point. Can you? I think that people are better off playing a real sport, such as baseball or soccer. At least people really run in that sport.

    다시 골프 이야기로 돌아가서, 많은 사람들이 이 바보 같은 운동 경기를 한다. 경기자는 기본적으로 금속 막대로 작은 공을 친다. 그리고는 걸어가서 공을 찾는다. 그들은 그 공을 쳐서 막대가 꽂힌 작은 구멍으로 넣으려고 노력한다. 나는 정말 이해할 수가 없다. 당신은 어떤가? 나는 사람들이 야구나 축구 같은 진짜 운동 경기를 하는 게 낫다고 생각한다. 최소한 그런 경기에서는 사람들이 실제로 달린다.

•• 해 설 ••
화자는 골프에 대해 부정적인 시각을 갖고 있다. "I can't really see the point. Can you"에서 "Can you?"는 정말 순수하게 묻고 있다기 보다는 당신도 이해가 안 가지 않느냐고 확인하는 것으로 봐야 한다. 이러한 맥락에 가장 가까운 답은 보기 중 (D)이다.

flag (국가·조직·소속 단체의) 기   see the point 요점을 알다, 이해하다

9. Human cloning or stem cell research has been a hot topic in most discussions lately. Of course, there are many issues that talk of ethics, 🎧 but we won't go into that now. What we're more interested in is how people can benefit from cloning. It is said that we might be able to cure many diseases that we previously could not. All we need is a sample of our own DNA. But we need to go to special clinics to get it. People are lining up outside specialized clinics, in case they become sick later on in their lives.

    인간복제 또는 줄기세포 연구는 최근 대부분의 토론에서 뜨거운 주제이다. 물론, 윤리에 관해 이야기하는 많은 이슈들이 있지만, 우리는 지금 그것을 다루지는 않겠다. 우리가 더 관심 있는 것은 복제로부터 사람들이 어떻게 이득을 볼 수 있을 지이다. 우리가 현재 치료하지 못했던 많은 질병들을 치료하게 될 수가 있을 것이라고 한다. 우리는 자신의 DNA 샘플만 있으면 된다. 그러나 그것을 얻기 위해서는 특수 진료소에 가야된다. 사람들은 살다가 나중에 아플 경우에 대비해서, 특수 진료소의 밖에 줄을 서고 있다.

•• 해 설 ••
"... there are many issues that talk of ethics, but we won't go into that now. What we're more interested in is how people can benefit from cloning."을 의역하자면 다른 여러 가지 도덕적 이슈가 있지만 이것들 말고 복제의 이득을 살펴보겠다는 뜻이 된다. "but we

won't go into that now."는 이번 시간에는 다루지 않겠다는 뜻이므로 오늘 주제는 도덕적 이슈가 아니고 다른 것임을 알 수 있다.

human cloning 인간복제   stem cell 줄기세포   ethics 윤리

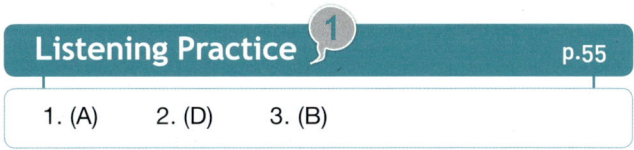

1. (A)   2. (D)   3. (B)

T: Does anyone believe in tarot cards or horoscopes?
M: Yes, I check my horoscope in the newspapers every day.
W: 🎧 That's silly. You know it's not true.
M: I know it's not real, but I find myself reading it all the time.
T: Well, who is to say if it's true or not? But fortune-telling, like crystal balls and palm readings, is widely accepted as being false.
W: So how come people still believe in fortune-telling?
T: A lot of it has got to do with psychology. We often find ourselves with problems in life. It is in our nature to find the reason for such problems. A lot of the problems are really our own fault, but our minds refuse to believe that. Instead, we want to look for some way to blame our problems on something else. This is where fortune-telling comes in. It gives us a way out of taking responsibility. It's easier to blame something that can't talk back, rather than a person.
M: So it's not very good for humans in the long run?
T: Yes. All we are doing is finding more excuses, instead of correcting ourselves. Therefore, we keep finding people or things to blame our problems on, even if they have nothing to do with them.

T: 타로카드나 별점을 믿는 사람 있나요?
M: 예, 저는 매일 신문에서 제 별점을 확인합니다.
W: 그건 바보 같은 거야. 사실이 아닌 거 알고 있잖아.
M: 사실이 아닌 건 알지만, 항상 읽게 되더라고.
T: 글쎄, 누가 그게 사실인지 아닌지 이야기할 수 있을까? 그렇지만, 크리스탈 공이나 손금 보기 같은 점술은 거짓이라고 널리 받아들여지고 있죠.
W: 그럼 어째서 사람들이 아직도 점을 믿는 거죠?
T: 그것이 대부분은 심리학과 관련이 있어요. 우리는 살다 보면 종종 문제를 겪게 되죠. 그런 문제의 이유를 찾는 것은 우리의 본성입니다. 대부분의 문제들이 우리 스스로의 잘못이지만, 우리의 생각은 그것을 믿길 거부합니다. 대신, 우리는 우리의 문제를 다른 것의 탓으로 돌릴 방법을 찾길 원하죠.

여기서부터 점이 시작된 것입니다. 그것은 우리에게 책임을 면할 길을 제공합니다. 사람에게보다는 말대꾸를 하지 않는 것의 탓으로 돌리는 것이 쉽죠.
M: 그럼 결국 사람들에게는 별로 안 좋겠네요.
T: 그래요. 우리가 하고 있는 것은 스스로를 바로잡는 대신에, 더 많은 핑계만 찾고 있는 것입니다. 즉, 우리의 문제와 관련이 없더라도 그 책임을 돌릴 사람이나 사물을 찾고 있는 것입니다.

•• 해설 ••

1. 점술이 사실이 아님에도 불구하고 널리 믿어지는 이유가 심리학과 관련이 있어서라는 것이 요지이다. 그러므로 답은 (A)이다.
2. 크리스탈 공이나 손금은 거짓이라고 받아들여지는 점의 예로써 언급되었다. 그러므로 답은 (D)이다.
3. "who is to say if it's true or not?"는 누가 그게 진실인지 아닌지 말할 수 있겠느냐 즉, 아무도 말할 수 없다는 뜻이다. 말할 수 있는 사람이 누구인지를 묻는 것이 아니다. 그러므로 답은 (D)가 아니라 (B)이다.

horoscopes 점성술, 별점   fortune-telling 점, 길흉(운세)
blame A on B A를 B의 탓으로 돌리다
in the long run (길게 보았을 때) 결국에는   have nothing to do with ~와 아무 관계가 없다

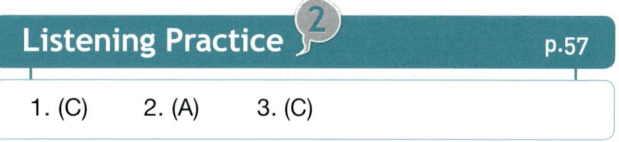

1. (C)   2. (A)   3. (C)

T: Hello, Tina. How are you? It's good to see you. What can I do for you?
W: 🎧 Hello. I'm fine, thank you. I have come to discuss something with you. I'm worried about my performance in class. I don't think I'm doing too well.
T: Well, you're right. Your test scores are fine, but you could probably improve your grade in class participation. Is there something I should know about? If something is bothering you, it's better to let it out.
W: No, it's nothing serious. It's a bit hard to say. I am not a shy person, but somehow I can't seem to talk well in class.
T: Is it because other students ask too many questions?
W: Yeah ... each time that I want to say something, someone speaks before me, and I feel like I don't ever get a chance to speak. I just find myself lost.
T: Hmm ... I see. So you find the guys talk too much and too quickly?

W: Yes. I feel so slow and dumb.

T: No, no. You should never feel like that. I sometimes feel that some of them actually disrupt the class with their endless questions. I have a suggestion. From now on, just look at me when you want to say something and I will call on you.

W: OK. I'm not sure whether you will be able to see me.

T: No. I will be looking out for you. I think a lot of people will be happy to hear what you have to say in class too.

T: 비나야. 안녕. 잘 지내니? 만나니까 정말 좋구나. 무엇을 도와 줄까?

W: 안녕하세요. 전 잘 지내요, 고맙습니다. 선생님과 상의할 게 있어서 왔어요. 저는 저의 수업 성취도가 걱정이 됩니다. 제가 잘 하고 있는 것 같지가 않아요.

T: 그래, 네가 맞아. 네 점수는 괜찮은데, 수업 참여를 통해서 점수를 더 올릴 수 있을 거야. 내가 알아야 될 것이 있는건가? 걱정되는 게 있으면 말하는 게 좋아.

W: 아니요, 심각한 것은 아니에요. 말씀 드리기가 좀 어려운데. 저는 부끄러움을 타는 사람은 아닌데, 어떻게 된 것인지 수업에서는 이야기를 잘 못하는 것 같아요.

T: 다른 학생들이 질문을 너무 많이 해서 그런가?

W: 예… 제가 말하려고 할 때마다 매번, 저보다 먼저 다른 애들이 이야기를 해요. 그래서 저는 말할 기회가 없을 것 같다고 생각이 되고요. 어찌 할 바를 모르겠어요.

T: 음… 알겠다. 그러니까 다른 녀석들이 말을 너무 많이, 빠르게 한다는 거지?

W: 예… 제가 너무 둔하고 바보 같다고 느껴져요.

T: 아니, 아니야. 그렇게 생각하면 안돼. 나는 가끔 개네 중 일부는 끝없는 질문으로 실제로 수업을 방해한다고 느껴. 제안을 하나 할게. 이제부터, 말하고 싶으면 그냥 나를 쳐다봐, 그럼 내가 널 부를게.

W: 좋아요. 선생님께서 절 보실 수가 있을지 모르겠네요.

T: 아니야. 꼭 너를 주시하고 있을게. 많은 사람들이 수업에서 네가 말하는 걸 들으면 좋아할 거라고 생각해.

•• 해 설 ••

1. "I have come to discuss something with you. I'm worried about my performance in class. I don't think I'm doing too well."라고 처음에 학생이 선생님을 찾아온 목적을 얘기했다. 기말고사나 프로젝트 혹은 레포트 때문이 아니라 수업 성취도가 걱정이 되어서 찾아온 것이다.

2. "I have a suggestion. From now on, just look at me when you want to say something and I will call on you."라고 선생님이 제안 했으므로 답은 (A)이다. 수업을 듣는 학생들 중에 말을 너무 많이, 빨리 하는 사람이 있다는 것이지 찾아온 학생보고 그렇게 변하라고 권하는 것이 아니므로 (C)는 답이 될 수 없다.

3. 선생님이 내가 알아야 할 뭔가가 있는 거냐고 묻는 의도는 학생이 갖고 있는 문제를 털어놓도록 유도하려는 것이다.

performance 실적, 성과   participation 참여   dumb 바보 같은
disrupt 방해하다

Listening Practice 3   p.59

1. (C)   2. (D)   3. (A)

Spain and Portugal came to dominate the seas after Columbus discovered America. 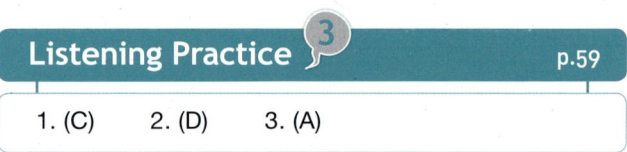 Basically, Spain and Portugal got to divide the world as they wished, and no one could really challenge their control of the seas. But unfortunately, Spain didn't keep its control of the seas for a long time.

There was one country in particular that was set to explore the world and conquer it. Under Queen Elizabeth I, England came to rule the seas. But first, it had to overcome the strong Spanish fleet.

Under King Philip II of Spain, Spain was a mighty sea power, dominating the Atlantic routes to the Americas. Elizabeth's response was to encourage her ships to attack the Spanish ships and claim their treasures for England. In the 1560s, Spain entered a war with the Netherlands. Elizabeth decided to support the Dutch. Spain responded by assembling a huge fleet, known as the Spanish Armada.

The English fleet of 200 boats was manned by less experienced sailors, but their boats were lighter and more agile than the Spanish ships. The Spanish fleet had a hard time moving, since it was big and heavy. They tried to escape, but unfortunately, they encountered a terrible storm that destroyed the remaining fleet. The defeat of the Spanish Armada marked the beginning of British power at sea.

스페인과 포르투갈은 콜롬버스가 아메리카를 발견한 후, 바다를 지배하게 되었다. 기본적으로, 스페인과 포르투갈은 그들이 원한대로 세계를 나누었고, 아무도 그들의 바다 지배에 실제로 도전할 수가 없었다. 그러나 불행하게도, 스페인은 바다의 지배를 오래 간직하지 못했다.

세계를 탐험하고 정복했던 특정한 한 나라가 있었다. 엘리자베스 1세 여왕 통치 하에, 영국은 바다를 지배하게 되었다. 그러나 처음에는 막강한 스페인 함대를 극복해야만 했다.

펠리페 2세 치하에서, 스페인은 아메리카로 향하는 대서양의 뱃길을 독점하는 강력한 해양 세력이었다. 엘리자베스의 대응은 그녀의 함선들을 북돋워 스페인 함선들을 공격하게 하고, 그들의 보물을 영국 것이라고 주장하는 것이었다. 1560년대, 스페인은 네덜란드와의 전쟁을 시작했다. 엘리자베스는 네덜란드를 지원하기로 결정했다. 스페인은 무적함대라고 불리는 대규모의 함대를

조직하는 것으로 대응했다.

200대의 함선으로 구성된 영국의 함대는 덜 훈련된 항해사들로 운용되었지만, 그들의 함선들은 스페인 함선들보다 가볍고 날렵했다. 스페인의 함대는 크고 무거웠기 때문에 이동하는 것이 어려웠다. 그들은 도망가려고 했지만, 불행히도 남은 함대를 파괴시켜 버린 끔찍한 태풍을 만나게 되었다. 스페인 무적함대의 패배는 바다에서의 영국 세력의 시작을 나타냈다.

•• 해 설 ••

1. 스페인의 무적함대가 영국에게 패하면서 바다의 지배권이 스페인에서 영국으로 넘어갔다는 것이 요지이다.

2. 강의에 따르면 엘리자베스 여왕은 스페인을 공격하여 결국 해상권을 차지했다. 여기서 그녀가 야심적 인물이라는 것을 추론 할 수 있다. (A)와 (C)는 틀렸고, (B)는 알 수 없다.

3. 바다에 대한 지배권이 스페인에서 다른 곳(영국)으로 옮겨갔다는 것을 알리기 위한 말이므로 답은 (A)이다. 강의를 끝내려는 것이 아니라 오히려 시작하려고 한 말이므로 (C)는 답이 될 수 없다.

dominate 지배하다   conquer 정복하다   overcome 극복하다
fleet 함대   mighty 강력한   assemble 집합시키다
agile 날렵한   encounter 마주치다, 맞닥뜨리다

iBT Practice   p.61

1. (A)   2. Yes: (A), (B), (E) / No: (C), (D)   3. (D)
4. (C)

Skin cancer has been steadily increasing in recent years due to tanning being popular. Although it might look good on some people, staying in the sun for long periods of time is not healthy for anyone. Too much tanning will cause the skin to turn red and become painful, because the blood vessels expand. The skin really turns brown because it is protecting itself from the UV rays of the sun. If we tan too long, then we can easily get skin cancer.

There are two types of skin cancer. One is non-melanoma. Non-melanoma cancers begin when UV radiation causes skin cells to form a tumor, while at the same time preventing our body from detecting the tumor. The signs of this type of skin cancer are varied. They include open sores that do not heal; a reddish patch that doesn't go away; a smooth, circular growth with a raised edge; a shiny bump or a pale mark. The cancer is curable in 95% of patients, and the tumor can be removed by doctors.

The other type of skin cancer is melanoma. Melanoma often has the appearance of a mole. It looks like a spilled ink spot. Melanoma is most likely to appear in persons who have fair skin, especially if they suffered occasional severe sunburns as children.

Regardless of the type of skin cancer, both can be fatal if we don't treat them quickly. Scientists explain that skin cancer can be avoided by taking a few precautions. 🎧 They suggest that people wear sunscreen not just for going to the beach, but on a daily basis. **I guess that's about it.** Tomorrow, we'll talk about other forms of cancer.

태닝(햇빛에 태우기)이 인기를 얻게 되면서, 최근에 피부암이 지속적으로 증가하고 있다. 어떤 사람들에게는 예쁘게 보일 수도 있지만, 햇빛 아래서 오랜 시간 동안 머무는 것은 누구에게나 건강에 좋지 않다. 너무 많은 태닝은 혈관의 확장으로 인해서 피부가 빨갛게 변하게 하고, 통증을 유발한다. 피부는 스스로 태양의 자외선으로부터 보호하기 위해 실제로 갈색으로 변한다. 너무 오랫동안 태울 경우에, 우리는 쉽게 피부암에 걸릴 수 있다.

피부암에는 두 가지 종류가 있다. 하나는 비흑색종이다. 비흑색종 피부암은 자외선 복사가 피부 세포를 종양으로 변화시키고, 동시에 우리의 몸이 종양을 탐지하는 것을 막을 때 발생하게 된다. 이런 종류의 피부함 징후는 다양하다. 그것에는 치유가 어려운 노출된 염증, 없어지지 않는 붉은 반점, 부풀어 오른 선단의 둥그런 확장, 윤이 나는 융기나 창백한 자국이 있다. 이 암은 환자의 95%에서 치료가 가능하며, 종양은 의사에 의해 제거될 수 있다.

다른 종류의 피부암은 흑색종이다. 흑색종은 종종 사마귀의 모습을 갖는다. 그것은 마치 잉크가 쏟아진 부분처럼 보인다. 흑색종은 특히 어렸을 때 때때로 심각한 정도로 햇볕에 탄 경험이 있는, 깨끗한 피부를 가진 사람들에게서 나타날 가능성이 크다.

피부암의 종류와는 상관 없이, 둘 모두 빨리 치료하지 않으면 치명적일 수 있다. 학자들은 몇 가지의 주의 사항을 지키면 피부암을 피할 수 있다고 설명한다. 그들은 자외선 차단제를 해변에 갈 때뿐만 아니라, 매일 바르라고 제안한다. 이 주제에 관해서는 여기까지 하도록 하고, 내일은 다른 형태의 암에 대해서 이야기할 것이다.

•• 해 설 ••

1. 피부암에 대한 강의이다. 도입부에서는 과도한 태닝이 피부암을 유발할 수 있다고 했고, 그 이후부터는 피부암의 두 가지 종류와 예방법이 제시되었다. 그러므로 이들 내용의 공통 분모는 피부암의 종류이다.

2. "The signs of this type of skin cancer are varied. They include open sores that do not heal; a reddish patch that doesn't go away; a smooth, circular growth with a raised edge; a shiny bump or a pale mark." 여기서 "this type"은 비흑색종(non-melanoma)을 일컬으므로 답은 첫째, 둘째, 다섯째 보기가 된다. 셋째와 넷째는 비흑색종(melanoma)의 증세이다.

3. "... that's about it."은 그 문제(피부암)에 관해서는 여기까지라는 뜻이므로 수업을 마무리 한다는 것을 알 수 있다. 이와 함께 "That's it for today." 역시 '오늘은 여기까지'라는 뜻으로 수업을 끝낼 때 자주 쓰이는

표현이므로 알아두자.

4. 도입부에서 "The skin really turns brown because it is protecting itself from UV rays of the sun"이라고 말했으므로 답은 (C)이다. 본론에서 피부암은 염증, 사마귀 등의 모습으로 나타난다고 했기 때문에 (A)는 답이 될 수 없다.

---

skin cancer 피부암   due to ~때문에   blood vessel 혈관
expand 확장 되다   protect A from B A를 B로부터 보호하다
UV rays 자외선   melanoma 흑색종   radiation 방사선
tumor 종양   prevent A from -ing A가 ~하는 것을 막다
sore 상처   patch 반점   bump 튀어나온 부분   pale 창백한
appearance 모습   suffer (질병·고통 등을) 겪다
sunburn 햇볕에 심하게 탐   fatal 치명적   treat 치료
precaution 예방 조치   on a daily basis 매일

Further Study   p.63

Topic : Skin cancer
- reason : too much tanning
- two types of skin cancer
  1. non-melanoma (non-melnm)
     – UV radiation : causes skin cells to form a tumor
     – open sores / reddish patch / raised edge / shiny bump / pale mark
  2. melnm
     – appearance of a mole
     – person with fair skin
- both can be fatal if not treated quickly
- precaution : to wear sunscreen on a daily basis

Word Review   p.64

1. (C)   2. (C)   3. (C)   4. (D)
5. in the long run   6. conquer
7. overcome   8. mighty
9. agile   10. radiation
11. fatal   12. precaution

Part B

4

Attitude

Sample Question   p.67

W: 지난 주에 너도 교수님 연구실에 불려갔었어?
M: 아니, 교수님이 너만 찾으셨던 것 같아. 뭐라고 하셨는데?
W: 내가 거의 모든 과목을 끝냈다고 하니까 좀 놀라셨어. 나는 졸업하려면 한 학기만 더 다니면 되거든.
M: 그거 대단하구나! 그런데 그게 어떻게 가능해? 너는 이제 2학년까지만 마친 거잖아.
W: 알아, 나도 좀 놀랐어. 근데 나는 한 학기에 여섯 과목씩 들었어. 시간 낭비하기 싫었거든.
M: 말도 안돼! 나는 매 학기에 최대 다섯 과목만 들을 수 있는 줄로 알았는데.
W: 네가 맞아. 그런데 나는 학기마다 한 과목씩 더 들을 수 있는 허가를 받았어. 힘들었지만, 내가 대학교를 거의 마쳤다는 게 기뻐.

Building Skills   p.68

Recognizing Tone of Voice

1. (A)   2. (B)

1. W: What are you reading, George?
M: I am looking for a part-time job.
W: Why do you need a job?
M: I have to earn some money for the next semester.
W: I thought you had a scholarship. Do you have something to buy?
M: No. The school decided to stop all the scholarships from the beginning of the next semester.
W: I'm sorry to hear that. Why did they decide to do that?
M: They are building a new library. I guess it's best for the school.
W: I'm glad that you have a positive attitude about it.

W: 조지야, 뭘 읽고 있어?
M: 아르바이트를 찾고 있어.
W: 왜 일을 하려고?
M: 다음 학기 때문에 돈을 좀 벌어야 해.
W: 너 장학금 받는 줄 알았는데. 뭐 살 게 있는 거야?

M: 아니. 학교에서 다음 학기 초부터 모든 장학금을 중단한대.
W: 그거 안 됐구나. 왜 그러기로 했대?
M: 새 도서관을 건설하나 봐. 학교로서는 최선인 것 같아.
W: 니가 그것에 대해서 긍정적인 자세를 가져서 다행이구나.

2. When dinosaurs walked the Earth, there were cockroaches. Even today, there are still many cockroaches. Just how have these insects lasted on this Earth without changing much of their shape at all?

The shape of their body is unique. It is very flexible, and allows them to crawl literally anywhere. They can also eat any type of food, including rubbish. In fact, cockroaches are the best adapted animal in the world. Scientists say that cockroaches would be the only survivors in a nuclear war.

공룡이 지구를 걸어 다닐 당시에, 바퀴벌레는 존재했었다. 오늘날, 아직까지도 많은 바퀴벌레들이 존재한다. 생김새를 거의 바꾸지 않고 도대체 어떻게 바퀴벌레들은 살아남은 것일까?

그것들의 몸통 생김새는 독특하다. 그것은 매우 유연하고, 말 그대로 어디라도 기어갈 수 있게 해준다. 그것들은 쓰레기를 포함한 어떤 종류의 먹이라도 먹을 수 있다. 사실, 바퀴벌레들은 세계에서 가장 적응력이 좋은 동물이다. 과학자들은 바퀴벌레들만이 핵 전쟁에서 유일하게 살아남을 것이라고 이야기한다.

Recognizing Degree of Certainty

1. (C)   2. (C)

1. Using computers is getting more common in schools and offices. Therefore, people are trying to learn how to use computers in a short amount of time. An effective way to use computers properly is typing quickly. Typing quickly can save working time so that we can use it later for something else. There are a few ways to improve our typing speed. Chatting with other people online is a fun way, and playing typing games is another. Typing without watching the keyboard can also be an effective way. The most important thing that you have to do is to find which way is the best for you.

학교나 사무실에서, 컴퓨터를 사용하는 것은 점점 더 일반적이 되고 있다. 그래서, 사람들은 짧은 시간 안에 컴퓨터를 사용하는 법을 배우기 위해서 노력한다. 컴퓨터를 제대로 사용하는 효율적인 방법은 타자를 빨리 치는 것이다. 타자를 빨리 치면, 업무 시간을 단축해 나중에 다른 일에 시간을 사용할 수 있다. 타자 속도를 높일 수 있는 방법들이 몇 가지 있다. 온라인에서 다른 사람들과 채팅을 하는 것이 재미있는 한 가지 방법이고, 타자 게임을 하는 것이 또 다른 방법이다. 키보드를 보지 않고 타자를 치는 것도 효과적인 방법이다. 가장 중요한 것은 어떤 방법이 당신에게 가장 잘 맞는지를 찾는 것이다.

2. Our voices are produced by air passing the vocal cords in our necks. Well, there can be many other things that affect the voice, but let's keep it simple today. Humans control the vibration of vocal cords to make meaningful sounds. People's voices change, depending on the size of the vocal cords. Children have the highest pitched voices, because their vocal cords are small and underdeveloped. Male adults usually have longer vocal cords; hence they have the lowest tone. Women are in between, as they have mid-sized vocal cords.

우리의 목소리는 목 안의 성대를 통과하는 공기에 의해서 생긴다. 그런데, 목소리에 영향을 주는 다른 많은 것들이 있지만, 오늘은 간단히 하자. 사람들은 의미있는 소리를 내기 위해 성대의 떨림을 제어한다. 사람들의 목소리는 성대의 크기에 따라서 달라진다. 아이들은 성대가 작고 충분히 발달되지 않았기 때문에, 가장 높은 목소리를 가진다. 어른 남성은 보통 더 긴 성대를 가졌다. 그래서 그들은 가장 낮은 음색을 갖는다. 여자들은 중간 크기의 성대를 가졌으므로, 그 사이에 있다.

Basic Drills   p.70

| 1. (D) | 2. (B) | 3. (A) | 4. (B) | 5. (C) |
| 6. (D) | 7. (B) | 8. (A) | 9. (C) | |

1.
W: Hey, what do you think of the new school logo?
M: Oh, I saw it, alright. I didn't think much of it.
W: Me neither. I think we should have voted on a few designs. I haven't met one person that says they like it.
M: That's what I told my teacher. But she said that the school paid a design company to design it. Besides, they already made the new signboards and printed new T-shirts with the logo.
W: I guess we don't have a choice. But that doesn't mean that I'm happy about it.

W: 야, 학교 새 로고에 대해서 어떻게 생각해?
M: 아, 그거 봤는데. 별로 좋아 보이지는 않더군.
W: 나도. 몇 가지 도안을 놓고 투표로 결정하면 좋았을 텐데. 그거 좋다고 하는 사람은 한 명도 못 만났어.
M: 나도 우리 선생님께 그렇게 말씀 드렸어. 그런데, 선생님은 학교에서 그 도안을 만들려고 디자인 회사에 돈을 주었다고 하시더라. 어쨌든, 벌써 새 간판하고 로고가 들어간 티셔츠도 만들었더라.
W: 우리한테는 선택이 없는 것 같아. 그렇지만, 그게 좋다는 뜻은 아니야.

•• 해설 ••

두 사람뿐만 아니라 다른 사람들도 새 학교 로고를 별로 좋아하지 않는다고 했다. 마지막에 "I guess we don't have a choice. But that doesn't mean that I'm happy about it."라는 말에서 선택의 여지가 없기 때문에 가만히 있는 것이지 로고를 좋아해서 그런 것은 아니라는 것을 알 수 있다. 처음에 남자가 "I saw it, alright."이라고 말한 부분이 있다. 이 말은 부정적인 상황에서 냉소적으로 하는 말이다. 괜찮게 봤다는 뜻이 아니므로 유의하자. 대화 전체에서 두 사람이 로고를 맘에 들어 하지 않음이 확연히 드러나 답은 (C)가 아니라 (D)이다.

think much of 중히 여기다   signboard 간판

2. Antonio Stradivarius was a master violin maker from Italy in the 17th century, and his violins are worth millions of dollars today. They are expensive because they sound better than any other violins in the world. However, many are now saying he was only lucky. Apparently, the trees in his backyard, which he used for his violins, just happened to be the best wood to make violins. I must say I don't see their point and cannot agree. It takes more than just great wood to make beautiful sounding violins.

안토니오 스트라디바리우스는 17세기 이탈리아의 바이올린 제작의 명인이었으며, 그의 바이올린들은 오늘날 수백만 달러의 가치를 지니고 있다. 이것들은 세계의 다른 어떤 바이올린보다 좋은 소리를 내기 때문에 비싼 것이다. 그런데, 많은 사람들은 그가 운이 좋았을 뿐이라고 이야기한다. 보아 하니, 그가 바이올린을 만드는데 사용한 뒷마당의 나무들이 그저 바이올린을 만들기 위한 최고의 나무였을 뿐이라는 것이다. 나는 그들의 말을 이해할 수 없고, 그래서 동의하지 않을 수 밖에 없다. 아름다운 소리를 내는 바이올린을 만드는 데는 좋은 나무이상의 것이 필요하다.

•• 해설 ••

어떤 사람들은 스트라디바리우스가 뒤뜰의 좋은 나무를 써서 최고의 바이올린을 만든 것일 뿐이라고 했지만 화자는 여기에 동의하지 않는다고 분명히 밝혔다. 음색이 좋은 바이올린을 만들기 위해서는 좋은 나무 외에도 필요한 것이 있다고 한 마지막 말은 스트라디바리우스가 바이올린에 대해 명인의 기술을 가졌다는 것을 함축한다. 그러므로 답은 (B)이다. (A)는 다른 사람들이 생각하는 바이다. (C)와 (D)는 틀린 말이다.

apparently 보아 하니

3. During World War II, there was something called the Holocaust. During this time, over 6 million Jewish men, women and children died. Hitler and his army, the Nazis, terrorized and killed as many Jews as they could from the countries that they invaded, such as Poland and other parts of Europe. Many of them were packed into trains that took them to a place called Auschwitz. There, the poor people were killed by putting them in gas chambers. It was a horrific piece of history that no one can or should forget.

제2차 세계 대전 동안, 홀로코스트라고 불리는 것이 있었다. 이 기간 동안, 6백만 명이 넘는 유대인 남자, 여자와 어린 아이들이 죽었다. 히틀러와 그의 군대 나치는 그들이 침공한 폴란드나 유럽의 다른 지역의 나라들에서 기능한 많은 유대인들을 공포에 떨게 하고, 죽였다. 그들 중의 다수는 기차에 실려져 아우슈비츠라는 곳으로 보내졌다. 거기서, 그 불쌍한 사람들은 가스실에 넣어져 학살당했다. 그것은 누구도 잊을 수 없고, 잊어서도 안 되는 끔찍한 역사의 일면이다.

•• 해설 ••

마지막 문장인 "It was a horrific piece of history that no one can or should forget."에서 선생님의 홀로코스트에 대한 태도가 나타나 있다.

terrorize 공포에 떨게 하다   invade 침공하다
pack into ~안에 집어 넣다   gas chamber 가스실
horrific 끔찍한

4. W: Don't you think that the chairs in our classes are uncomfortable?
M: Yes, you're right. The chairs are very hard and uncomfortable.
W: It's much worse for me because I have a bad back. I can't seem to get comfortable no matter what I do.
M: I know what you mean. I hate my physics class because Professor Jackson has very long lectures.
W: That sounds terrible. I think we should write a letter to the school about it.
M: You're right. Let's go and do that right now.

W: 우리 교실 의자가 불편하다고 생각 안 하니?
M: 어. 맞어. 의자가 너무 딱딱하고 불편해.
W: 나는 등이 아파서 훨씬 안 좋아. 어떻게 해도 편하게 안 되더라.
M: 무슨 말인지 알겠어. 잭슨 교수님이 수업을 너무 길게 하셔서 나는 물리학 수업이 너무 싫어.
W: 정말 끔찍하겠다. 우리가 학교에다가 편지를 쓰는 게 좋겠어.
M: 그래. 가서 지금 바로 그러자.

•• 해설 ••

남자는 여자의 말에 동의하고 있다. 의자가 불편한 것이 큰 문제가 되는 이유는 여자가 개인적으로 허리가 안 좋기 때문이다. 남자 역시 긴 수업을 들

어야 하기 때문에 의자가 불편한 것이 더욱 문제가 되는 것이다. 즉, 두 사람은 의자가 개선되어야 하는 이유를 가진 같은 입장에 서 있다.

5. The Underground Railroad is a large part of black history in America. But unlike the name, it does not involve trains or stations. It was the name of a movement in the 1800s to help runaway slaves reach the northern states, where slavery was banned. In those days, helping a runaway slave meant big trouble. Still, freed slaves, like Harriet Tubman, as well as other non-black Americans, helped many runaway slaves. Thanks to the Underground Railroad, thousands of blacks were free, and they, in turn, helped other runaway slaves. Without the Underground Railroad, the US might be a very different country today.

지하철은 미국의 흑인역사에서 큰 부분을 차지하고 있다. 그러나 그 이름과 달리, 그것은 기차나 역과는 관련이 없다. 그것은 1800년대에, 탈출한 노예들이 노예제가 금지되었던 북쪽의 주로 가는 것을 돕기 위한 운동의 이름이었다. 그 시대에, 탈출한 노예를 돕는 것은 엄청난 위험이 뒤따랐다. 그래도, 해리엇 터브만과 같이 자유의 몸이 된 노예들과 흑인이 아닌 다른 미국인들은 많은 도망 노예들을 도왔다. 지하철 덕에, 수천 명의 흑인들이 자유롭게 되었고, 그들은, 차례로, 다른 도망 노예들을 도와주었다. 지하철이 없었더라면, 미국은 오늘날 매우 다른 나라가 되었을 수도 있다.

•• 해설 ••

"The Underground Railroad is a large part of black history in America."라고 처음에 나와있다. (A), (B), (D)는 틀린 내용이다.

black history 흑인역사   runaway 달아난   ban 금지하다

6. W: Have you been to India?
   M: No, I haven't. I heard that there is nothing to see over there.
   W: You heard wrong. I just got back from India. It's a big country, and there are many things to see and experience.
   M: Really? What did you see while you were there?
   W: I went to the Taj Mahal, and then the Ganges River. There were so many people, and it was still very beautiful. After that, I went to a city called Bangalore. You really should go there too.
   M: Yes, I think I should, too. I've not seen you this happy before.

   W: 인도에 가본 적 있어?
   M: 아니, 없어. 거기엔 볼 게 없다고 하던데.
   W: 잘못 들은 거야. 내가 방금 인도에서 돌아왔거든. 인도는 매우 큰 나라고, 구경하고 경험할 것도 많아.
   M: 정말? 거기 있을 때 뭘 구경했었는데?
   W: 타지마할에 갔었고, 그 다음에는 갠지스강에도 갔었어. 사람이 엄청나게 많았는데, 그래도 정말 아름다웠어. 그 다음에는, 방갈로라는 도시에 갔어. 거기도 꼭 가봐야 해.
   M: 그래, 나도 가봐야 될 것 같아. 네가 이렇게 좋아해 하는걸 본 적이 없는걸.

   •• 해설 ••

   인도 여행을 방금 하고 돌아온 여자는 인도가 볼 것도 많고 아름다운 곳이라며 꼭 가볼 것을 권한다. 그러므로 답은 (D)이다.

7. George Orwell was the British writer who wrote *Animal Farm*. It is an interesting story of how a few animals chase a bad farmer away and try to run the farm themselves. In the end, the farm becomes even worse because of a bad leader. The book is really talking directly about Russia, and highlighted Stalin's mistakes. The Communist system probably became very unpopular because of the book. It became a classic, and is great to read at any time.

   조지 오웰은 「동물농장」을 쓴 영국의 작가였다. 그것은 몇 마리의 동물이 어떻게 나쁜 농장주를 몰아내고 농장을 스스로 운영하기를 시도했는지에 대한 재미있는 소설이다. 결국에, 농장은 나쁜 지도자 때문에 더 악화된다. 책은 실제 러시아에 대해 직접적으로 이야기하고 있고, 스탈린의 실패를 강조했다. 아마도 이 책 때문에 공산주의 체제는 점점 인기가 없어지게 되었다. 이것은 고전이 되었고, 언제 읽어도 좋은 책이다.

   •• 해설 ••

   처음에 "It is an interesting story ..."라고 했고 마지막에 "It became a classic, and is great to read at any time."이라고 했으므로 답은 (B)이다.

   chase away ~을 쫓아내다   Communist system 공산주의 체제

8. W: I don't know if I should stay in the dorms or if I should move out.
   M: I think it's great to stay in the dorms.
   W: Why do you think so? It's cheaper to live outside the campus.
   M: 🎧 Think about it. You're still new in school, aren't you?
   W: Well, I am still a freshman until the end of the year. I haven't made that many friends yet.
   M: That's reason enough, don't you think?
   W: I see what you mean. I've gotten a lot of help from my neighbors.

W: 기숙사에 남아야 할지, 이사를 해야 할지 모르겠어.
M: 내 생각엔 기숙사에 남는 게 좋을 것 같은데.
W: 왜 그렇게 생각해? 학교 밖에서 사는 게 더 싸잖아.
M: 생각해봐. 너는 아직 학교에서 새내기잖아, 안 그래?
W: 하긴, 연말까지는 아직 1학년이지. 아직 친구들도 많이 못 만들었고.
M: 그거면 충분한 이유가 되잖아, 안 그렇게 생각해?
W: 무슨 얘긴지 알겠어. 주변 친구들이 도움도 많이 주고 좋지.

•• 해 설 ••

여자가 일학년이고 아직 친구를 많이 못 사귀었다고 했을 때, 남자가 그 이유면 충분하다면서 계속 기숙사에 머물 것을 권한다. 그렇다면 기숙사에 사는 것이 친구를 사귀기에 좋다는 추론을 해 볼 수 있다.

9. T: What do you think are some easy languages to learn?
W: That's easy. I say Chinese, because the largest number of people use it.
M: Are you sure about that? I don't think that means it is easy to learn. Besides, Chinese writing is so difficult to learn.
T: The two of you have a good point. But when I said language, I meant both spoken and written forms. I guess I should have been clear on that.
W: Oh. I was only thinking of the spoken form.
M: In that case, I have no idea what the easiest language is.

T: 배우기 쉬운 언어에는 어떤 것들이 있을까요?
W: 그건 쉽죠. 저는 중국어 같아요. 왜냐면 가장 많은 사람들이 쓰는 말이니까요.
M: 정말 그렇게 생각해? 나는 그렇다고 그게 배우기 쉽다는 뜻은 아닌 것 같은데. 게다가, 중국 글자는 배우기 너무 어려워.
T: 두 사람 모두 일리가 있어요. 하지만 내가 언어라고 말한 것은 음성언어와 문자언어 모두를 의미한 거예요. 좀 더 정확히 말할 걸 그랬나?
W: 아. 저는 음성언어만 생각하고 있었어요.
M: 그런 경우라면, 저는 제일 쉬운 언어가 무엇인지 모르겠습니다.

•• 해 설 ••

배우기 쉬운 언어에 대해 말하는 도중 남자와 여자의 대화가 엇갈리는 이유는 언어의 음성언어와 문자언어를 구분하지 않은 채 자기 생각을 말했기 때문이다. 선생님은 음성언어와 문자언어를 모두 포함한다고 확실히 말했어야 한다며 자신의 잘못을 시인하고 있다.

Listening Practice 1 p.73

1. (A), (C)   2. (C)   3. (B)

M: Hello. How may I help you?
W: Hi. I have a few questions about studying abroad. I have been thinking about going abroad for a long time but can't make up my mind about where to go.
M: Well, have you at least chosen a continent or do you want to travel the world?
W: No … I want to go to Europe but I just can't decide which country. I am wondering if I should go to a country where I don't have any problem with the language or go to a place where I will have to learn the language.
M: Alright. I am guessing that England is one of your choices. So what are your other choices?
W: I know a little French and less Italian. If I chose either country, I would have to take language courses first.
M: What is your major?
W: I am an English major. But I also have taken a course on French cinema and one on Italian art. Since I am a literature major, I am leaning more towards going to France and studying French literature.
M: That's not a bad idea. I think going to Italy is a great idea too, but I want to suggest you go somewhere that is going to help you with your studies. French literature is very important and you will benefit if you study it. So, as hard as French is, it might be worth it.
W: Yes, thank you. You really have been a great help.
M: Glad to have helped. Take care and let me know of your decision.

M: 안녕하세요. 어떻게 도와드릴까요?
W: 안녕하세요. 유학에 대해서 몇 가지 궁금한 점이 있어요. 오랫동안 해외에 있을 계획인데, 어디로 가야 할지 결정을 못하겠어요.
M: 그렇다면, 최소한 대륙은 결정하셨나요. 아니면 세계를 돌아다니실 생각이신가요?
W: 아니요… 저는 유럽으로 가고 싶은데, 단지 어떤 나라로 갈지를 못 정하겠어요. 언어 문제가 없는 나라로 가야 할지 아니면 새로 언어를 배워야 되는 곳으로 가야 할지 의문이에요.
M: 그래요. 영국이 하나의 선택이 될 수 있을 것 같군요. 그럼 또 다른 선택은 뭐가 있을까요?
W: 프랑스어를 조금 할 줄 알고, 이탈리아어는 거의 못해요. 어느 나라를 고르더라도, 언어 강의를 먼저 들어야 될 거예요.
M: 전공은 뭐죠?
W: 저는 영어 전공이에요. 하지만 프랑스 영화에 대한 강의랑 이탈리아 미술에 관한 강의도 들었어요. 제가 문학 전공자이기 때문에, 프랑스에 가서 프랑스 문학을 공부하는 쪽으로 더 기울고 있어요.
M: 그것도 나쁜 생각은 아니죠. 이탈리아에 가는 것도 좋은 생각이지만, 저는 학생이 공부하는데 도움이 되는 곳으로 가는 것을 제안하고 싶군요. 프랑

스 문학은 아주 중요하고, 그걸 공부하면 유익할 거예요. 그러니까, 프랑스어가 어렵겠지만, 그것이 그만큼의 값을 할 거예요.
W: 네, 고맙습니다. 정말 도움이 많이 됐어요.
M: 도움이 돼서 기쁩니다. 잘 지내시고, 학생의 결정에 대해서 저한테도 알려주세요.

•• 해설 ••

1. 전공이 뭐냐는 질문에 "I am an English major. But I also have taken a course on French cinema and in Italian arts."라고 답했다.

2. 여자는 유학을 어디로 가야 할지 몰라서 남자를 찾아온 것이다. 최소한 어느 대륙으로 갈 지는 결정했냐는 남자의 말을 통해 장소가 우선 결정이 되어야 한다는 것을 알 수 있다. 무엇을 공부할지는 그 다음에 나온 얘기다. 그러므로 가장 먼저 결정해야 할 것은 (C)의 여자가 가고 싶은 나라이다. 여자가 외국에서 공부하려는 것은 확실하므로 (B)는 답이 될 수 없다.

3. 남자는 여자가 유학을 가는 데에 필요한 여러 가지 조언을 해주고 있다. 여자가 유학을 어디로 가야 할지 모르겠다고 하자 그렇다면 구체적이지는 않더라도 어느 방향으로 가고 싶은지 대강의 생각을 알고 싶은 것이다. 그래야 거기에 맞춰서 여자를 도와줄 수 있다. 그러므로 답은 (B)이다.

continent 대륙   literature 문학   benefit 유익하다

Listening Practice 2   p.75

1. (D)   2. Yes: (B), (C) / No: (A), (D)   3. (D)

Violins are popular in classical music, and famous classical music composers have all used violins in their music at one time or another. It is considered to be one of the hardest instruments to play, yet the most beautiful sounding. Players use a bow made of horsehair, and drag it on any of the 4 strings. Different tones are made by pressing the string to the fingerboard with our fingers. So what makes the violin sound so special?

The first answer might be obvious to some. It is the overall shape of the violin. The two long f-shaped holes on each side of the strings allow sound waves to vibrate the top plate just enough. The holes also limit the sound waves from escaping too quickly. As a result, the overall shape of the violin body, the size and placement of the holes are all highly important in making sure that violins sound beautiful.

🎧 Since violins rely on vibrating the body, getting the correct balance of thickness is very important. If the body is too thick, it will not vibrate properly. On the other hand, if the body is too thin, the sound waves might shake the body too much and cause unwanted noise, not to mention a very weak violin. In addition, different wood has different strength and different vibration characteristics.

바이올린은 서양 클래식음악에서 널리 쓰이는 악기이고, 유명한 서양 클래식음악 작곡가들은 모두 그들의 음악에서 바이올린을 한번이나 그 이상 사용했다. 그것은 연주하기 가장 어려운 악기 중 하나로 여겨지지만, 가장 아름다운 소리를 낸다. 연주자들은 말총으로 만든 활을 사용해 4개의 현을 문지른다. 서로 다른 음색은 손가락으로 현을 지판에 눌러 닿게 함으로써 만들어진다. 그렇다면 무엇이 바이올린의 소리를 특별하게 만드는 걸까?

첫 번째 답은 일부에게는 명백할 수 있다. 그것은 바이올린의 전체적 생김새이다. 현 양쪽의 긴 f자 모양으로 생긴 두 개의 구멍은 음파가 상판을 충분히 진동시킬 수 있도록 해준다. 그 구멍은 또한 음파가 너무 빨리 새어 나가는 것을 막아준다. 결과적으로, 몸통의 전체적인 생김새, 구멍의 크기와 위치는 모두 바이올린의 소리를 아름답게 만드는데 있어 아주 중요하다.

바이올린의 소리는 몸통의 진동이 매우 중요하기 때문에, 두께의 적당한 균형을 유지해야 한다. 몸통이 너무 두꺼우면, 제대로 진동하지 않을 것이다. 반면에, 몸통이 너무 얇으면, 아주 약한 바이올린은 말할 나위도 없이, 음파가 몸통을 너무 많이 흔들어서, 원하지 않은 소음을 발생시키게 된다. 덧붙이자면, 서로 다른 종류의 목재는 서로 다른 강도와 서로 다른 진동 특성을 갖는다.

•• 해설 ••

1. 구멍의 역할은 크게 두 가지이다. 하나는 음파가 상판을 충분히 진동시킬 수 있도록 해주는 것이고 다른 하나는 음파가 너무 빨리 새어나가는 것을 막는 것이다. "The hole also limits the sound waves from escaping too quickly."라고 말했으므로 답은 (D)이다.

2. 첫 문단에서 무엇이 바이올린의 소리를 특별하게 만드는가 하는 의문을 던지자 다음 문단들에서 그 답을 준다. 하나는 둘째 문단에 나온 바이올린의 전체적 생김새이고, 다른 하나는 셋째 문단에서 제시된 나무 두께의 적당한 균형이다.

3. 나무 두께에 대한 설명을 하다가 나무마다 강도나 진동의 특성이 다르다는 말을 덧붙였다. 즉, 나무의 특성에 따라 바이올린의 소리가 달라진다는 뜻이다. 그러므로 답은 (D)이다. 나무마다 특성이 다르다고 했으므로 같은 종류의 나무를 사용해야 한다는 (B)는 답이 아니다.

composer 작곡가   instrument 악기   bow 활
drag 천천히 움직이다   string 현   fingerboard 지판

Listening Practice 3   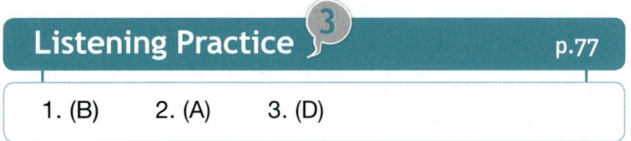   p.77

1. (B)   2. (A)   3. (D)

Hello, class. Today we are going to talk about a well known country, Japan. You all know about the big electronics giants. What about Japanese carmakers? Right now, they are world-class, but I can remember a time when Americans were against buying Japanese cars. People started campaigns to make people buy cars made in the USA. Now, things are different. Many Americans own Japanese cars.

Japan and the US have always had an awkward relationship. This is so because Americans felt threatened by the Japanese long ago. This was mainly due to the sudden attack on Pearl Harbor. During the war, Americans didn't trust Japanese-Americans, fearing that they were spying for Japan.

After World War II, the US became the most powerful country in the world. They had won the war and had become rich through the war. But many things slowed down the US, such as the Vietnam War. Americans wasted a lot of money, energy and effort in the Vietnam War. In the 1980s, Japan emerged as a major superpower with powerful companies that slowly but surely overtook many industries.

Americans were desperate to find out the Japanese formula for success, and in the process also made fun of them. They ridiculed them as robots who didn't know how to enjoy life. It was racist of Americans to characterize Japanese in such a way.

I see that we don't have any more time. We will continue our discussion next week.

여러분 안녕하세요. 오늘 우리는 잘 알려진 나라인 일본에 대해서 이야기를 하겠어요. 여러분은 모두 거대한 전자 대기업들을 알고 있어요. 일본의 자동차 제조사들은 어떻죠? 현재 그들은 세계 수준이지만, 저는 미국인들이 일제 자동차 구입에 반대하던 때가 기억이 나는군요. 사람들은 미국에서 만들어진 차를 구입하게 하려는 운동을 시작했죠. 이제 모두가 달라졌어요. 많은 미국 사람들이 일제 자동차를 갖고 있죠.

미일관계는 늘 어색했어요. 이것은 미국인들이 오래 전 일본인들로부터 위협을 느꼈었기 때문이죠. 이는 주로 진주만의 기습 때문이에요. 전쟁 중에, 미국인들은 일본계 미국인들이 일본을 위해 간첩 활동을 하고 있다고 염려해서 그들을 믿지 않았었죠.

제2차 세계 대전 후, 미국은 세계에서 가장 강력한 국가가 되었습니다. 그들은 전쟁에서 승리했고, 전쟁을 통해 부강해졌습니다. 그러나 베트남 전쟁과 같은 많은 것들이 미국의 성장에 방해가 됐어요. 미국인들은 많은 돈, 에너지를 베트남 전쟁에서 낭비했어요. 1980년대에, 일본의 기업들이 느리지만 확고하게 여러 산업을 장악하면서 일본은 주요 강대국으로 부상하기 시작했습니다.

미국인들은 일본의 성공 비결을 몹시도 알아내고 싶었고, 동시에 일본인들을 조롱하기도 했습니다. 그들은 일본인들을 인생을 즐길 줄 모르는 로봇들이라고 조롱했죠. 그런 식으로 일본인들을 판단한 걸 보면 미국인들도 인종 차별주의적인 편견으로 가득차 있었죠.

시간이 없는 것 같군요. 토론은 다음 주에 계속하겠습니다.

•• 해설 ••

1. 미국과 일본의 관계에 관한 강의인데 (C)와 (D)는 일본만 나와 있으므로 답이 아니다. (A)는 너무 광범위한 데다가 본 강의의 핵심을 담고 있지 않다. 미국과 일본이 어색한 관계를 갖게 된 연유를 역사적 배경을 들어 설명하고 있으므로 (B)가 답이다.

2. "Americans felt threatened by the Japanese long ago. This was mainly due to the sudden attack on Pearl Harbor."을 통해 (A)가 답임을 알 수 있다.

3. "They(Americans) ridiculed them(Japanese) as robots who didn't know how to enjoy life. It was racist of Americans to characterize Japanese in such a way."를 통해 선생님은 일본인에 대한 미국인의 행동이 옳지 않았다고 생각한다는 것을 알 수 있다.

awkward 어색한, 불편한   slow down (속도·진행을)늦추다
emerge 부상하다   desperate to 간절히 원하는
formula 공식, 방식   ridicule 조롱하다   racist 인종 차별주의적인

iBT Practice   p.79

1. (A)   2. (D)   3. (C)   4. (D)

M: Hey, Wilma. I got a question for you.
W: What is it?
M: 🎧 I heard someone mention something about urban legends. What are they?
W: They are short and mostly untrue stories, made to scare other people.
M: Why would anyone want to do that?
W: I don't know what to tell you. But there are many of them.
M: Could you tell me one?
W: Sure. Here's one that I just heard. If you put a human tooth in a glass, fill it with cola and leave it for one week, the cola will melt the tooth.
M: Yes, isn't that true? I heard that cola is like acid. It might even kill us.
W: No, it's not. It's totally false. Many people tried it, but no one has managed to do it. Cola is no worse than normal candy. It can't even change the color of the tooth to black.
M: Are you serious? That's news to me. Tell me another one.

W: Alright. Hmm ... Did you hear about the alligator living in the sewers of New York City?
M: I think I did. Didn't they catch a really big alligator down there? They said it was nearly 5 meters long!
W: That's another false story. Nobody caught any alligator in the sewers of New York, or any other sewage system.
M: Wow, and I thought all those stories were true. How do these urban legends spread?
W: There are many ways, but the most popular way is, of course, the internet. People send urban legends to other friends, thinking that they are real. Soon, the whole world thinks that a made-up story is real.

M: 얘, 윌마. 너한테 물어볼 것이 있어.
W: 뭔데?
M: 누가 도시전설이라는 것에 대해서 언급하는 걸 들었어. 그게 뭐야?
W: 짧고, 대부분 거짓인 이야기들이야. 사람들을 겁주려고 만든거지.
M: 왜 그런 걸 하고 싶어할까?
W: 어떻게 말해줘야 할지 모르겠다. 하여튼, 그런 전설은 많이 있어.
M: 하나만 얘기해 줄 수 있어?
W: 그래. 나도 최근에 들은 거야. 사람의 이를 잔 속에 넣고, 콜라로 채운 다음 한 주 동안 놔두면, 콜라가 이를 녹여버린대.
M: 그래, 그거 사실 아니야? 나는 콜라가 산 같은 거라고 들었는데. 그럼 우릴 죽일 수도 있겠다.
W: 아니, 사실이 아니야. 완전히 잘못된 거야. 많은 사람들이 해 봤는데, 아무도 성공을 못했어. 콜라는 보통 사탕보다도 해롭지 않아. 이의 색깔을 검정으로 바꾸지도 못 해.
M: 정말이야? 나한테는 새로운데. 다른 것도 얘기해주라.
W: 그래. 음… 뉴욕 시(市) 하수도에 사는 악어에 대해서 들어 봤어?
M: 들은 것 같아. 그 밑에서 정말 큰 악어가 잡히지 않았었나? 거의 5미터 길이라고 했어!
W: 그것 또한 잘못된 얘기야. 아무도 뉴욕의 하수도나 다른 곳의 하수도에서 악어를 잡은 적이 없어.
M: 와, 나는 그런 얘기들이 사실인줄 알았는데. 이런 도시전설들이 어떻게 퍼지는 걸까?
W: 여러가지 방법이 있는데, 가장 흔한 방법은, 당연히 인터넷이야. 사람들은 진짜인 줄 알고 도시전설을 다른 친구들한테 보내. 곧 있으면, 전 세계가 지어낸 얘기를 진짜인 줄로 알게 되지.

•• 해설 ••

1. M: Hey, Wilma. I got a question for you.
   W: What is it?
   M: I heard someone mention something about urban legends. What are they?
   남자는 도시 전설이 무엇인지 물어보려고 여자에게 말을 걸었으므로 답은 (A)이다.

2. 콜라 속에 일주일 동안 이를 담가 놓으면 이가 녹는다는 것은 도시 전설의 예로서 전혀 사실이 아니라고 말한다. 콜라는 이의 색깔을 검정으로 바꾸지도 못하며 당연히 사람을 죽이지도 않는다. 그러므로 (A), (B), (C)는 모두 틀린 답이다. "Cola is no worse than normal candy."라고 했으므로 답은 (D)이다.

3. 왜 사람들을 겁주려고 도시 전설을 만드냐는 질문에 여자는 뭐라고 답해야 할지 모르겠다고 말했다. 말 그대로 잘 모르기 때문에 대답하기가 곤란한 것일 뿐이다. (D)와 같은 다른 이유가 있었는데 표면적으로 그렇게 대답한 것이라면 그 근거가 대화에 드러나 있어야 한다.

4. "There are many ways, but the most popular way is, of course, the internet"이라고 말했다.

urban 도시의   legend 전설   melt 녹이다   acid 산
that's news to me 금시초문이다   alligator 악어
sewer 하수구   spread 퍼지다   made-up 지어낸

Further Study   p.81

Topic : Urban legends
= short and mostly untrue stories

– Purpose : to scare other people
– Examples :
  • Putting a human tooth in cola
  • Alligator living in the sewers of NY
– How they spread : through the internet

Word Review   p.82

1. (D)   2. (A)   3. (C)   4. (C)
5. apparently   6. horrific
7. runaway   8. continent
9. literature   10. awkward
11. racist   12. urban

Part C 5. Organization

Sample Question   p.87

뱀은 파충류과에 속해있다. 그러나 뱀은 진화라고 불리는 과정을 통해 다리를 잃었다. 그것과는 상관없이, 뱀은 아직도 거친 피부와 긴 혀, 그리고 꼬리를 갖고 있다. 그런데, 그들은 먹이를 잡는 방법에 있어서 다르다.

대부분의 뱀은 먹이를 잡는데 입을 사용한다. 그들은 날카로운 이빨을 사용해 동물을 문다. 많은 뱀들은 독액을 갖고 있어서, 동물을 물 때 독을 주입한다. 그 독액은 동물의 심장을 멈추게 하고, 뱀은 먹이를 천천히 먹을 수 있게 된다.

아나콘다들은 약간 다르다. 그들 역시도 큰 이빨을 갖고 있고, 가끔은 입으로 공격한다. 그러나, 아나콘다는 먹이를 졸라 죽이는 뱀이다. 그것들은 독액이 없다. 이것은, 아나콘다가 물어서 독액을 주입하는 대신에, 동물의 둘레에 그 두꺼운 몸통을 감아서 조른다는 것을 의미한다. 그것들은 동물이 숨을 못 쉬어 빨리 죽도록 매우 세게 조른다.

Building Skills   p.88

Understanding Relationships

1. (B)   2. Q1. categorization
          Q2. definition
          Q3. exemplification

1. W: Did you bring your jogging shoes?
   M: Are there special shoes for jogging?
   W: Of course. There are many different types of shoes now.
   M: I don't understand.
   W: Take a look at soccer, for example. They need to run on grass, right? So they have spikes on their shoes.
   M: But that's only one sport. How about others?
   W: Oh, there's more. There are different shoes for ballet, for instance. I remember another one. Basketball shoes are very comfortable and light.
   M: Now that you mention it, I guess you're right. I think my shoes are basketball shoes.

   W: 너 조깅화 가져왔어?
   M: 조깅용 신발이 따로 있어?
   W: 당연하지. 요즘에는 신발 종류가 얼마나 많은데.
   M: 나는 이해가 안 되는데.
   W: 예를 들어서, 축구를 봐. 잔디 위에서 뛰어야 되잖아, 그렇지? 그래서 그 사람들은 스파이크가 달린 신을 신는 거야.
   M: 그건 겨우 한 가지 예 밖에 없어? 다른 종목들은?
   W: 아, 더 있지. 예를 들면, 발레용 신발도 있어. 또 다른 것도 생각난다. 농구화는 아주 편하고 가벼워.
   M: 네 말을 들으니, 맞는 것 같다. 내 신발은 농구화인 것 같아.

2. There are literally billions of animals in the world, including insects and bugs. But we can group them into three categories, depending on what they eat. The three groups are called herbivores, carnivores and omnivores. Herbivores are animals that only eat plants. Many of these animals have multiple stomachs. Carnivores are animals that only eat meat. Lions and tigers are well-known carnivores. Omnivores are animals that eat both meat and plants. Most humans are omnivores, although some only eat plants. We call them vegetarians.

   곤충과 벌레들을 포함해, 지구에는 말 그대로 수십억 종류의 동물이 있다. 그러나 우리는 그들이 먹는 먹이에 따라 세 집단으로 나눌 수 있다. 그 세 집단은 육식동물, 초식동물, 잡식동물이라고 불린다. 초식동물은 식물만을 먹는 동물이다. 많은 초식동물들이 여러 개의 위를 갖고 있다. 육식동물은 동물성 먹이만을 먹는 동물이다. 사자와 호랑이가 잘 알려진 육식동물이다. 잡식동물은 동물성과 식물성 먹이를 모두 먹는 동물이다. 비록 일부 사람들은 채소만을 먹지만, 대부분의 사람은 잡식성이다. 우리는 그런 사람들을 채식주의자라고 부른다.

Understanding Purpose in Organization

1. Q1. (A)   2. Q1. (B)
   Q2. (D)   Q2. (A)

1. W: Did you read *Native Son*?
   M: No, what is it?
   W: It's an American classic. A very famous African American named Richard Wright wrote the book.
   M: What kind of person was he?
   W: His grandparents were slaves. He wanted to tell the world that it was hard living in America as an African American.
   M: So how did he get famous?
   W: He participated in a story writing competition. He wrote many short stories and sent them in. Most of his stories are classics even today.

W: 「흑인의 아들」읽어봤니?
M: 아니. 그게 뭔데?
W: 미국의 명작이야. 리차드 라이트라는 유명한 아프리카계 미국인이 그 책을 썼어.
M: 그 사람이 어떤 사람이었는데?
W: 그 사람의 조부모가 노예였어. 그는 미국에서 아프리카계 미국인으로 사는 것이 어렵다는 것을 세계에 이야기하고 싶어했지.
M: 그럼 그가 어떻게 유명해진 거야?
W: 문예 창작 대회에 나갔었대. 짧은 소설을 많이 써서 보냈어. 그 소설 대부분들은 오늘날에도 명작으로 평가받지.

2. Gilbert Stuart is a famous American painter. He painted people's faces very well. He used good brushwork and bright colors in his paintings. His most famous painting is the head of George Washington.

Now, Gilbert's life was unusual. He was born in America, and later he studied in London. After 6 years, he came back and opened a gallery. It was successful, but he wasted his money away in just 5 years. He went to Ireland and came back to America when he was 41 years old. Only then did he become America's most famous portrait painter.

길버트 스튜어트는 유명한 미국 화가이다. 그는 사람들의 얼굴을 잘 그렸다. 그는 그의 그림에서 뛰어난 붓 놀림과 밝은 색깔들을 사용했다. 그의 그림 중의 가장 유명한 것은 조지 워싱턴의 초상이다.

그런데. 길버트의 삶은 약간 특이했다. 그는 미국에서 태어나서 이후에 런던에서 공부했다. 6년 후. 그는 돌아와서 화랑을 열었다. 성공적이었지만. 그는 그의 돈을 5년 만에 탕진해버렸다. 그는 아일랜드로 갔다가 마흔 한 살에 미국으로 돌아왔다. 그때서야 그는 미국에서 가장 유명한 초상화가가 되었다.

Basic Drills   p.90

1. (B)   2. (D)   3. (D)   4. (C)   5. (A)
6. (A)   7. (C)   8. (D)   9. (C)

1. W: I learned about symbiosis today.
M: What's that?
W: It's where different animals help each other, like partners. Take a look at alligators. Have you seen one before?
M: Sure. I've seen them on television.
W: Well, do you remember seeing birds around alligators? They help each other.
M: How can such small animals help such big and mean animals?
W: When alligators open their mouth, the birds eat the food between their teeth.
M: And the alligator doesn't eat the bird?
W: No. The birds are so helpful that the alligators only protect the birds.

W: 오늘 공생에 대해서 배웠어.
M: 그게 뭐야?
W: 서로 다른 동물들이 동반자처럼 서로를 돕는 거야. 악어를 봐. 악어 본 적 있어?
M: 물론. 텔레비전에서 봤지.
W: 그럼. 악어 주변의 새들을 본 기억은 나? 그들은 서로를 돕는다구.
M: 어떻게 그렇게 작은 동물이 그렇게 크고 사나운 동물을 도울 수 있지?
W: 악어가 입을 벌리면. 새들이 이빨 사이의 음식을 먹는 거야.
M: 그리고 악어는 새들을 안 잡아먹고?
W: 응. 새들이 너무 많은 도움이 되니까 악어들은 새들을 보호해줄 따름이야.

•• 해 설 ••
공생을 설명하기 위해 악어와 새를 예로 들었다.

symbiosis 공생

2. Computers are one of the most important machines that we use today. They are everywhere. However, computers were not popular in the beginning.

Long ago, computers were big and expensive calculators. Then, people started using them to store information. They used an old punch card system instead of keyboards. As computers started getting cheaper, many companies started buying them for their business. Soon, computers were used to make video games. Finally, computers were cheap enough for many people to buy and use at home.

컴퓨터는 오늘날 우리가 사용하는 가장 중요한 기계들 중의 하나이다. 그것들은 널리 사용되고 있다. 그러나. 초기에 컴퓨터는 대중적이지 않았다.

오래전. 컴퓨터는 거대하고 비싼 계산기였다. 이후. 사람들은 정보를 저장하기 위해 그것들을 사용하기 시작했다. 그들은 키보드 대신에 구식의 천공카드 방식을 사용했다. 컴퓨터의 값이 싸지게 되면서. 많은 회사들이 업무에 사용하기 위해 그것들을 구입하기 시작했다. 곧. 컴퓨터는 비디오 게임을 만드는데 사용되었다. 결국. 컴퓨터는 많은 사람들이 구입해 집에서 사용할 수 있을 정도로 충분히 값이 내리게 되었다.

•• 해 설 ••
과거와 현재에 따른 컴퓨터의 변화를 설명하고 있다. 단순히 컴퓨터의 종류를 열거한 것이 아니라 어떻게 변화되었는지를 말하고 있으므로 (C)는 답이라고 보기 어렵다.

3. The concept of business is really easier than what people think. We will talk about how the prices of things are determined. It all depends on two things called supply and demand. Supply is controlled by the companies. Demand is controlled by the buyers. We can draw them on a graph. When these two lines meet on the graph, the price is chosen. Popular products have a high demand, so prices rise.

비지니스의 개념은 사람들이 생각하는 것보다 정말 쉽다. 우리는 어떻게 가격이 결정되는지에 대해서 이야기할 것이다. 가격은 공급과 수요라는 두 가지에 의해서 결정된다. 공급은 기업들에 의해서 조절된다. 수요는 구매자들에 의해서 조절된다. 우리는 그것들을 한 그래프에 그릴 수 있다. 이 두 선들이 그래프 상에서 만나면, 가격이 결정된다. 인기 있는 상품들은 높은 수요를 가지고, 따라서 가격이 오른다.

•• 해설 ••

가격은 수요와 공급이 만나는 지점에서 결정된다고 했다. 그래프를 언급한 이유는 이를 통해 학생들이 개념을 더 쉽게 이해할 수 있게 하려는 것이다. 학생들을 테스트하려는 것도, 다른 개념을 소개하려는 것도, 기업의 중요성을 강조하려는 것도 아니므로 (A), (B), (C)는 답이 아니다.

determine 결정하다   supply 공급   demand 수요

4. W: Did you go to sleep last night?
M: No, I didn't. I stayed up all night studying for the history test.
W: Me too. I think everyone is worried about the test. I have trouble remembering the names of old Egyptian kings.
M: What do you mean, Egyptian kings? Rebecca told me that the test will be about England.
W: Oh, I think you heard it wrong. Mr. Green reminded us to remember the Egyptian names for the test. You know, like King Tutankhamen.
M: Oh, no. I am in so much trouble now.

W: 어제 밤에 잠은 잤니?
M: 아니. 역사 시험 공부하느라고 밤을 샜어.
W: 나도 그랬어. 내 생각에는 다들 그 시험 걱정하는 것 같아. 나는 고대 이집트 왕들 이름 외우는 것이 힘들어.
M: 이집트 왕이라니 무슨 소리야? 리베카가 말하기로는 시험은 영국에 대해서라던데?
W: 아, 네가 잘못 들은 걸 거야. 그린 선생님이 시험에 대비해서 이집트 이름을 외우라고 일러주셨거든. 투탕카멘 왕 같이.
M: 아, 안돼. 나는 이제 큰일 났다.

•• 해설 ••

두 사람은 시험 범위에 대해 얘기하고 있다. 남자가 시험이 영국에 관해서 나온다고 하자 여자가 그렇지 않다고 말한다. 여자는 선생님이 투탕카멘 같은 이집트 왕 이름을 외우라고 했다면서 자신의 의견을 주장한다.

5. Every child in the world goes to school. But the opening season of school can be a little different. For instance, students in US schools start a new school year in September, after the summer holiday. But Korean students start a new school year in March, after the winter holiday. The holidays are also longer just before the start of the new school year. Korean students rest longer during winter, and US students rest more in the summer.

세계의 모든 어린이들은 학교에 간다. 그러나 학교의 개학 시기는 약간씩 다를 수 있다. 예를 들어, 미국 학교의 학생들은 새 학년을 여름 방학 후인 9월에 시작한다. 그러나 한국 학생들은 겨울 방학 후인 3월에 새 학년을 시작한다. 새 학년 직전의 방학은 또한 더 길다. 한국 학생들은 겨울에 더 오래 쉬고, 미국 학생들은 여름에 더 오래 쉰다.

•• 해설 ••

세계의 모든 아이들이 학교에 가지만 학교 시스템은 각기 다르다는 것을 말하고 있다.

6. T: Everyone knows petroleum is energy. But does anyone know other types of energy?
W: Yes, my calculator runs on solar power.
M: What's that?
W: It means that it gets power from the sun and not from batteries.
T: That's right. The calculator has a small panel called a solar cell. The cell converts light into energy.
M: That's great. It means free energy.
T: Well, yes, it's free. Unfortunately, solar cells are very expensive. They also take time to make power. But one day, we might use light as energy more than petroleum.

T: 모든 사람들은 석유가 에너지라는 것을 알고 있습니다. 그런데 다른 종류의 에너지를 아는 사람이 있습니까?
W: 예, 제 계산기는 태양 에너지로 작동돼요.
M: 그게 뭐지?
W: 태양으로부터 전력을 얻는다는 뜻이야.
T: 맞습니다. 계산기에는 태양전지라고 불리는 작은 판들이 있습니다. 이 전지들이 빛을 에너지로 변환하죠.
M: 와 그거 대단하네요. 공짜 에너지잖아요.

T: 글쎄. 그렇죠. 공짜예요. 불행히도, 태양전지는 매우 비쌉니다. 전력을 만드는데 시간도 걸리고요. 그러나 언젠가는 석유보다도 빛을 에너지로 더 많이 사용하게 될 겁니다.

•• 해 설 ••

태양 에너지의 장점과 단점을 설명하고 있으므로 답은 (A)이다. 장점은 공짜라는 것이고 단점은 설비가 비싸고 전력을 만들기까지 시간이 걸린다는 점이다. (C)를 보자면 태양전지를 배터리와 비교한 것이 아니라 태양전지 자체의 특징을 설명한 것이므로 답이 아니다.

solar 태양의   panel 판   convert 변환하다

7. W: How do speakers make noise?
   M: That's easy. Music is electrical signals. The audio amplifiers change music to electric signals. This goes to the speaker's voice coil. They are really just wires in circles. Electricity passes from one end to the other end.
   W: Then what happens?
   M: The magnets will push and pull on the voice coil, depending on the electric signal.
   W: So is that sound?
   M: Yes, sort of. The voice coil is on the speaker cone. The cones move very quickly and push the air. Moving air quickly makes sound.
   W: Wow, that's so interesting!

   W: 스피커는 어떻게 소리를 낼까?
   M: 쉬워. 음악은 전기적 신호야. 오디오 증폭기가 음악을 전기적 신호로 바꾸지. 이것이 스피커의 음성코일로 이동해. 그건 그냥 둥글게 되어 있는 전선이야. 전기가 한쪽 끝에 서 다른 쪽 끝으로 전달돼.
   W: 그 다음에는 어떻게 돼?
   M: 자석들이 전기 신호에 따라서 음성코일 위에서 밀거나 당기지.
   W: 그럼 그게 소리야?
   M: 어, 그렇다고 할 수 있어. 음성코일은 스피커 콘 위에 있어. 콘이 매우 빨리 움직여서 공기를 밀어내서 소리를 만들지.
   W: 와, 그거 참 신기하다!

•• 해 설 ••

남자는 스피커가 음악을 어떻게 소리로 바꾸는지 단계를 차례대로 설명하고 있으므로 답은 (C)이다. 여성이 "Then what happens?"를 묻는걸 보아도 시간적 순서로 설명하고 있음을 알 수 있다.

amplifier 증폭기   depending on ~에 따라

8. Spiders live in many different places around the world. There are even spiders that live under water. The water spider or the diving bell spider builds a house under water. Their house looks like a bell, and the spider brings fresh air into the house by trapping air between the hairs on its body.
   The spider sits in the bell-shaped house, looking for food. When the spider catches food, the spider brings food back to the bell and eats in the house. They don't need to come up to the surface much at all!

   거미는 세계 곳곳의 여러 다른 장소에서 서식한다. 심지어 물 속에 사는 거미도 있다. 물거미, 즉 잠수종 거미는 수중에 집을 짓는다. 그 집은 종처럼 생겼고, 거미는 몸의 털 사이에 신선한 공기를 가둬서 집까지 가져온다.
   거미는 종처럼 생긴 집에 앉아서 먹이를 찾는다. 먹이를 잡으면, 거미는 집까지 먹이를 가지고 가서 먹는다. 그것들은 표면으로 올라올 필요가 거의 없다!

•• 해 설 ••

물 속에 사는 거미들이 어떻게 사는지 설명했으므로 (D)가 정답이다. 거미가 먹는 음식의 종류나 왜 거미가 물 속에 살아야 하는지는 언급이 없으므로 (A)와 (C)는 답이 될 수 없다. 물 속 거미의 특성을 설명했을 뿐 다른 거미들과 비교한 바는 없기 때문에 (B) 역시 답이 아니다.

trap 가두다

9. T: Writing a diary on the internet, or blogging, is a popular activity. How many have a blog?
   W: I do. I write in it every day. I share my blog with many people.
   M: I don't like blogs. I think they are silly.
   W: Why? There's nothing wrong with expressing ourselves.
   M: It's not people expressing themselves that bothers me.
   T: Then what don't you like about blogging?
   M: Well, it gives me the feeling that I am checking up on other people.
   W: Don't be silly. People write on blogs because they want others to see.
   M: Still, you don't know who is looking at your blogs.
   T: You have a point. Some people do not like writing blogs because it takes away their privacy.

   T: 인터넷에 일기를 쓰는 것, 즉 블로깅은 인기 있는 활동입니다. 몇 명이나 블로그를 갖고 있나요?
   W: 저요. 저는 매일 써요. 여러 사람들하고 블로그를 공유합니다.
   M: 저는 블로그가 싫어요. 제 생각에는 바보 같아요.
   W: 왜? 스스로를 표현하는 거는 잘못된 것이 아니야.

M: 나는 스스로를 표현하는 것이 신경 쓰이는 게 아닌데.
T: 그럼 블로깅의 어떤점이 싫은가요?
M: 글쎄. 다른 사람을 조사하고 있다는 느낌이 들게 해요.
W: 바보같이 굴지마. 사람들은 다른 이들에게 보여주려고 블로그에 글을 쓰는 거야.
M: 그렇다 해도, 네 블로그를 누가 보고 있는지는 모르잖아.
T: 일리가 있군요. 어떤 사람들은 사생활을 침해 당한다며 블로그에 글을 쓰는 것을 좋아하지 않습니다.

•• 해 설 ••

남자는 블로깅을 싫어하는 이유가 누군지도 모르는 사람들이 자기 글을 읽는 게 싫어서라고 말했다. 선생님은 이를 마지막에 잘 요약하고 있다. 즉, 몇몇 사람들은 사생활 침해를 우려하여 블로깅을 싫어한다고 말이다. 다시 말해, 사생활은 블로깅의 문제점을 잘 지적한 단어이다.

express oneself 자신을 표현하다
check up on somebody (비밀리에) ~에 대한 정보를 알아내다

Listening Practice 1 p.93

1. (C)   2. (B)   3. (C)

M: Did you get a locker this semester?
W: Yes, I did. I got a half-sized locker.
M: Me, too. Which floor is your locker on?
W: It is on the second floor. Why do you ask?
M: I asked for a locker about two months ago, but I got a locker on the 5th floor.
W: So what's wrong with that?
M: All my classes this semester are on the ground floor. It'll be a problem because I hurt my legs last month. I can't walk up the stairs all the time.
W: Oh, that's terrible. Did you complain to the school?
M: Of course I did, but they said there was nothing that they could do. All the lockers are full. I'll have to wait for the next semester.
W: Oh, that is terrible. Oh, wait a minute. I have many classes on the 4th floor. Do you want to change lockers?
M: Wow, that's a great idea! Are you alright with that?
W: Sure, I don't mind it at all. Let's go and do it now while we have time.
M: Thanks so much. You're the best!

M: 이번 학기에 사물함 받았어?
W: 응. 받았어. 나는 반 크기 사물함 받았어.
M: 나도야. 네 사물함은 몇 층에 있어?
W: 2층에 있어. 왜 묻는데?
M: 두 달 정도 전에 사물함 신청을 했는데, 5층에 있는 사물함을 받았어.
W: 그게 뭐가 잘못됐는데?
M: 이번 학기 수업은 전부 다 1층이란 말이야. 그게 문제가 될 거야. 왜냐하면 지난 달에 다리를 다쳤거든. 항상 계단을 올라갈 수는 없어.
W: 아, 끔찍하다. 학교에다 건의를 해봤어?
M: 당연히 했지. 그런데 그들이 할 수 있는 것이 없더라는. 모든 사물함이 다 차서. 다음 학기까지 기다려야 될 거야.
W: 아, 정말 끔찍한데. 오, 가만 있어봐. 나는 4층 수업이 많은데. 사물함을 바꿀까?
M: 와, 그거 좋은 생각이다! 그래도 괜찮아?
W: 당연하지. 나는 괜찮아. 지금 시간 있을 때 가서 하자.
M: 진짜 고마워. 네가 최고야!

•• 해 설 ••

1. 남자는 다리를 다쳤고 수업이 모두 1층에서 이루어지기 때문에 낮은 층에 위치한 사물함이 필요하다. 그러나 남자의 사물함이 5층에 있어 문제가 된다.

2. 남자가 자신의 문제를 말하자 여자는 "Do you want to change lockers?"라고 물어봤고 즉시 자신의 사물함과 남자의 사물함을 바꾸자고 한다.

3. 남자가 다리를 다친 것을 말한 이유는 자신의 상황을 잘 설명하기 위해서이다. 만일 남자의 수업이 모두 1층에서 진행되고 사물함이 5층에 있다는 것만 말했다면 여자는 그리 큰 문제라고 생각하지 않았을지 모른다. 남자가 다리를 다친 것은 남자가 현재 처한 문제의 큰 비중을 차지한다.

ground floor 1층   I don't mind 괜찮아요   not at all 전혀

Listening Practice 2 p.95

1. (A)   2. (C)   3. (A), (C)

All living things in this world have children, or what are called offspring. Plants also have offspring, but unlike animals, do not have mobility. Mobility means the ability to move around. Plants have roots that are buried deep in the ground. But the plants still need to share their pollen or get their seeds far away. So instead of moving around, plants use insects and animals to help them.

Some plants use bees to help them share with other plants. They attract bees and other insects by sharing sweet liquid called nectar. When the bees sit on the flower to get the nectar, the pollen sticks on the bees' legs. The bees then look for another flower for nectar. Some pollen will drop off, and new pollen will stick on their legs. This is why most bees have yellow legs.

Some fruit plants rely on big furry animals to spread their seeds. They have seeds that have little hooks. They attach to the fur of animals when they pass by the plant. Later, the animal will shake the seed off. This way, the seed will have traveled very far.

이 세상의 모든 생물에게는 자녀, 즉 새끼라고 불리는 것들이 있다. 식물들도 자손이 있지만, 동물들과 다르게 이동성이 없다. 이동성은 움직여 다닐 수 있는 능력을 의미한 다. 식물은 땅속에 묻혀있는 뿌리를 갖고 있다. 그럴더라도 식물들은 꽃가루를 나누거나, 씨앗을 멀리까지 퍼뜨려야 한다. 따라서, 움직여 다니는 대신에, 식물들은 곤충이나 동물의 도움을 받는다.

어떤 식물은 다른 식물들과 나누는데 도움을 얻기 위해 벌들을 이용한다. 그들은 꿀이라고 불리는 달콤한 액체를 나눠줌으로써 벌이나 다른 곤충을 불러들인다. 벌들이 꿀을 얻기위해 꽃에 앉으면, 꽃가루가 벌들의 다리에 묻는다. 그리고 벌들은 꿀을 위해 또 다른 꽃을 찾는다. 일부의 꽃가루는 떨어지고, 새로운 꽃가루가 다리에 묻는다. 이것이 많은 벌들이 노란 다리를 갖고 있는 이유이다.

어떤 열매 나무들은 씨앗을 퍼뜨리기 위해 크고 털로 덮인 동물에 의존한다. 그들은 작은 고리가 있는 씨를 갖고 있다. 동물이 식물 곁을 지나갈 때, 그것들이 동물의 털에 달라붙는다. 나중에, 동물은 씨를 털어 내게 된다. 이런 식으로, 씨가 멀리까지 이동할 수 있는 것이다.

•• 해 설 ••

1. 식물은 이동성이 없지만 동물의 도움을 받아 꽃가루와 씨를 퍼뜨린다는 것이 주요 내용이다. 그러므로 꽃가루와 씨앗을 퍼뜨리는 방법이라는 (A)가 답이다.

2. 번식을 위해 어떻게 식물들이 꽃가루나 씨앗을 퍼뜨리는지 그 방법이 제시되었다. 식물은 이동성이 없기 때문에 대신 동물의 힘을 빌리는 것이다. 즉, 어떻게 동물들이 식물을 돕는 지 설명한다는 (C)가 답이 된다. 동물들이 꽃가루와 씨앗을 옮긴 뒤의 상황은 나와있지 않으므로 (B)는 답이 아니다.

3. 꽃가루를 다리에 묻힌 벌들이 다른 꽃에 앉으면서 퍼뜨리거나, 고리가 달린 씨가 털이 많은 동물에게 달라붙은 뒤 털어낼 때 떨어지는 방법이 있다.

| offspring 새끼 | bury 묻다 | pollen 꽃가루 | seed 씨앗 |
| furry 털로 덮인 | hook 고리 | | |

Listening Practice 3   p.97

1. (C)   2. (D)   3. (B)

M: My science teacher told us that cows have four stomachs. Is that true? I can't believe it.
W: Of course. A lot of animals that only eat vegetables have multiple stomachs.
M: A lot? What other animals have so many stomachs?
W: Well, animals in the cow family all have four stomachs. The ox and buffalo both have many stomachs. Even deer have many stomachs.
M: Why do they need to have so many stomachs?
W: Plants and grass have very little energy. They need different stomachs to absorb as much energy as they can when they digest food.
M: This all sounds fascinating. But are they the only animals with many stomachs?
W: Oh, I remember another animal. Camels also have many stomachs. They need them to digest thorny food.
M: Thorny food? What do you mean?
W: They eat sticks and dry branches. Their stomachs can digest them easily.
M: It sounds like animals waste a lot of time just eating a meal. They must get so tired.
W: Oh, I'm sure that the animals are used to eating that way.

M: 우리 과학 선생님이 소는 위가 네 개 있다고 하셨어. 정말일까? 믿을 수가 없어.
W: 당연하지. 채소만 먹는 많은 동물들이 여러 개의 위를 갖고 있어.
M: 많은 동물들? 또 어떤 동물들이 위를 그렇게 많이 갖고 있는데?
W: 글쎄, 소과의 동물들은 모두 위를 네 개씩 갖고 있어. 소나 버팔로 모두 위를 많이 갖고 있지. 사슴 역시도 여러 개의 위를 갖고 있어.
M: 왜 위가 그렇게 많이 필요한 거지?
W: 나무나 풀에는 에너지가 아주 적어. 먹이를 소화시킬 때 최대한의 에너지를 흡수하기 위해서 여러 다른 위가 필요한 것이야.
M: 그거 다 진짜로 흥미로운데. 그런데, 위를 여러 개 가진 동물은 그것들이 전부야?
W: 아, 다른 동물이 생각났어. 낙타도 위가 여러 개 있어. 가시가 있는 먹이를 소화하기 위해서 필요하지.
M: 가시가 있는 먹이? 무슨 얘기야?
W: 낙타들은 나무토막이랑 마른 가지를 먹어. 그들의 위는 그걸 쉽게 소화시킬 수 있어.
M: 동물들이 한 끼 먹이를 먹는데 시간을 많이 낭비하는 것 같아 보여. 정말 피곤할 거야.
W: 아, 내가 보기엔 동물들은 그런 식으로 먹는 것에 익숙해져 있을 게 분명해.

•• 해 설 ••

1. 처음에 남자가 여자에게 "My science teacher told us that cows have four stomachs. Is that true? I can't believe it."이라고 말했다. 즉, 남자는 소가 네 개의 위를 갖고 있는지 의문이 들었고 정말 그런지 이를 확인 받고 싶었던 것이다.

2. 초식동물들이 위가 여러 개 필요한 이유는, 나무나 풀에는 에너지가 매우

적기 때문에 먹이를 소화시킬 때 최대한 많은 에너지를 흡수하기 위해서이다.

3. 소과의 동물들이 왜 여러 개의 위를 가지게 되었는지 그 이유가 제시되었다. 나머지 (A), (C), (D)는 언급이 없다.

multiple 여러 개의, 복수의   buffalo 버팔로, 물소
absorb 흡수하다   digest 소화하다   thorny 가시가 있는

iBT Practice   p.99

1. (C)   2. Yes: (B), (D) / No: (A), (C)
3. (A)   4. (C)

During World War II, Hitler's army from Germany flew towards Britain. They thought nobody knew that they were coming. But when they got there, Britain was ready to fight. The shocked Germans flew back. How did the British know that the Germans were coming? The answer is radar.

Radar is actually a two-part system. One machine, called the transmitter, sends powerful radio waves into the sky. The radio waves can go very far and fast, until they bounce off objects. The objects are usually planes, helicopters and missiles. Clouds are water vapor, so radars do not detect them. The waves fly back to something called a receiver. The receiver looks like a very big dish. The reason why the dish is so big is because the bounced signal can be very weak. The farther away the plane, the weaker the signal will be when it comes back to the dish.

Radars are now used in a lot of places, not just for planes. Even police use radar to check cars on the road. Radar guns can tell us how fast we are going. Scientists use radars to study space. There are even radar telescopes that are much more powerful than normal telescopes.

It is interesting to note that the radar systems in airports are a little different. They are not true radar systems because they do not have transmitters. The transmitters are on the planes. In fact, every commercial plane in the world must have a transmitter. Airports only have receivers in their systems. Therefore, if the airplane switches off the transmitter, the radar system computer cannot see the plane.

제 2차 세계 대전 동안, 히틀러의 독일군은 영국을 향해 날아갔다. 그들은 아무도 그들이 가고 있다는 것을 모를 거라고 생각했다. 그러나 그들이 거기에 도착했을 때, 영국은 싸울 준비가 되어있었다. 놀란 독일군은 퇴각했다. 그런데 어떻게 영국은 독일군들이 오고 있다는 것을 알 수 있었을까? 정답은 레이더에 있다.

레이더는 사실 두 부분으로 된 시스템이다. 송신기라고 부르는 한 기계가 하늘로 강력한 전파를 보낸다. 전파는 물체에 부딪쳐 산란하기 전까지 아주 멀리 빠르게 갈 수 있다. 그 물체들은 대부분 비행기, 헬리콥터, 그리고 미사일들이다. 구름은 수증기이므로, 레이더는 그것들을 탐지하지 않는다. 전파는 수신기라고 불리는 것을 향해 날아 돌아 온다. 수신기는 매우 큰 접시처럼 생겼다. 그 접시가 매우 큰 이유는, 반사된 전파는 매우 약할 수 있기 때문이다. 비행기가 더 멀리 있을수록, 접시로 되돌아 올 때의 전파는 더 약할 것이다.

레이더는 오늘날에는 비행기뿐만 아니라 많은 곳에서 사용된다 경찰들까지도 도로에서 자동차를 검사하기 위해 레이더를 사용한다. 레이더건은 얼마나 빨리 움직이고 있는지를 알려준다. 과학자들은 우주를 연구하기 위해서 레이더를 사용한다. 심지어 보통의 망원경보다 훨씬 강력한 레이더 망원경도 있다.

공항의 레이더 시스템은 조금 다르다는 것은 흥미로운 사실이다. 그것들은 송신기가 없기 때문에, 진짜 레이더 시스템이 아니다. 송신기는 비행기에 장착되어 있다. 사실, 세계의 모든 상업 항공기는 송신기를 장착해야 한다. 공항의 시스템에 는 수신기만 있다. 그러므로, 항공기가 송신기의 전원을 차단하면, 레이더 시스템의 컴퓨터는 비행기를 볼 수가 없다.

•• 해 설 ••

1. "But when they got there, Britain was ready to fight. The Shocked Germans flew back"라고 분명히 말했다.

2. 영국군이 독일군 비행기가 오고 있다는 것을 감지할 수 있었던 것은 레이더 때문이었으므로 두 번째 보기는 답이 된다. 레이더의 수신기는 반사된 신호를 받는 것이지 신호를 반사시키는 것이 아니므로 첫번째 보기는 답이 아니다. 경찰들은 레이더건을 이용하여 과속차량을 감시하므로 네 번째 보기가 답이다.

3. 도입부에서 화자는 독일군의 2차 세계대전 이야기를 하며 흥미를 유발하고 이번 시간에 다룰 주제인 레이더를 소개한다.

4. 마지막 단락에서 공항 레이더 시스템과 진짜 레이더 시스템의 중요한 차이점에 대해 설명하고 있다. 서로 대조시키기 위해 공항 레이더 시스템에 대한 이야기를 했다.

radar 레이더; 전파탐지기   transmitter 송신기   radio wave 전파
bounce off 부딪혀 산란하다   object 물체   water vapor 수증기
receiver 수신기   normal 보통의, 평범한   commercial 상업의

Further Study   p.101

Topic : Radar

* Two-part system = transmitter + receiver
1. transmitter
   - send powerful radio waves into the sky
     → bounce off objects → fly back to a receiver
2. receiver = very big dish to receive weak signal

* Use of radar
- planes
- police : check cars – radar guns
- scientists : study space – radar telescopes
- airports : only have receivers, transmitters are on planes

Word Review   p.102

1. (A)   2. (A)   3. (A)   4. (D)
5. supply   6. solar
7. offspring   8. multiple
9. digest   10. normal
11. object   12. commercial

Part C

Connecting Content

Sample Question   p.105

M: 제인, 너 천문학 공부하지, 안 그래?
W: 응, 맞아. 왜 묻는 건데?
M: 행성에 대해서 써야 하는데, 네가 나를 도와주면 좋겠어.
W: 그러지 뭐. 뭘 알고 싶어?
M: 행성에 대한 아무것이면 돼. 학교 도서관에 갔었는데, 도움이 안 되더라.
W: 목성은 어때? 태양계에서 제일 큰 행성이야. 아주 커서, 지구를 포함한 태양계의 나머지 8개의 행성이 다 들어갈 정도라고.
M: 와, 그 정도로 큰 지는 몰랐어. 목성에 대해서 다른 흥미로운 건 없을까?
W: 목성은 63개의 위성을 갖고 있어. 아, 목성은 거대 가스형 행성 중 하나야.
M: 왜 그렇게 부르는데?
W: 과학자들은 그것이 가스로 가득 차 있대, 고체의 암석 표면 없이. 색깔이 항상 변하고 있는 이유지.
M: 그래, 필요한 것 보다 더 많이 안 것 같아. 알려줘서 고마워!

Building Skills   p.106

Connecting Content in Comparison

1. Notebook: easier to carry to class
   Desktop: can't type fast

2. (A) B
   (B) K
   (C) K

1. W: Can you help me out for a minute? I can't decide whether to buy a notebook computer or a desktop computer.
   M: Sure. Do you plan to use the computer in your room?
   W: I would say a fair bit. But I also want to take it to class to take notes.
   M: Well, notebook computers are easier to carry than desktops. But do you type quickly?
   W: No, I type very slowly. I don't know how to use all of my fingers.
   M: Then don't waste your time with notebook

computers. I think you should buy a desktop computer.
W: 잠깐만 도와줄 수 있어? 노트북을 살 지 데스크톱 컴퓨터 살 지 결정을 못 하겠어.
M: 그러지 뭐. 컴퓨터는 네 방에서 쓸 거야?
W: 거의 그럴 거야. 그런데 필기하려고 수업에도 갖고 가고 싶어.
M: 음, 내가 봐도 노트북이 데스크톱 컴퓨터보다 갖고 다니기 쉬워. 그런데 너 타자 잘 하니?
W: 아니. 나 타자 느린데. 어떻게 손가락 전부를 다 쓰는지 모르겠다.
M: 그럼 노트북으로 시간 낭비하지 마. 내 생각엔 데스크톱을 사는 게 나을 것 같아.

2. M: I'm thinking about taking up a sport.
W: That's good. What did you have in mind?
M: I am interested in kickboxing and boxing.
W: Aren't they the same?
M: No, they are very different. Boxing only uses the hands. Kickboxers can use their hands, legs, knees and elbows.
W: Oh, so the rules of the game are very different?
M: That's right. They are completely different sports.
W: It sounds interesting. Maybe I should join too.

M: 운동을 좀 하려고 생각 중이야.
W: 그거 잘 됐네. 어떤 걸 하려는데?
M: 킥복싱하고 권투에 관심이 가.
W: 그 둘이 같은 거 아니냐?
M: 아니, 많이 달라. 권투는 손만 사용해. 킥복싱 하는 사람들은 손, 다리, 무릎 그리고 팔꿈치까지 쓸 수 있어.
W: 아, 그럼 경기 규칙도 많이 달라?
M: 그래 맞아. 둘은 완전히 다른 운동이라니까.
W: 재미있을 것 같아. 나도 해봐야겠다.

Connecting Content in Process

1. (A), (D), (B), (C)   2. (B), (C), (A)

1. M: Can you tell me how to get to the main building?
W: Sure. Are you in a hurry, or do you like walking?
M: I'm not in a hurry. I like walking.
W: Walk down this road until you reach a junction. Turn right and walk up all the way to the end of the hill. You'll see the main tower about another 10 minutes away.
M: I changed my mind. I don't want to walk that far.
W: Alright. You can wait for the shuttle bus here. It comes around very often.
M: Thank you.

M: 본부 건물로 어떻게 가는지 좀 알려주시겠어요?
W: 물론이죠. 바쁘세요, 아니면 걷는 걸 좋아하세요?
M: 안 바빠요. 걷는 걸 좋아하구요.
W: 교차로가 나올 때까지 이 길을 따라 가세요. 오른쪽으로 돌아서 언덕 끝까지 죽 올라가세요. 10분 정도 더 가시면 본부 탑이 보일 겁니다.
M: 생각이 바뀌었어요. 그렇게 멀리까지는 걷기가 싫군요.
W: 그래요. 여기서 셔틀 버스를 기다리셔도 돼요. 자주 오거든요.
M: 고맙습니다.

2. Before there was the internet, companies only had phones to send and receive messages.
It was the only way to get in contact with people. Then, a typewriter system called the telex was introduced. It looked like a normal typewriter. However, it sent typed messages through the telephone lines. The receiving telex machine would type the message out automatically. Finally, many companies started using fax machines during the '80s. They still used telephone lines, but they could also send pictures to other fax machines. In fact, companies still use fax machines today. They play a big role in companies, sending and receiving important documents to one another.

인터넷이 있기 전에는, 기업들이 메시지를 보내고 받기 위해서는 전화선 밖에 없었다.
그것이 다른 사람들과 연락을 유지하기 위한 유일한 수단이었다. 그 후, 텔렉스라고 불리는 타자 시스템이 나왔다. 그것은 일반적인 타자기처럼 생겼다. 그러나, 그것은 타자된 메시지를 전화선을 통해 전송했다. 수신하는 텔렉스 기계는 그 메시지를 자동으로 타자했다. 결국, 80년대에는 많은 기업들이 팩스 기계를 사용하기 시작했다. 그것은 역시 전화선을 사용했지만, 다른 팩스 기계로 사진도 보낼 수 있었다. 실제로, 기업들은 오늘날에도 팩스 기계를 사용한다. 기업들끼리 중요한 문서를 보내고 받는데에 있어서 큰 역할을 하고 있다.

Basic Drills   p.00

1. Yes: (A), (C) / No: (B), (D)   2. (A)-(B)-(C)-(D)
3. Warm-Blooded: (A) / Cold-Blooded: (B), (C), (D)
4. Computer Systems: (A), (C) / Business IT: (B), (D)
5. Yes: (A), (C) / No: (B), (D)
6. Yes: (B), (D) / No: (A), (C)
7. (B)-(D)-(C)-(A)   8. Yes: (B), (D) / No: (A), (C)
9. Seahorses: (B), (C), (D) / Other animals: (A)

1. W: I think I am going to drop math. It's getting too hard

for me. I can't understand what is going on.
M: I think you're mistaken. You can't drop math. That's a required subject. You cannot drop all the subjects that you want.
W: What do you mean? I thought we could quit any 2 subjects that we wanted.
M: Yes, but not some subjects, such as English, math and science.
W: Are you kidding? I can't continue learning math. It's too difficult.

W: 수학 수업 취소 할까 봐. 나한테 점점 더 어려워져. 뭐가 어떻게 되고 있는 건지 모르겠어.
M: 나는 네가 잘못 생각한 것 같아. 수학은 취소할 수가 없어. 필수 과목이잖아. 원하는 과목을 다 취소할 수는 없다고.
W: 무슨 소리야? 나는 원하는 아무 과목 2개는 취소할 수 있는 줄 알았는데.
M: 그래. 영어, 수학이나 과학 같은 필수 과목은 빼고.
W: 진짜야? 수학은 더 못 배우겠어. 너무 어렵단 말이야.

•• 해 설 ••
여학생은 수학이 어려워 수업취소를 고려하고 있었지만, 학교 규정을 잘못 이해하고 있었다. 영어, 수학, 과학은 취소가 불가능한 필수 과목이다.

drop (수업을) 취소하다

2. Countries around the world need something called petroleum. We need it in cars and buses. So where do we get petroleum?
The first step is to get something called crude oil. We pump it from the ground. Then, we boil the oil slowly, so it will not catch fire. Special machines collect the gas from the boiling oil. The gas is cooled and turned into liquid. Finally, companies deliver the liquid to petrol stations around the world. The liquid can be a few types, such as petrol or diesel.

세계 여러 나라들은 석유라고 불리는 것을 필요로 한다. 우리는 자동차나 버스에 석유가 필요하다. 그렇다면 우리는 어디서 석유를 얻는 걸까?
첫 번째 단계는 원유라고 불리는 것을 얻는 것이다. 우리는 땅 속에서 그것을 퍼 올린다. 그리고, 불이 붙지 않도록 그 기름을 천천히 끓이고, 특별한 장비로 끓는 기름에서 가스를 추출해 낸다. 그 가스는 식혀져서 액체로 바뀌게 된다. 마지막으로, 회사들이 세계 곳곳의 주유소로 그 액체를 배달한다. 이 액체는 휘발유나 디젤유 등 다양한 종류가 있다.

•• 해 설 ••
Signal words가 순서대로 정보를 나열시켜준다. "The first step is …" "Then …" "Finally …".

crude oil 원유   catch on fire 불붙다   petrol 휘발유

3. Humans have a body temperature that does not change very much. This is because humans and most mammals are warm-blooded animals. There are also many cold-blooded animals. Reptiles, such as snakes and lizards, are cold-blooded animals. Their body temperature can be very different. When cold-blooded animals are in a cold area, their body temperature becomes the same temperature with the outside. Therefore, they need to sit in the sun for a long time to get a warmer temperature in their body.

인간의 체온은 거의 변하지 않는다. 이것은 사람과 대부분의 포유동물들이 온혈동물이기 때문이다. 냉혈동물들 또한 많이 있다. 뱀이나 도마뱀 같은 파충류는 냉혈동물이다. 그들의 체온은 변화가 심하다. 냉혈동물이 추운 지역에 있을 경우, 그들의 체온도 외부온도와 같아진다. 그러므로, 그들은 몸의 온도를 따뜻하게 높이기 위해서는 햇볕을 오랫동안 쬐야 한다.

•• 해 설 ••
온혈동물은 체온이 잘 변하지 않는다. 반면에 뱀과 도마뱀을 포함한 냉혈동물들은 주위환경에 따라 체온이 변하며 따뜻하게 하기 위해 햇볕을 쬐야 한다고 설명하고 있다.

body temperature 체온   mammal 포유동물   reptile 파충류

4. W: Have you decided on a major yet?
M: No, not yet. I still can't decide whether to study computer systems or business IT.
W: They sound pretty similar. Is there a big difference between the two majors?
M: Yes, there is a big difference. Students that major in computer systems learn a lot about computer networks and different hardware.
W: How about business IT students?
M: They learn a lot more about economics, management and accounting.
W: Both sound like interesting majors. I hope you make the right decision.
M: I hope so, too.

W: 전공은 결정했어?
M: 아니, 아직. 컴퓨터 체계를 공부할지, 경영정보기술을 공부할지 아직도 결정을 못하겠어.
W: 둘 다 비슷한 것 같은데. 두 전공 사이에 큰 차이가 있어?
M: 응. 큰 차이가 있지. 컴퓨터 체계를 전공하는 학생들은 컴퓨터 네트워

크랑 갖가지의 하드웨어도 배워.
W: 경영정보기술 학생들은 어때?
M: 그들은 경제와 경영, 회계에 대해서 더 많이 배우지.
W: 둘 다 재미있는 전공 같은데, 옳은 결정을 할 바래.
M: 나도 그랬으면 좋겠어.

•• 해 설 ••

컴퓨터 시스템을 전공하면 컴퓨터 네트워크와 여러 가지 하드웨어를 배우는 반면, 경영, 정보기술은 경영과 회계에 대해 배운다.

management 경영 **accounting** 회계

5. Everyone is talking about how to be healthy. People are trying to lose weight and eat well-being foods. But before we simply buy any well-being food that we see, we should always learn about it before trying it. We need to control our food slowly. Being healthy does not mean losing weight all of a sudden. We also need to start exercising bit by bit. It can be very dangerous to have a sudden change in our body or daily life.

모든 사람들이 어떻게 건강해질 지에 대해서 이야기한다. 사람들은 몸무게를 줄이고 웰빙 음식을 먹으려고 한다. 그러나 아무 웰빙 음식이나 보이는 대로 소비하기 보다는, 우리는 먹어 보기 전에 항상 그것에 대해서 알아야 한다. 우리는 서서히 음식을 조절해야 한다. 갑자기 몸무게를 줄인다고 건강해지는 것은 아니다. 우리는 또한 조금씩 운동을 시작해야 한다. 우리의 몸이나 일상에서의 갑작스런 변화는 매우 위험할 수 있다.

•• 해 설 ••

웰빙음식이라도 조사해 본 후에 먹으라고 선생님은 말한다. 갑작스러운 변화를 주며 빨리 체중을 줄이기보다는 천천히 운동과 식이요법을 시작해야 한다고 당부하고 있다.

6. The Amazon River is the second longest river in the world. It also gets a lot of rainfall. This is why it holds the largest amount of water in one place. However, the Amazon has recently been facing droughts. A lot of fish and animals have been dying because of the disappearing water. This is a very big problem, as many people depend on the waters of the Amazon. Scientists do not really know why this is happening, but they suspect global warming and pollution are the main problems.

아마존 강은 세계에서 두 번째로 긴 강이다. 거기에는 비도 많이 내린다. 이는 그것이 한 곳에서 가장 많은 수량을 지니는 이유이다. 그러나, 아마존은 최근에 가뭄에 시달리고 있다. 물이 사라지고 있기 때문에 많은 물고기와 동물들이 죽고 있다. 이것은 많은 사람들이 아마존의 물에 의존하기 때문에 매우 큰 문제이다. 학자들은 왜 이런 일이 발생하는지에 대해서 잘 모르지만, 주원인으로 지구 온난화와 오염을 주요인으로 의심한다.

•• 해 설 ••

아마존 강은 세계에서 2번째로 긴 강이며, 수량이 가장 많은 강이기도 하다. 최근에 아마존 강이 가뭄에 시달리고 있는데, 많은 사람들이 강물에 의존하고 있기 때문에 매우 큰 문제라고 강의에서 언급되어 있다.

drought 가뭄 **suspect** 의심하다 **global warming** 지구 온난화 **pollution** 오염

7. Cavemen drew on walls with branches. They dipped the branch into the ink and painted. In the middle ages, people used big feathers called quills. People cut and shaped the thick end of the feather. They were still not pens, because people still had to carry ink separately.

Then, the fountain pen was born. This time, the ink was inside the pen. But this was also a problem. The ink often leaked or dried up. Thankfully, the ballpoint pen changed all that. It had a metal ball on the tip of the pen. The ink did not dry up or leak. People could use it easily.

혈거인(동굴에 사는 사람)들은 나뭇가지로 벽에 그림을 그렸다. 그들은 나뭇가지에 잉크를 담가서 칠했다. 중세 시대에는, 사람들은 깃펜이라고 불리는 커다란 깃털을 사용했다. 사람들은 깃펜의 두꺼운 쪽을 잘라서 모양을 냈다. 그래도 사람들이 잉크를 따로 갖고 다녀야 했기 때문에, 그것은 아직 펜이 아니었다.

그 후, 만년필이 태어났다. 이번에는, 잉크가 펜 속에 들어있었다. 그러나 이것은 또한 문제점이기도 했다. 잉크는 종종 새거나 말라버렸다. 고맙게도, 볼펜은 그 모든 것을 바꿨다. 볼펜의 끝에는 금속 볼이 들어 있었다. 잉크가 말라버리거나 새지 않았다. 사람들은 쉽게 그것을 사용할 수 있었다.

•• 해 설 ••

혈거인들은 나뭇가지로 그림을 그렸고, 그 후 중세 시대 사람들이 깃털을 이용했다. "Then, ..."이 다음 사건인 만년필의 개발을 암시한다. 그리고 마지막으로 볼펜이 탄생되었다.

caveman 혈거인 **dip** 담그다 **quill** 깃펜 **leak** 새다

8. Colors, shapes and sounds around us can make a big difference in our minds. Let's take an example of fast food restaurants. In most fast food restaurants, the common colors on their logo and inside of their restaurants are red, yellow and white. This is because many people feel hungry when they see those colors. The seats and tables are rounded. Round seats are uncomfortable. Finally, the music in fast food restaurants is upbeat. They play fast and exciting music so that people will eat quickly and leave.

우리 주변의 색, 모양과 소리는 우리의 생각에 큰 차이를 가져올 수 있다. 패스트푸드 식당의 예로 들어 보자. 대부분의 패스트푸드 식당에서, 로고와 식당 안에서 흔한 색깔은 빨강, 노랑 그리고 하얀색이다. 이것은 사람들이 이런 색깔을 보면 배고픔을 느끼기 때문이다. 의자와 식탁은 둥글게 되어 있다. 둥근 의자는 불편하다. 마지막으로, 패스트푸드 식당의 음악은 흥겹다. 그들은 빠르고 신나는 음악을 틀어서 사람들이 빨리 먹고 나가게 만든다.

•• 해 설 ••

패스트푸드 식당에서는 빨강, 노랑, 하얀색과 같은 밝은 색을 이용해 사람들의 식욕을 자극시킨다. 또한 불편한 둥근 테이블과 의자를 사용하고, 빠른 음악을 틀어 사람들이 빨리 식사하고 나가게 만든다고 선생님이 설명하고 있다.

upbeat 흥겨운, 긍정적인

9. Seahorses do not look like most other animals. In fact, there are many differences between seahorses and other animals. But the biggest difference is how male seahorses take care of their children.

Most male animals eat or sleep while mothers take care of the children. However, male seahorses are always around their children. They always look around for danger. They do not even eat while taking care of their offspring. The male seahorse has a pouch at the bottom of his body. The babies swim and hide inside the pouch if there is danger.

해마는 대부분의 다른 동물들과 생김새가 다르다. 사실, 해마와 다른 동물들 사이에는 많은 차이점이 있다. 하지만 가장 큰 차이는 수컷 해마가 새끼들을 보살피는 방법이다.

대부분의 수컷 동물들은 어미가 새끼들을 보살피는 동안 먹거나 잔다. 그러나 수컷 해마는 항상 새끼들의 주변에 있다. 그들은 항상 위험에 대비해 주위를 살핀다. 그들의 자손을 돌보고 있을 때는 먹지도 않는다. 수컷 해마는 몸통 아랫 부분에 주머니를 갖고 있다. 위험이 발생하면, 새끼들은 그 주머니로 헤엄쳐 와서 숨는다.

•• 해 설 ••

대부분의 수컷 동물들은 어미가 새끼를 돌보는 동안 잠을 자는데, 수컷 해마는 항상 새끼 주변을 지키며, 새끼를 돌보고 있을 땐 밥도 안 먹는다. 또한 위험이 발생하면 새끼를 주머니에 숨긴다고 설명하고 있다.

seahorse 해마   pouch 주머니

Listening Practice 1   p.111

1. (C)   2. (B)
3. Uri Geller: (A), (D) / James Randi: (B), (C)

There are many people around the world that claim to have certain powers of the mind. Sometimes they insist that they can do supernatural things, like bending spoons simply by using their mind or making things float in the air. But it is unclear if special mind powers really exist.

Uri Geller is one of the most famous people that claim to have supernatural powers. He showed off his power on television, and the whole world quickly heard about him. He bent spoons and fixed watches on television to show the strength of his mind power. After watching his show, most people thought that he really had great mind powers. He soon traveled around the world to show off his powers and tell people about the power of the mind. However, there were some people that did not believe in his powers.

James Randi was a famous magician. Unlike Uri, James tried to show everyone that there is no such thing as mind power. He came on television many times to tell everyone that mind power is not real. He claimed on television that he would give $1 million to anyone who can prove that they have supernatural powers. He first offered it in the 1970s, but nobody has won the money. Randi and Uri continue to argue with each other and try to prove each other wrong.

세계에는 특별한 영적 능력을 갖고 있다고 주장하는 사람들이 많이 있다. 그들은 염력을 통한 숟가락 구부리기나 사물들이 공중에 뜨게 하는 초자연적인 일들을 할 수 있다고 주장하기도 한다. 그러나 특별한 영적 능력이 실제로 존재하는지는 확실하지 않다.

유리 겔러는 초능력을 가졌다고 주장하는 가장 유명한 사람들 중의 한 명이다. 그는 텔레비전에서 그의 능력을 자랑했고, 전 세계는 곧 그에 대해서 듣게 되었다. 그는 영적 능력의 힘을 보여주기 위해 텔레비전에서 숟가락을 구부리고, 시계를 고쳤다. 그의 쇼를 본 뒤 대부분의 사람들은 그가 정말로 대단한 영적 능력을 갖고 있다고 생각했다. 그는 곧 그의 능력을 자랑하기 위해 세계 곳곳을 여행했고, 사람들에게 영적 능력에 대해서 이야기했다. 그러나, 그의 능력을 믿지 않은 사람들도 있었다.

제임스 랜디는 유명한 마술사였다. 겔러와 다르게, 랜디는 모두에게 영적 능력 같은 것은 없다는 것을 보여주려고 했다. 그는 모든 이들에게 영적 능력이 허구라는 것을 보여주기 위해 여러 번 텔레비전에 출연했다. 그는 텔레비전에서 초능력을 증명할 수 있는 사람에게는 1백만 달러를 주겠다고 단언했다. 그는 1970년대 처음 그런 제의를 했으나, 아무도 그 돈을 타지는 못했다. 랜디와 겔러는 계속 싸우면서 서로가 틀리다는 것을 증명하려고 노력하고 있다.

•• 해 설 ••

1. 초능력의 유무에 대한 내용이다. 유리 겔러는 초능력이 존재한다고 주장했고, 제임스 랜디는 아니라고 주장했다. 그러므로 답은 (C)이다. (A), (B)는 전체를 포괄하지 못한다.

2. 유리 겔러는 초능력이 존재한다고 믿었다. 이에 맞서 초능력이 존재하지 않는다고 주장하는 인물로 제임스 랜디를 언급했다. 이와 같이 두 사람은 대조 되므로 (B)가 답이다.

3. 숟가락을 구부리고 시계를 고치며 초능력이 있다고 주장한 사람은 유리 겔러였고, 초능력이 존재하지 않는다고 주장한 유명 마술사는 제임스 랜디였다.

insist 주장하다, 우기다 bend 구부리다 float 뜨다
exist 존재하다 show off 자랑하다 offer 제의하다

Listening Practice 2   p.113

1. (C)   2. (B)   3. Yes: (A), (C) / No: (B), (D)

T: Modern doctors go through many years of studies and testing. When they are finished, they take something called the Hippocratic Oath. Hippocrates made the oath for doctors to take before they became doctors.
W: Who's Hippocrates?
T: Hippocrates was a famous Greek philosopher. Many call him the father of modern medicine. He taught many people about helping sick people get better.
M: So why must doctors take the oath?
T: The oath basically states that doctors should do everything to help sick people, and make them comfortable.
M: I think that's a great oath. Do doctors still take the Hippocratic Oath?
T: Of course they do. It changes bit by bit as the years go by, but the overall meaning is still the same. However, not all doctors take the oath.
W: Really? What kinds of doctors do not take the oath?
T: Veterinarians, for example. They only treat and heal pets or animals. So they do not need to take the oath. Apparently, the oath is only valid for humans.
W: That's strange. Pets also need the love and care of doctors. I heard that pet medicine and human medicine are the same.
T: Well, the oath is really a formality. When a person becomes any sort of doctor, they will naturally help others in the best way that they can.

T: 현대의 의사들은 여러 해 동안의 공부와 시험을 거칩니다. 그것이 끝나면, 그들은 히포크라테스의 선서라는 것을 하게 됩니다. 히포크라테스는 의사들을 위해 의사가 되기 전에 하는 선서를 만들었습니다.
W: 히포크라테스가 누구예요?
T: 히포크라테스는 유명한 그리스 철학자였습니다. 많은 사람들이 그를 현대 의학의 아버지라고 부르죠. 그는 아픈 사람들을 낫도록 도와주는 것에 대해서 많은 사람들을 가르쳤습니다.
M: 그럼 왜 의사들은 꼭 선서를 해야 하나요?
T: 그 선서는 무엇보다도 의사는 아픈 사람을 돕기 위해서 어떠한 일이라도 해야 하며, 그들을 편하게 해야만 한다고 말하고 있어요.
M: 그거 정말 좋은 선서 같은데요. 아직도 의사들은 히포크라테스의 선서를 합니까?
T: 물론 합니다. 시간이 흐름에 따라서 조금씩 바뀌기는 하지만, 전체적인 뜻은 그대로입니다. 그렇지만, 모든 의사들이 그 선서를 하는 것은 아니에요.
W: 정말이에요? 그럼 어떤 종류의 의사들이 선서를 안 하나요?
T: 예를 들어서, 수의사들. 그들은 오직 애완동물이나 동물들만을 치료하고 낫게 하죠. 그래서 그들은 선서를 하지 않습니다. 듣자 하니 그 선서는 사람들에게만 유효해요.
W: 그건 이상한데요. 애완동물들도 역시 의사의 사랑과 보살핌이 필요하잖아요. 제가 듣기로는 애완동물 약과 사람의 약이 같다고 하던데요.
T: 글쎄, 선서는 사실 형식적 의례입니다. 어떤 사람이 어떠한 종류의 의사라도 된다면, 그는 자연히 그가 할 수 있는 모든 방법으로 다른 이들을 도울 겁니다.

•• 해 설 ••

1. 히포크라테스 선서에 관한 내용이다. 그 유래와 선서 내용, 선서 대상자(수의사를 제외한 의사) 등이 다루어졌다. 그러므로 보기 중 가장 가까운 답은 (C)이다. 히포크라테스라는 인물의 언급이 있었지만 이는 선서의 창시자로서 언급된 것일 뿐 전체가 그의 얘기라고는 볼 수 없으므로 (D)는 답이 아니다.

2. "Hippocrates was a famous Greek philosopher. Many call him the father of modern medicine." 라고했다. 보기 중 히포크라테스를 가장 잘 나타낸 것은 (B)이다. 히포크라테스는 수의사가 아니었으므로 (A)와 (D)는 틀린 답이다.

3. 히포크라테스 선서는 의사가 되기 전에 해야 하는 선서로 시간이 지나면서 조금씩 내용이 변했지만 전체적인 의미는 동일하다. 하지만 이 선서는 오직 사람에게만 해당되기 때문에 모든 의사들이 하지 않는다. 모든 생명체가 아닌 사람들에게만 해당 되기때문에 (B)는 Yes가 될 수 없다.

oath 선서 bit by bit 조금씩 valid 유효한
formality 형식적 의례

Listening Practice 3
p.115

1. (D)　　2. (B)　　3. Yes: (B), (C) / No: (A), (D)

M: Do you know of any vehicle that can travel by air, water and land?
W: I don't think that there's any vehicle that can use all three surfaces. It can't be a boat, plane, or a car.
M: You're right. It's none of the three. But there is something called a hovercraft that can really travel on all three.
W: What's a hovercraft?
M: Hovercrafts are vehicles that use airpower to float just above the surface. They have very powerful fans that blow air underneath the hovercraft. It looks like a car, but it doesn't have wheels.
W: What does it have instead?
M: 🎧 It has something called an air skirt. It keeps the air underneath the hovercraft. When running, the hovercraft is sitting on a layer of air.
W: So what is that good for?
M: Are you kidding? It means that it can go on water or land without a problem.
W: That is amazing, I must say. But why don't we see a lot of hovercrafts around?
M: There are a few reasons. Hovercrafts turn and stop very gently, I mean very slowly. They are also very noisy and vibrate a lot. Still, they are good for some things. Until the Channel Tunnel was built in Europe, big hovercrafts used to carry many people across the English Channel.

M: 공중, 수상, 그리고 육상에서 움직일 수 있는 교통수단 중에 아는 거 있어?
W: 세 가지 표면을 다 쓸 수 있는 교통수단은 없는 것 같은데. 배나 비행기도, 그렇다고 자동차도 아니잖아.
M: 맞아. 그 셋 중에서는 아니야. 그런데 실제로 그 세 군데 모두에서 사용할 수 있는 호버크라프트라고 불리는 것이 있어.
W: 호버크라프트가 뭐야?
M: 호버크라프트는 표면 바로 위에 떠 있기 위해서 공기의 힘을 이용하는 교통수단이야. 호버크라프트에는 공기를 아래쪽으로 분사하기 위한 강력한 송풍기가 달려 있어. 자동차처럼 보이지만 바퀴가 없지.
W: 대신에 뭐가 달려 있는 거야?
M: 공기 스커트라는 것이 달려 있어. 호버크라프트의 아랫쪽에 공기를 가두지. 움직이는 동안 호버크라프트는 공기 층 위에 떠 있는 거야.
W: 그게 어떻게 좋은데?
M: 정말 몰라서 묻니? 문제없이 물이나 땅 위를 다닐 수 있다니까.
W: 그거 참 신기하네. 그런데 왜 주변에 호버크라프트가 별로 안 보이는 거야?
M: 몇 가지 이유가 있어. 호버크라프트는 회전과 정지를 매우 부드럽게, 그러니까 느리게 해. 또 그건 엄청 시끄럽고 진동도 크지. 그렇지만, 어떤 경우에는 좋을 때도 있어. 유럽에 해협 터널이 건설되기 전까지, 영불해협에서 대형 호버크라프트들이 많은 사람들을 실어 날랐지.

•• 해설 ••

1. 공중, 수상, 육상에서 움직일 수 있는 호버크라프트를 설명하고 있다. 그러므로 호버크라프트의 특징이라고 한 (D)가 답이다. (A)와 (B)는 부분적인 설명이므로 주제어가 될 수 없다.

2. 남자는 여자가 호버크라프트의 장점을 모르고 있다는 것에 놀라움을 표현하고 있다. 앞뒤 문맥을 봤을 때 여자가 농담을 언급 한 적도 없기 때문에 (A) 와 (C)는 답이 될 수 없다.

3. 호버크라프트는 바퀴 없이 표면 바로 위에 떠다니기 때문에 공중, 수상, 육상에서 움직일 수 있고 회전과 정지를 매우 부드럽게 할 수 있다. 그러므로 육상과 수상에서만 움직일 수 있다는 보기 (D)는 Yes가 될 수 없다.

vehicle 교통수단　　surface 표면　　vibrate 진동하다

iBT Practice
p.117

1. (B)　　2. (D)　　3. (D)　　4. (D)-(B)-(A)-(C)

T: How do you think companies test their medicine?
W: I'm not very sure. Don't they make the medicine and just sell it?
M: I heard that they test it on animals first.
T: You're partly right. Medicine companies do test their medicine on animals first. Most of them use mice. But that's not the end.
W: What do you mean? If the animal is safe, then can't humans take the medicine?
T: Well, many think that animal testing is the end. But medicine is actually tested even on humans.
M: Wow, isn't that dangerous?
T: Of course, there is some danger. But since the medicines are safe on animals, humans are usually safe too.
W: So how do humans test the medicine?
T: It's a very simple process. Doctors choose about 100 people in hospitals. Then, they give half of them the real medicine, and half of them fake medicine.
M: What do you mean by fake medicine?
T: Pills that do not really contain any medicine. Then,

they study the people for a couple of years. When the results get back, they will know if the medicine was an effective medicine.
M: Why do they give half the people fake medicine?
T: Some people take fake medicine and think they are getting better. It's called a placebo effect. They feel better because they think that the medicine works.
W: So how will we know if the medicine is effective?
T: The medicine must be effective to people who took the real medicine. If the number is similar to people who took the fake medicine, then the medicine is not effective.
W: Wow, that's a simple process.
T: Yes, it is a rather simple process, but the only problem is that it takes a lot of time, and it is expensive.

T: 회사들이 약을 어떻게 실험할까요?
W: 잘 모르겠는데요. 약을 만들어서 그냥 파는 것 아닌가요?
M: 저는 먼저 동물에 대해서 실험한다고 들었습니다.
T: 어느 정도는 맞습니다. 제약회사들은 그들의 약을 먼저 동물에게 실험합니다. 대부분이 쥐를 사용하죠. 그렇지만 그게 끝이 아닙니다.
W: 무슨 말씀이에요? 동물이 안전하다면, 사람이 그 약을 먹을 수 있지 않나요?
T: 글쎄요. 많은 이들이 동물 실험이 끝이라고 생각합니다. 그렇지만 약은 실제 사람들에게도 실험됩니다.
M: 와, 위험하지 않나요?
T: 물론, 어느 정도의 위험은 있어요. 하지만 동물에게 약이 안전하면, 사람들한테도 보통은 안전하죠.
W: 그럼 사람들은 어떻게 약을 실험하나요?
T: 그것은 정말 아주 간단한 과정이에요. 의사들이 병원들에서 약 100 명의 사람을 선발합니다. 그리고, 그들의 반에게는 진짜 약을 주고, 나머지 반에게는 가짜 약을 주죠.
M: 가짜 약이라니 무슨 뜻입니까?
T: 약이 실제로 들어 있지 않은 알약이에요. 그 후에, 그들은 그 사람들을 몇 년 동안 연구합니다. 결과가 나오면, 약이 효과가 있는지 알 수 있지요.
M: 왜 반에게는 가짜 약을 줍니까?
T: 어떤 사람들은 가짜 약을 먹고 나아지고 있다 생각합니다. 플라시보 효과라고 불리는 거죠. 그 약이 작용한다고 생각하기 때문에 나아지는 것으로 느끼는거죠.
W: 그러면, 어떻게 약이 효과가 있는지 아는 거에요?
T: 그 약은 진짜 약을 먹은 사람에게 효과적이어야 하죠. 만약 가짜 약을 먹은 사람들과 수가 비슷하다면, 약은 효과가 없는 것이죠.
W: 와, 그거 간단한 과정이네요.
T: 예, 꽤 간단한 과정이죠. 단, 너무 오래 걸리고 비싸다는 것이 유일한 문제입니다.

•• 해 설 ••

1. 약을 어떻게 실험하는가가 주요 내용이다. 그러므로 답은 (B)이고 나머지 (A), (C), (D)는 지엽적인 설명이다. 왜냐하면 처음에 동물에게 약을 시험한 뒤 사람에게도 시험한다는 내용과, 가짜 약을 먹은 절반의 실험 대상자가 약효가 있다고 느끼는 플라시보 효과가 (B)에 포함되기 때문이다.

2. 의약품이 정말 효과가 있는지를 보려면 플라시보 효과가 아닌지를 검증해 봐야 한다. "The medicine must be effective to people who took the real medicine. If the number is similar to people who took the fake medicine, then the medicine is not effective."를 보면 알 수 있다.

3. 선생님은 대화 마지막에 "Yes, it is a rather simple process, but the only problem is that it takes a lot of time and it is expensive"라고 말하면서 실험 방법이 꽤 간단하긴 하지만 시간과 돈이 많이 든다고 말했다.

4. 선생님은 약을 실험하는 방법을 차례대로 설명한다. 우선 동물들에게 실험을 먼저 해보고 안전하면 100여명의 사람들을 고른다. 그 중 반에게는 진짜 약, 그리고 나머지에게는 가짜 약을 주고 약을 준다. 그렇게 해서 약이 진짜 효과가 있는지 확인하는 것이 마지막 단계이다.

medicine 약 fake 가짜의 pill 알약 effective 효과적인
placebo effect 플라시보 효과(속임약 투여에 의한 심리 효과로 실제로 호전되는 일)

Further Study p.119

Topic : Medicine Testing
• first, animals → then, humans
  – some danger but usually safe
✱ Testing Process on humans
• choose 100 → half, real medicine vs. half, fake medicine → results
• reasons for fake medicine
  – psych. problem, "placebo effect"
• effective medicine
  – people took real medicine > fake medicine
• simple process, but takes time and is expensive

Word Review   p.120

1. (B)   2. (D)   3. (A)   4. (D)
5. bend   6. float
7. show off   8. oath
9. valid   10. formality
11. surface   12. fake

Part C

7

Inference

Sample Question   p.123

W: 가을에 대학 입학하는 거 신나지 않니? 날씨도 멋질 거고, 많은 사람들이 어느 대학을 갈 지 고르고 있을 거야.

M: 응. 그런데 나는 그렇게나 많은 걸 준비해야 하는지 몰랐어.

W: 그래? 벌써 입학 지원서 보냈어?

M: 음, 나 TOEFL 시험 봤어. 거의 모든 대학교에서 필요하다더라. 시험 결과를 대학교들에 보냈어, 입학 지원 에세이도 같이.

W: 그럼 이제 또 뭘 해야 돼? 아니면 결과를 기다리는 중이야?

M: 아직 안 끝났어. 우리 선생님들로부터 추천서를 세 장 받아서 보내야 돼. 두 장은 받았는데, 지난 학기 생물학 선생님한테는 아직 못 받았어.

W: 선생님 사무실에 가보지 그래? 깜빡 잊으신 게 분명해.

M: 응, 그러려고 하고 있어.

Building Skills   p.124

Making Inferences

1. Q1. T   2. Q1. (A)
   Q2. F   Q2. (B)
   Q3. T

1. Shaolin is a form of martial arts from a temple in China. It is considered to be the oldest form of martial art in human history. It was made by a group of monks that wanted to protect themselves from invaders. It follows the movements of animals and reptiles. The movement looks gentle but is, in fact, very effective because it targets the weakest points of the human body. People still practice shaolin, and it is even spreading into the western world.

   소림권은 중국의 절에서 유래된 무술의 한 형태이다. 그것은 인류 역사상 가장 오래된 동양 무술의 형태라고 여겨진다. 그것은 외적으로부터 스스로를 지키고자 했던 한 승려 집단에 의해 만들어졌다. 그것은 동물과 파충류의 움직임을 따른다. 그 움직임은 부드러운 것 같지만, 사람 몸의 가장 약한 부분을 표적으로 하기 때문에 사실은 매우 효과적이다. 사람들은 현재도 소림권을 연습하며, 그것은 서양으로까지 퍼지고 있다.

2. W: We learned about Mt. Rushmore today. It was more

interesting than I thought.
M: Really? Tell me about it. I only know that it has the faces of four US presidents.
W: Well, people do not realize how big the faces really are.
M: How big are they?
W: The nose of Abraham Lincoln is about 2 meters. That is taller than you.
M: Wow, that is huge.
W: Yes, and it took over 14 years to complete the four faces. Since the faces were so big, they even used dynamite.

W: 우리 오늘 러시모어산에 대해서 배웠어. 생각보다 더 흥미롭더라.
M: 정말? 얘기해줘. 나는 거기에 미국 대통령 네명 얼굴이 있다는 것만 아는데.
W: 그런데, 사람들은 그 얼굴이 얼마나 큰 지를 실감을 못 해.
M: 얼마나 큰데?
W: 에이브러햄 링컨의 코가 약 2미터야. 네 키보다도 크지.
M: 와, 엄청 크다.

Gathering Information

1. (A)   2. (A), (B), (C)

1. W: Why can't we borrow more than 5 books from the library? I need more to finish my assignment.
M: Calm down. Why do you need so many books anyway?
W: I'm writing an essay for English literature, and a report about shooting stars.
M: Wow, that's going to be tough. So how many more books do you need to borrow?
W: I really need to borrow 2 more books on Edgar Allan Poe.
M: Hmm, let me help you, then. I can borrow 4 more books from the library. Just remember to return them on time. You know how expensive the fine is for late returns.

W: 왜 도서관에서 책을 5권 밖에 못 빌리는 거지? 숙제 하려면 더 필요한데.
M: 진정하라구. 그런데 책이 왜 그렇게 많이 필요해?
W: 영문학에 대한 글도 써야 되고, 유성에 대해서도 보고서를 써야 돼.
M: 와, 그거 힘들겠다. 책을 몇 권이나 빌려야 되는데?
W: 에드거 앨런 포우에 대한 책 두 권만 더 빌리면 돼.
M: 음, 그럼 내가 도와줄게. 나는 도서관에서 책을 4권 더 빌릴 수 있으니까. 제 시간에 반납하는 것만 기억해. 연체 벌금이 얼마나 비싼지 알잖아.

2. Most think that a bird's nest is made of leaves and branches. But a swallow's nest is different. The birds use their saliva to build their nest. The saliva hardens like cement. The nests are usually found on cave walls and look like small cups. Nest hunters have to climb very high in order to get the nests. It is a very hard and dangerous job. This is why the nests are rare and expensive.

대부분의 사람들은 새의 둥지가 나뭇잎과 나뭇가지로 만들어졌다고 생각한다. 그러나 제비의 둥지는 다르다. 새들은 둥지를 짓는데 침을 이용한다. 침은 시멘트처럼 굳어진다. 둥지는 보통 동굴 벽에서 발견되고, 작은 컵 모양으로 생겼다. 제비집 사냥꾼들은 제비집을 채집하기 위해서는 매우 높은 곳까지 벽을 타고 올라가야 한다. 그것은 매우 힘들고 위험한 작업이다. 이것이 바로 제비집이 그렇게 진귀하고 비싼 이유이다.

Basic Drills   p.126

1. (B)   2. (D)   3. (C)   4. (A)   5. (C)
6. (B)   7. (C)   8. (A)   9. (D)

1. Hydrogen is the most common element because it is a part of water. This is why scientists work hard to separate it from water and use it as energy. The most popular forms of energy are petroleum and gas. These forms of energy are produced easily compared to hydrogen, but they cause air pollution. Once we can find easier ways to produce hydrogen from water, air pollution from cars and buses will be a thing of the past.

수소는 물의 요소이기 때문에 가장 흔한 원소이다. 과학자들이 수소를 물로부터 분리해 내고 그것을 에너지로 사용하려고 열심히 연구하는 것은 바로 이 때문이다. 에너지의 가장 흔한 형태는 석유와 가스이다. 이런 형태의 에너지는 수소에 비해서 쉽게 생산되지만, 대기 오염을 유발한다. 물에서 수소를 생산해 내는 더 쉬운 방법을 발견한다면, 자동차와 버스로부터 생기는 대기 오염은 지난 날의 일이 될 것이다.

•• 해 설 ••

"Once we can find easier ways to produce hydrogen from water ..."를 통해 수소를 물에서부터 분리해 내는 것이 쉽지 않다는 것을 추론할 수 있다. (A)와 (C)는 본문을 통해 알 수 없다. (D)는 석유와 가스에 해당하는 얘기다.

hydrogen 수소   element 원소

2. W: I'm going on a field trip for the weekend in astronomy class. I remember that you said you were interested in going.
   M: Oh, yes. I really want to go, but I think I have to meet with the members of my music club.
   W: That's a pity. We are planning to go to the planetarium, and then see the stars at night.
   M: That sounds wonderful. Tell you what, I will call them and push the meeting to another day.

   W: 이번 주말에 천문학 수업에서 견학 갈 거야. 너도 참가에 관심 있다고 했던 걸로 기억하는데.
   M: 어, 맞아. 정말로 가고 싶은데. 음악 동아리 친구들을 만나야 돼서.
   W: 안됐다. 우리는 플라네타리움(천체투영실)에 갈 계획이고, 밤에는 별도 볼 거야.
   M: 그거 정말 대단하겠는데. 있잖아. 애들한테 전화해서 모임을 다른 날로 미뤄야겠어.

   •• 해 설 ••

   마지막에 남자가 "I will call them and push the meeting to another day." 라고 한 말에서 남자가 음악 동아리 모임을 취소할 것임을 알 수 있다.

   field trip 견학   astronomy 천문학
   planetarium 플라네타륨; 천체투영실

3. W: I'm so tired. I was awake the whole night.
   M: What's wrong?
   W: I have a chemistry test in the afternoon. I'm so nervous that I can't remember what I studied.
   M: Do you always get tense before an exam?
   W: I think I do. Do you know how I might be able to relax?
   M: As a matter of fact, I have a book that can help you. It's about stress relief. Let me go get it for you.
   W: Thanks. I'll return it when I'm done with the book.

   W: 정말 피곤해. 밤새 깨어있었다니까.
   M: 뭐가 문제인데?
   W: 오후에 화학 시험이 있어. 그런데 너무 초조해서 공부했던 걸 기억을 못 하겠어.
   M: 시험 전에는 항상 긴장하니?
   W: 그런 것 같아. 어떻게 하면 긴장을 풀 수 있는지 알아?
   M: 사실은, 너한테 도움이 될만한 책이 한 권 있는데. 스트레스 완화에 대한 거야. 가서 가져다 줄게.
   W: 고마워. 책 다 읽으면 돌려줄게.

   •• 해 설 ••

   "... I have a book that can help you. Let me go get it for you." 라고 남자가 말했으므로 남자가 여자에게 책을 빌려줄 것이다.

   chemistry 화학   tense 긴장한

4. M: May I borrow your bike?
   W: Of course you can. It's downstairs. Mine is the blue one. What do you need it for, though? You live in the dormitory.
   M: It's because of my classes. I only have five minutes to get to the next class, but it takes me more than that.
   W: Oh, I know what you mean. I got an idea. Feel free to use my bike except on the weekends.
   M: Really? Thank you so much.

   M: 자전거 좀 빌려도 될까?
   W: 물론 되지. 아래층에 있어. 내 건 파란색이야. 근데, 뭐 때문에 필요한 거야? 너는 기숙사에 살잖아.
   M: 수업 때문에. 다음 수업에 들어갈 때까지 5분 밖에 없는데. 그것보다 더 걸리거든.
   W: 아, 무슨 말인지 알아. 나한테 좋은 생각이 있는데. 주말 빼고는 언제라도 편하게 내 자전거 써도 돼.
   M: 진짜? 정말로 고맙다.

   •• 해 설 ••

   "Feel free to use my bike except on the weekends." 라고 여자가 말한 것을 보아, 여자가 주중이 아닌 주말에만 자전거를 사용함을 알 수 있다. 그러므로 답은 (A)이다. (B), (C), (D)는 틀린 내용이다.

   feel free to 부담 없이 ~하다

5. Biscuits and potato chips are always in airtight bags. There are good reasons for this. 🎧 The most obvious one is so that they do not fall out of the bag. But another reason is to keep the food fresh as long as possible. Bacteria need air to make food go bad, so preventing fresh air from going into the packet can extend freshness. Also, a bag full of air stops the potato chips and biscuits inside from breaking.

   비스켓과 감자칩은 언제나 밀폐된 봉지에 들어있다. 여기에는 타당한 이유들이 있다. 가장 분명한 것은, 내용물이 봉지 밖으로 빠져 나오지 못하도록 하기 위함이다. 또 다른 이유는, 최대한 오랫동안 음식을 신선하게 보관하기 위함이다. 박테리아가 음식을 상하게 하려면 공기가 필요하기 때문에, 포장 속으로 신선한 공기가 들어가는 것을 막음으로써 신선함을 연장

시킬 수 있다. 또한, 공기로 가득 찬 봉지는 그 안의 감자칩이나 비스켓이 부서지는 것을 막아 준다.

•• 해 설 ••

공기가 팽팽하게 밀폐된 봉지에 비스켓이나 감자칩이 들어있는 이유가 우선은 내용물이 밖으로 나오지 않게 하려는 것임은 두 말할 나위 없이 당연한 것이다. 이 외에도 다른 특별한 이유가 있다는 것을 말하기 위해 언지를 준 것이라고 봐야 한다.

airtight 밀폐된   bacteria 박테리아; 세균   extend 연장하다

6. People are sensitive to smell. Smell can even make a person seem attractive. As a result, many people use perfumes. But what goes into perfumes? Long ago, perfumes were made of all natural things. This included parts of animal scents and flower oils. The animal scents mostly came from male deer or big whales. But people who were allergic to these animals couldn't use the perfumes. Therefore, companies now mix chemicals to make perfumes smell great.

사람들은 냄새에 민감하다. 냄새는 사람을 매력적으로 만들어 줄 수도 있다. 그래서 사람들은 향수를 쓴다. 그렇다면, 향수에는 무엇이 들어갈까? 오래전, 향수는 자연적인 것들로 만들어졌다. 이것은 동물의 향과 꽃의 기름을 포함한다. 대부분의 동물의 향기는 수컷 사슴이나 큰 고래에서 얻었다. 그런데, 어떤 사람들은 동물 알레르기가 있어, 향수를 사용할 수가 없었다. 그래서, 기업들은 이제 향기 좋은 향수를 만들기 위해서 화학물질들을 섞는다.

•• 해 설 ••

동물의 향을 채취하여 만든 자연적 향수에 알레르기 반응을 보이는 사람들이 있어서 이제는 화학 물질을 섞는다고 말했다. 그러므로 화학물질은 동물의 향보다는 사람들에게 알레르기 반응을 덜 일으킨다고 추론해 볼 수 있다.

sensitive (to) ~에 민감한   attractive 매력적인
allergic 알레르기가 있는

7. W: I just bought a new history book from the university website.
   M: I don't trust the internet with money. I heard that a lot of bad people steal your money.
   W: That's old news. Most people shop on the internet. It's very safe now. Besides, it's so much easier to shop on the internet than to go to shops and waste time.
   M: Really? Maybe it's time I started trusting the internet. I'll give it a try tonight.
   W: Good for you.

W: 방금 대학교 웹사이트에서 새로 나온 역사책 샀어.
M: 나는 돈과 관련해서는 인터넷을 안 믿어. 많은 나쁜 사람들이 돈을 훔친다고 들었어.
W: 그건 옛날 일이야. 대부분의 사람들이 인터넷에서 쇼핑을 한다구. 이제는 아주 안전해. 또, 직접 가서 쇼핑을 하고 시간을 낭비하는 것보다 인터넷에서 쇼핑하는 것이 훨씬 더 쉬워.
M: 정말? 인터넷을 믿어도 될 때가 되었나봐. 오늘밤에 한 번 해보지 뭐.
W: 잘났네.

•• 해 설 ••

"Maybe it's time I started trusting the internet. I'll give it a try tonight."라고 남자가 마지막에 말했는데 여기서 시도해 보겠다고 하는 대상은 인터넷 쇼핑이다. 그러므로 인터넷으로 물건을 구매할 것이라는 (C)가 답이 된다. 나머지 (A), (B), (D)는 반대로 쓰여져야 옳다.

that's old news 그건 옛날 일이야

8. SUVs are large sized cars that people enjoy driving around on roads. People drive them because they feel safe and comfortable in these cars. But there has been talk about banning SUVs on the road, as some people think they are too dangerous. When smaller cars are involved in accidents with SUVs, the smaller cars suffer a lot of damage. In fact, much of the damage could be avoided if SUVs weren't so large. As a solution, car companies are looking into making SUVs that cause less damage to other cars in crashes.

SUV는 사람들이 도로에서 타고 돌아다니기를 즐기는 큰 크기의 자동차이다. 사람들은 그 차 안에서는 안전하고 편안하다고 느끼기 때문에 SUV를 운전한다. 그런데 일부의 사람들이 SUV가 너무 위험하다고 생각하는 만큼, 도로에서 그것을 금지하는 것에 대한 이야기가 있어왔다. 소형차가 SUV와 사고를 낼 경우에 소형차의 피해가 매우 크다. 사실, SUV가 그렇게 크지 않았다면, 피해를 많이 줄일 수 있었을 것이다. 해결책의 하나로, 자동차 회사들은 SUV가 충돌할 때 다른 차들에게 덜 손상을 주는 SUV를 만들려고 하고 있다.

•• 해 설 ••

"... much of the damage could be avoided if SUVs weren't so large."로부터 SUV의 크기가 너무 커서 안전 문제가 있었다는 것을 추론할 수 있다.

damage 피해   crash 충돌사고

9. *Lord of the Flies* is the name of a very famous book.

It was written by William Golding, who won the Nobel Prize in literature for the book. The book talks about a group of boys on an island. They soon part into two groups, and one of them turns violent and vicious. The book is really telling us how humans can change when left alone. The book won a Nobel Prize, and many schools use this book in English literature classes.

「파리대왕」은 매우 유명한 책의 제목이다. 그것은 그 책으로 노벨 문학상을 수상한 윌리엄 골딩에 의해서 쓰여졌다. 그 책은 한 섬의 남자 아이들 무리에 대해 이야기한다. 그들은 곧 두 무리로 나뉘고, 그 중 한 무리는 폭력적이고 잔인하게 변해버린다. 이 책은 사람이 홀로 남겨질 경우 어떻게 변할 수 있는가 얘기해 주고 있다. 이 책은 노벨 문학상을 받았고, 많은 학교에서 이 책을 영문학 수업에서 사용한다.

•• 해설 ••

「파리대왕」은 인간이 혼자 남겨졌을 때 어떻게 할 수 있는지를 다룬, 영문학 수업에 이용되는 책이므로 교육적일 것이라고 추론할 수 있다. 그러므로 답은 (D)이다. 나머지 (A), (B), (C)는 정답과 매우 거리가 멀다.

vicious 잔인한

Listening Practice 1   p.129

1. (D)   2. (B)   3. Yes: (A), (D) / No: (B), (C)

M: I have to write a long essay about an emergency rescue service. It can't be about fire, rescue, police or the ambulance. I don't know any more than those. Can you help me out?
W: Sure. Let me see … Well, there's the coast guard. I'm sure that you would have a lot to write about.
M: What can I write about them? I don't know anything about them, except that their uniform is red and white.
W: There are so many things you can write about. They have the same power and work as police officers on the streets do. They catch bad people, make sure that there's no trouble, and so on. The big difference is that they patrol the sea.
M: Is that all? Then there's not much difference between police officers on the street and on the sea.
W: No, coast guards are also like lifeguards on beaches and swimming pools. They train very hard to rescue people in the water. They must always be healthy, and even learn to swim in the sea during dangerous storms.
M: Wow, they are more interesting than I thought. How wrong I was. I think I'll write about them after I find out more about them in the library. Thanks for helping me out.

M: 비상 구조 활동에 대한 긴 글을 써야 돼. 화재, 구조, 경찰이나 앰뷸런스에 대해서는 안 된대. 그것들 말고는 모르겠어. 좀 도와줄 수 있니?
W: 그래. 어디 보자… 그래, 해안경비대 있잖아. 분명히 쓸 게 많이 있을 거야.
M: 그들에 대해서 뭘 쓸 수 있어? 제복이 빨갛고 하얗다는 것 말고는 하나도 모르는데.
W: 쓸 수 있는 건 아주 많지. 그 사람들의 권한이나 업무는 도로에서의 경찰과 같아. 나쁜 사람들을 잡고, 아무 문제가 생기지 않도록 하는 등등. 차이가 있다면, 해안 경비대는 바다를 순찰한다는 것이지.
M: 그게 다야? 그럼 도로에서의 경찰관들이랑 바다에서나 별 차이가 없는걸.
W: 아니, 해안경비대는 해변이나 수영장의 인명구조원들하고도 비슷해. 그들은 수중에서 사람들을 구조하기 위해서 아주 열심히 훈련하지. 언제나 건강해야 되고, 위험한 폭풍우 속에서도 수영을 하는 것까지도 배워야 돼.
M: 우와, 내가 생각했던 것 보다 더 재미있네. 내가 잘못 알고 있었구나. 도서관에서 더 찾아보고 글을 써야 될 것 같다. 도와줘서 고마워.

•• 해설 ••

1. "I have to write a long essay about an emergency rescue service. It can't be about fire, rescue, police or the ambulance. I don't know any more than those. Can you help me out?"라고 처음에 남자가 말했다. 즉, 에세이를 쓰는 것에 대해 도움을 얻고자 여자에게 말을 건 것이다.

2. "I think I'll write about them after I find out more about them in the library."라고 마지막에 남자가 말했다. 여기서 "them"은 해안 경비대를 가리킨다. 그러므로 해안 경비대에 관해 글을 쓸 것이라는 (B)가 답이 된다.

3. 해안 경비대가 경찰과의 가장 큰 차이점은 바다를 순찰하는 것이다. 또한 물에 빠진 사람을 구하기 위해 폭풍우 속에서도 수영하는 법을 배운다고 했으므로 굳은 날씨 중에도 사람들을 돕는다고 할 수 있다. 해안 경비대가 남을 훈련시키는 것이 아니라 스스로 훈련하는 것이므로 둘째 보기는 틀리며 또한 경찰과 함께 일하는 것이 아니라 경찰과 같은 권한과 업무를 갖는 것이라고 했으므로 셋째 보기도 답이 아니다.

emergency 비상 (사태)   rescue 구조   patrol 순찰하다
lifeguard 인명구조원

Listening Practice 2   p.131

1. (B), (C)   2. (C)   3. (A)

The early 1900s saw a big advancement in air travel. Soon after the Wright brothers performed their first flight, people started inventing new ways to fly. Many tried to make flying aircraft, but an airship called the Zeppelin was the most popular aircraft during the early years of flight.

The Zeppelin was like a floating balloon. It had a very large tube at the top, filled with hydrogen. Hydrogen was used because it was much lighter than air. So, like helium balloons, the Zeppelin floated easily. Small propellers were used to change direction of the airship.

The benefits of Zeppelins seemed endless. The passenger compartment was below the tube, and although it was very slow, it was very quiet and stable. Planes during that time were very expensive. On the other hand, people could travel in Zeppelins for a very cheap price. However, the Zeppelins could not carry as much weight as other planes. Regardless, during both World Wars, the Germans used the Zeppelins as spy planes and to carry bombs.

Unfortunately, the Zeppelins had a sad and quick ending. A very large Zeppelin called the *Hindenburg* crashed and burned very quickly, due to the dangerous hydrogen in the big tubes. The accident happened on a trip to the US, and it killed hundreds of people. It was the last Zeppelin to carry many people at once. There are still a handful of airships around today, but only for advertisements.

1900년대 초, 항공 교통에는 큰 진보가 있었다. 라이트 형제가 그들의 첫 비행을 시연하고 얼마 뒤, 사람들은 날 수 있는 다른 수단을 발명하기 시작했다. 많은 사람들이 날 수 있는 항공기를 만들려고 했지만, 체펠린 비행선이라고 불리는 비행선이 비행의 초기 시대에 가장 인기 있는 항공기였다.

체펠린 비행선은 떠 있는 풍선과 같았다. 그것의 윗부분에는 수소로 가득 찬 매우 큰 관이 있었다. 공기보다 훨씬 가볍기 때문에 수소가 사용되었다. 따라서, 헬륨 풍선처럼, 체펠린 비행선은 쉽게 떴다. 비행선의 방향을 바꾸기 위해서 작은 프로펠러들이 사용되었다.

체펠린 비행선의 용도는 무궁무진해 보였다. 객실은 관 밑에 아래쪽에 위치했고, 비록 매우 느렸지만, 아주 조용하고 흔들림이 없었다. 비행기들은 당시에 매우 비쌌다. 반면에, 사람들은 아주 싼 값에 체펠린 비행선으로 여행할 수 있었다. 그러나, 체펠린 비행선은 비행기만큼 많은 무게를 싣지는 못했다. 그럼에도, 두 번의 세계 대전 동안 독일인들은 체펠린 비행선을 정찰기와 폭탄을 실어 나르는 데에 이용했다.

불행히도, 체펠린 비행선은 슬프고 빠른 종말을 맞았다. 힌덴부르크라고 불리던 초대형의 체펠린 비행선이 대형 통 안의 위험한 수소 때문에 추락한 후 엄청나게 빨리 전소되어버린 것이다. 그 사고는 미국으로의 비행 중에 일어났고, 수백 명의 사람을 죽게 했다. 그것은 한번에 많은 사람을 싣는 마지막 체펠린 비행선이었다. 오늘날 세계 곳곳에는 아직도 소수의 비행선이 남아있지만, 오직 광고를 위한 것들이다.

•• 해 설 ••

1. 체펠린 비행선의 장단점이 제시되었다. 장점은 매우 조용하고 흔들림이 없다는 것, 그리고 가격이 싸다는 것이다. 단점은 많은 무게를 싣지 못하고 수소로 인해 위험할 수 있다는 것이다. 그러므로 장점은 둘째, 셋째 보기이다.

2. 힌덴부르크호의 사고 이후에는 체펠린 비행선이 더 이상 운송수단으로 운행되지 않고, 광고용으로만 사용되고 있다고 했다.

3. 세계대전 중 정찰기나 폭탄을 실어 나르는 데에 체펠린 비행선이 이용되었다는 언급을 한 이유는 이 비행선이 여러 가지 중요한 용도로 사용되었다는 것을 보여주기 위함이나. 여기에 가장 가까운 답은 (A)이다.

advancement 진보 hydrogen 수소 compartment 객실
stable 흔들림 없는, 안정된 regardless 그럼에도, 어쨌든
at once 한번에

p.133

1. (B)   2. (C)   3. (C)

W: Hey, Derek. I need to ask you about a few things.
M: Sure. How can I help?
W: I remember that you used to work for the school newspaper for some time. Was it good working there?
M: Yes, it was a lot of fun. It's a pity I had to quit because of my studies, because I would still love to do it.
W: Good. I asked you because I'm thinking of getting into the school newspaper myself.
M: That's great. I really encourage you to try it.
W: Yes, but as you know, I'm a first year student, and I don't know if I am qualified.
M: I didn't think about that. I was a second year student, so I can't say if it's possible or not. You'll have to ask the editor-in-chief about it first. But personally, I don't see why first year students can't become reporters.
W: I'm glad to hear about it, thanks. Oh, could I ask you another question?
M: Of course you can. What else would you like to know?
W: Must I sit through a test before I can work there? I want to be prepared for anything that I might have to do.
M: Yes, the editors will test your writing skills. When you pass that, then you will be tested on speaking. That's all I can remember. Then, if your results are good enough, you'll be hired as a junior reporter. I suggest that you go and meet with the editor-in-chief.
W: Thanks a lot. I think I'll do that right now.

W: 데릭 안녕. 너한테 몇 가지 좀 물어봐야겠어.
M: 그래, 무슨 일이야?
W: 네가 학보사에서 얼마 동안 일한적 있던 것이 기억나는데. 거기서 일하는 거 좋았어?
M: 응. 아주 재미있었어. 아직도 정말 일하고 싶은데. 공부 때문에 그만둬야만 했으니 안타깝지.
W: 그렇구나. 내가 학보사 기자로 들어갈까 생각중이거든.
M: 그거 잘됐다. 한번 해봐.
W: 응. 그런데 알다시피. 나는 1학년이잖아. 그래서 내가 자격이 되는지 모르겠어.
M: 그건 생각 못했네. 나는 2학년이었으니까. 그게 가능한지 아닌지는 말 못 하겠다. 먼저 편집장한테 물어봐야 될 거야. 근데 개인적으로는, 왜 1학년은 기자가 될 수 없는지 이해할 수 없어.
W: 그 얘기를 들으니까 좋다. 고마워. 아, 다른 것 하나 물어봐도 돼?
M: 당연히 물어봐도 되지. 또 뭘 알고 싶은 거야?
W: 거기서 일하려면 시험을 치러야 하는거니? 준비해야 될 것이 있으면 준비하고 싶은데.
M: 응. 편집자들이 너의 작문 실력을 시험할거야. 그걸 통과하면, 말하기도 시험 볼거야. 기억나는 것은 그게 다야. 그 다음에, 네 시험 결과가 충분히 좋으면, 부(副)기자로 고용될 거야. 가서 편집장을 만나보는 게 좋을 것 같다.
W: 정말 고마워. 지금 만나뵈야 겠어.

•• 해 설 ••

1. "I asked you because I'm thinking of getting into the school newspaper myself."를 통해 여자가 학보사에 기자로 들어가려고 하는데 전에 거기서 일했던 데릭에게 몇 가지 물어보기 위해 말을 걸었다는 사실을 알 수 있다. 남자와 인터뷰를 한다거나 토론을 하려는 것은 아니다. 그러므로 답은 (B)이다.

2. 마지막에 데릭이 편집장을 만나보라고 권했고 여자는 당장 그렇게 하겠다고 했으므로 답은 (C)이다.

3. 학보사 기자가 되려면 시험에 합격해야 하는데 시험은 작문과 말하기 시험의 순서로 있다고 말해주었다. 그러므로 답은 (C)이다. 남자가 신문사 시험을 교내 다른 시험과 비교한 적 없고, 시험에 나올 문제를 알려준 적도 없으므로 (B)와 (D)는 답이 될 수 없다.

qualified 자격이 되는   editor-in-chief 편집장

iBT Practice p.135

1. (A)   2. (A)   3. (B), (D)   4. (B)

T: Hello. Today we are going to talk about a famous European figure as a great soldier, general and fierce leader. Do you have any idea whom I am talking about?
M: Hmmm ... Are you talking about Napoleon?
T: Yes. As you know, Napoleon was a French general. He was not from royalty, and he wasn't even French. He was born in Corsica, a little island off the coast of Italy, and the French invaded the island and made it part of France. His family was poor, but the father was able to go to Paris and see the beauty of the city. He wanted his son Napoleon to succeed and managed to get him enrolled in an excellent school in France.

  It would have been impossible for a foreigner with no money and friends, like Napoleon, to succeed in France. But history changed, and so did Napoleon's life. The French Revolution happened, and the government granted full rights of citizenship to people who were not French. Because of this historical event, Napoleon participated in French politics and was able to demonstrate his skill.

  Napoleon was very ambitious, and he wanted to conquer the whole of Europe. He nearly succeeded, but other European countries fought back fiercely and did not allow him to carry out his dreams. The French soon got tired of fighting. Despite the constant battles, Napoleon is not remembered just for his fighting. While he conquered Egypt, he ordered scholars to research into Egyptian culture and art, and succeeded in reading the ancient Egyptian picture writing called hieroglyphics. He also established the Napoleonic Code, which is a set of civil codes or civil laws. Many of the European countries copied the Napoleonic Code.

  Well, time is over. See you next time.

T: 안녕하세요. 오늘은 위대한 군인이자, 장군, 그리고 용맹스러운 지도자로서 유명한 유럽의 한 인물에 대해서 이야기해 보겠습니다. 제가 누구에 대해서 말하는 것인지 알겠나요?
M: 음… 나폴레옹 말씀이신가요?
T: 그래요. 아시다시피, 나폴레옹은 프랑스의 장군이었습니다. 그는 왕족도 아니었고, 프랑스 사람도 아니었어요. 그는 이탈리아 연안의 작은 섬으로, 프랑스인들이 침공해 프랑스령으로 만들었던 코르시카섬에서 태어났습니다. 나폴레옹의 가족은 가난했지만 그의 아버지는 파리로 가서 그 도시의 아름다움을 볼 수 있었죠. 그는 나폴레옹이 성공하기를 원했고 결국 그를 프랑스의 일류 학교에 입학시키는데 성공했습니다.

  나폴레옹처럼 돈도 친구도 없는 외국인이 프랑스에서 성공하기는 불가능했을 수도 있습니다. 그러나 역사는 바뀌었고, 나폴레옹의 삶도 그랬습니다. 프랑스 혁명이 일어났고. 정부는 프랑스인이 아닌 사람들에게도 시민권의 완전한 권리를 승인했습니다. 이 역사적 사건 덕분에. 나폴레옹은 프랑스의 정치에 참여해 그의 수완을 보여줄 수 있었습니다.

  나폴레옹은 매우 야심적이었고. 그는 유럽 전체를 정복하고자 했습니

다. 그는 거의 성공했지만, 유럽의 다른 나라들이 맹렬히 반격했고 그의 야망을 이루도록 허락하지 않았습니다. 프랑스인들은 곧 전쟁이 지긋지긋해졌죠. 계속된 전쟁에도 불구하고, 나폴레옹은 그의 전쟁 때문에 기억되는 것만은 아니에요. 이집트를 정복하는 동안 그는 학자들에게 이집트의 문화와 예술을 연구하라고 명령해서 상형문자라고 불리는 고대 이집트의 그림 글자를 해석하는데 성공했습니다. 그는 또한 민사 판례나 민법을 모은 나폴레옹 법전을 제정했어요. 유럽의 많은 나라들이 나폴레옹 법전을 모방했습니다.

자, 시간이 다 됐군요. 다음 시간에 봅시다.

•• 해 설 ••

1. 선생님이 수업 처음에 '위대한 군인이자, 장군 그리고 용맹스러운 지도자로 유명한 유럽의 한 인물에 대해 얘기하겠다'고 말했다. 그 인물은 나폴레옹이므로 나폴레옹의 인생과 업적이라는 (A)가 답이다.

2. "... history changed, and so did Napoleon's life. The French Revolution happened ..."을 보면 프랑스 혁명으로 나폴레옹의 인생이 바뀐 것을 알 수 있다. 이 역사적 사건으로 프랑스인이 아니었던 나폴레옹이 시민권을 가질 수 있었고 정치에 참여할 길이 트인 것이다.

3. "... Napoleon is not remembered just for his fighting." 이 문장 뒤에 나폴레옹이 성취한 두 가지가 제시되었다. 하나는 학자들로 하여금 이집트 상형문자를 해석하게 한 것이고, 다른 하나는 나폴레옹 법전을 제정한 것이다.

4. 선생님은 "Despite the constant battles, Napoleon is not remembered just for his fighting"이라고 말하며, 나폴레옹의 다른 업적의 예를 든다. 이집트 문화에 대한 이야기를 하긴 하지만 나폴레옹의 다른 업적이 핵심내용이기 때문에 정답이 (D)라고 보기 힘들다.

> figure 인물   general 장군   fierce 용맹스러운, 격렬한   royalty 왕족   manage to 성공하다, 간신히 해내다   enroll 입학시키다   grant 승인하다   citizenship 시민권   participate in 참여하다   demonstrate 보여주다   ambitious 야심적인   conquer 정복하다   despite ~에도 불구하고   constant 계속되는, 끊임없는   scholars 학자   hieroglyphics (고대 이집트의) 상형문자

Further Study   p.137

Napoleon : great soldier, general, fierce leader

- He was not from royalty, and not French either
- Historical event : French Revolution
  ∴ He got citizenship from the govt.
- Napoleon's achievements : • Egyptian research
  • Napoleonic Code

Word Review   p.138

1. (C)   2. (D)   3. (D)   4. (C)
5. sensitive   6. emergency
7. patrol   8. advancement
9. regardless   10. qualified
11. manage   12. constant

Actual Test ① p.142

1. (B)	2. (A)	3. (C)	4. (A)	5. (D)
6. (D)	7. (A)	8. (B)	9. (C)	10. (C)
11. (D)	12. (B)	13. (D)	14. (B)	15. (C)
16. (D)	17. (B)			

1-5.

M: Excuse me. Do you offer any computing classes in this lab?
W: I'm sorry. We don't have actual classes to teach computers to students, but perhaps I can help you. Are you new to computers?
M: Yes. It's really hard telling someone this, but I've never used a computer in my life.
W: That's alright. There are many people that are new to computers. But if you're uncomfortable learning from courses, then you might want to try learning it by yourself. Our computer labs have very easy instructions on the bulletin boards. It is easy enough for beginners to try for themselves. Also, there is a computer assistant that works part-time in there. He can help you if you have any problems. He's a student here, and you might even know him.
M: I was hoping that I could learn from a stranger. I feel that I won't be shy to ask questions to strangers.
W: 🎧 I don't know about that. The assistants know how to teach beginners because they know what they are talking about, but I'm not so sure with complete strangers.
M: I guess you have a point. Is there any other way that I might be able to learn computers easily?
W: There are so many ways. Oh, I just remembered something. I bought my dad this book about using computers for beginners. You see, he's a beginner in computers, just like you, and he said that the book was very helpful. I'm not sure if they still sell it in the bookstore. Maybe the book will help you out, too. So, what would you like to do? Do you want the assistant's contact?
M: Perhaps I'd better get that too. Thank you. You've been so much help.

M: 실례합니다. 이 연구실에서 컴퓨터 수업을 제공하나요?
W: 죄송합니다. 저희는 실제로 학생들에게 컴퓨터를 가르치는 수업은 안 하는데요. 아마 제가 도와드릴 수 있을 것 같아요. 컴퓨터는 처음이신가요?
M: 예. 누군가에게 이런 얘기를 하기는 정말 어렵지만, 저는 평생 동안 컴퓨터를 한 번도 안 써봤어요.
W: 괜찮아요. 컴퓨터에 처음인 사람들도 많이 있거든요. 그런데, 수업으로 컴퓨터를 배우는 것이 불편하면, 스스로 배워볼 수도 있어요. 저희 연구실의 게시판에는 아주 쉬운 사용법들이 있어요. 초보자들이 직접 해볼 수 있을 정도로 쉬워요. 또, 거기에서 시간제로 일하는 컴퓨터 조교도 있습니다. 문제가 있으면 그가 도와줄 거에요. 그는 여기 학생이고, 아는 사람일 수도 있겠네요.
M: 낯선 사람한테서 배웠으면 좋겠는데요. 모르는 사람이라면 질문하는 데도 부끄럽지 않을 것 같아요.
W: 그것은 모르겠군요. 조교들은 잘 알기 때문에 초보자들을 어떻게 가르치는지 아는 거고요. 그렇지만 완전히 모르는 사람들이 그러할지는 확실하지 않네요.
M: 일리가 있는 것 같아요. 컴퓨터를 쉽게 배울 수 있는 다른 방법은 없나요?
W: 여러 가지 많은 방법이 있지요. 아, 방금 뭐가 생각났네요. 제가 아버지께 컴퓨터 사용에 관한 초보자들을 위한 책을 사 드렸거든요. 그 분은 학생처럼 컴퓨터 초보자였는데, 그 책이 아주 도움이 됐다고 하시더군요. 아직도 서점에서 파는 지는 모르겠네요. 아마 그 책이 학생에게도 도움이 될 거에요. 그럼. 어떻게 하시겠어요? 조교의 연락처를 원하세요?
M: 아마 그것도 받는 게 좋을 것 같아요. 감사합니다. 정말 많은 도움이 됐어요.

lab 연구실 bulletin board 게시판

6-11.

T: Whales are the largest creatures on Earth. Naturally, they must eat a tremendous amount to store up plenty of energy. And whales move to warmer waters when the waters get cold.
W: Why do they need to do that? I thought that whales do not get affected by cold weather.
T: Q11 🎧 Most whales move to warmer waters. Why they need to do this is debatable. There is a theory that says whales move in order to save their energy.
M: That doesn't make much sense to me. Aren't they wasting a lot of energy just by swimming around?
T: You brought up a very good point. Logic tells us that whales are doing something foolish. They use up a lot of energy by moving their huge body. Still, they somehow know that once they reach warmer waters, they can get much more energy. I personally think that this theory is believable. It's quite amazing, if you think about it.
M: What do you mean by that?
T: Warmer waters have more food than colder waters

for the whales to eat. It's only natural that more small animals live in warmer waters than ice cold waters. The whales seem to know this.

W: You mean that the whales are intelligent enough to make such decisions?

T: Maybe, maybe not. So far, people think it's more towards instinct than intelligence. After all, it's all theories. Q9 🎧 But what is amazing is the fact that whales seem to have a map of the world's oceans in their head. They almost always end up safe in warmer waters. This theory looks like it's worth studying more about.

T: 고래는 지구상에서 가장 큰 생물입니다. 자연히, 그들은 많은 에너지를 저장하기 위해서 엄청난 양을 먹어야 하죠. 그리고 고래들은 수온이 낮아지면 따뜻한 물로 이동합니다.

W: 왜 그래야 하는 겁니까? 저는 고래는 찬 날씨에 영향을 안 받을 거라고 생각했는데요.

T: 대부분의 고래들이 따뜻한 물을 찾아 이동합니다. 왜 그래야 하는지는 논쟁의 여지가 있어요. 고래가 에너지를 저장하기 위해서 이동한다는 설도 있습니다.

M: 저한테는 별로 수긍이 안 가는데요. 그냥 수영만 해도 많은 에너지를 낭비하는 것 아닌가요?

T: 좋은 지적을 했어요. 논리로 보자면 고래들이 바보 같은 짓을 하고 있는 것이죠. 그들은 그 큰 몸을 움직임으로써 많은 에너지는 소모합니다. 그래도, 그들은 따뜻한 물이 있는 곳에 닿으면, 더 많은 에너지를 얻을 수 있다는 것을 어떻게든 알고 있는 것이죠. 개인적으로는 이 설이 믿을만하다고 생각됩니다. 생각해 보면 그건 꽤 놀라워요.

M: 무슨 뜻이에요?

T: 따뜻한 물에는 찬 물보다 고래들이 먹을 수 있는 먹이가 더 많아요. 얼음처럼 찬 물보다 따뜻한 물에 더 많은 작은 동물이 사는 것은 당연한 것이죠. 고래들은 이것을 알고 있는 것 같습니다.

W: 고래들이 그런 결정을 내릴 만큼 똑똑하다는 뜻인가요?

T: 그럴 수도 있고, 아닐 수도 있죠. 지금까지, 사람들은 그것이 지능보다 본능에 가깝다고 생각해요. 아무튼, 그것은 모두 가설이죠. 그렇지만, 놀라운 것은 고래들이 전세계 바다의 지도를 머릿속에 가지고 있는 것 같다는 겁니다. 그들은 거의 언제나 따뜻한 바다에 안전하게 있죠. 이 가설은 충분히 더 연구해 볼만한 가치가 있는 것 같습니다.

creature 생물   tremendous 엄청난, 거대한   store up 저장하다
debatable 논쟁의 여지가 있는   logic 논리   intelligent 똑똑한

12-17.

Greenhouses are used by farmers in cold climates. They allow plants to get sunlight and trap heat. The result is warm air inside the greenhouse. Scientists use them as an example to explain a big problem on our planet. It is global warming. The theory is that the whole world is becoming hotter because of what humans are doing on Earth. They say that humans are polluting the environment and making tall buildings that are bad for the environment.

Different gases absorb heat bounced off the Earth. Most of the heat is supposed to go back into space. But too much gas in our atmosphere, such as carbon dioxide, means that a lot of the heat will remain on Earth. The gases act like a plastic roof in greenhouses. They prevent the heat from escaping. This can lead to higher temperatures. Although we might not feel it, the world has become hotter in the last 100 years by about 0.6 degree Celsius. At this rate, in 1,000 years, the world would be 6 degrees hotter. It would be a huge disaster to the world. If the icebergs of the world were to melt, the whole Earth will be flooded.

Another reason why scientists think humans are to blame for global warming is because of our buildings. Everything on Earth is supposed to absorb some heat, as color absorbs heat. But big, tall buildings in large cities have very shiny and silver windows, almost like mirrors. They do not absorb much heat. Instead, they reflect as much heat as possible. The heat, instead of going back to space, gets trapped in the gases. Experts think that this cycle is making Earth hotter.

온실은 찬 기후 지방의 농민들이 사용한다. 그것들은 식물이 햇빛을 받을 수 있게 하고, 열을 가두도록 해 준다. 그 결과가 온실 안의 따뜻한 공기이다. 과학자들을 지구의 큰 문제를 설명하기 위해서 이 예를 사용한다. 그것은 바로 지구온난화(global warming)이다. 그 학설은 사람들이 하는 일로 인해서, 지구 전체가 더워지고 있다는 것이다. 그들은 사람들이 환경을 오염시키고 있고, 높은 건물을 건설하는 것이 환경에 좋지 않다고 말한다.

여러 종류의 기체가 지구에서 방출되는 열을 흡수한다. 대부분은 열은 우주 밖으로 되돌아가야 한다. 그러나 이산화탄소 같은 기체가 대기 속에 너무 많이 존재하면, 많은 열이 지구상에 그대로 남게 된다. 이러한 기체들이 온실의 비닐 지붕 역할을 한다. 그것들이 열이 빠져나가는 것을 막는다. 이것은 높은 온도를 유발시킬 수 있다. 우리가 느끼지 못할 수도 있지만, 지구의 온도는 지난 100년간 섭씨 0.6도만큼 올랐다. 이런 속도라면, 1,000년 후에, 지구는 6도만큼 더워질 것이다. 그것은 세계에 있어서 엄청난 재난이 될 것이다. 세계의 빙산이 녹게 된다면, 지구가 전체가 물에 잠기게 된다.

과학자들이 사람들을 지구온난화의 원인으로 지적하는 또 다른 이유는 우리의 건물 때문이다. 지구상의 모든 것들은 색깔이 열을 흡수하는 것처럼, 일부의 열을 흡수하게 되어있다. 그러나, 대도시들의 거대하고 높은 건물들은 거의 거울같이 매우 번쩍거리는 은빛의 창문을 갖고 있다. 그것들은 열을 별로 많이 흡수하지 못한다. 대신에, 가능한 많은 열을 반사시킨다. 우주 밖으로 배출되는 대신, 열은 기체 속에 가두어진다. 전문가들은 이런 순환 과정이 지구를 점점 더 덥게 만들고 있다고 생각한다.

greenhouse 온실   climate 기후   pollute 오염시키다
atmosphere 대기   carbon dioxide 이산화탄소   iceberg 빙산
reflect (빛·열·음을) 반사하다

Actual Test ❷

p.148

1. (A)	2. (B)	3. Yes : (A), (C) / No : (B), (D)
4. (D)	5. (A)	6. (C)	7. (B)	8. (A)
9. (D)	10. (B)	11. (A)	12. (A)	13. (C)
14. (D)	15. (C)	16. (A)	17. (B)

1-5.

M: I was wondering if you could help me with something.

W: Sure. What seems to be the problem?

M: 🎧 Well, I'm looking for a book that I need to use in my English class this semester. It's called *Introduction to the English Language*.

W: Are you kidding? The semester started over a month ago.

M: Yes, I know, but I lost it last week. I left it on the subway.

W: That's too bad. Anyway, let me see if we have another copy in our database. No, I'm sorry. That book is all out. It looks like the students have bought the last of them. And it looks like there are no plans to order them in yet.

M: Oh, no. I really need that book. Could you please check it again? I can't finish the course without this book.

W: Keep your hopes up. You might still be able to get it somehow.

M: Really? How?

W: Well, first is to get your professor to request another copy of the book for you. Second is to try another bookstore outside the school. Third is to put up a note on the message board in the cafeteria. Someone might have an old copy that they might not need anymore.

M: Alright, I'll try the last option. Erm ... how do I get to the cafeteria from here?

W: You can take the stairs just outside the shop, but it's a long way down. Instead, turn left outside the store, walk to the end of the corridor, and you'll see the lift. Take the lift and go down all the way to B1. The whole underground floor is the cafeteria.

M: 저를 좀 도와주실 수 있는지 생각하고 있었어요.

W: 물론이죠. 뭐가 문제에요?

M: 음. 이번 학기 영어 수업 시간에 쓸 책을 찾고 있어요. 「영어학입문」이라는 책입니다.

W: 정말이예요? 한 달도 더 전에 학기가 시작됐는걸요.

M: 예, 알아요. 그런데 지난 주에 잃어버렸어요. 지하철에다 두고 내렸거든요.

W: 안됐군요. 어쨌든, 우리 데이터 베이스에 다른 권이 있는지 찾아볼게요. 이런, 죄송합니다. 전부 다 나갔어요. 학생들이 마지막 것들까지 사간 것 같은데요. 그리고 새로 주문할 계획도 아직 없는 것 같고요.

M: 아, 안돼요. 그 책이 정말 필요해요. 다시 한 번 확인해 주실래요? 이 책 없이는 수업을 끝까지 들을 수가 없어요.

W: 희망을 버리지 말아요. 그래도 어떻게 하면 구할 수 있을 거에요.

M: 정말이요? 어떻게요?

W: 음, 첫 번째는 교수님께서 학생 대신에 그 책을 새로 한 권 주문해달라고 하는 거고요. 두 번째는 학교 밖의 다른 시점에서 구해보는 거에요. 세 번째는 카페테리아의 게시판에 메모를 남기는 거지요. 누군가는 이제 필요 없는 옛 책을 가지고 있을 수 있어요.

M: 좋아요, 마지막 선택을 택할게요. 음… 여기서 카페테리아는 어떻게 가죠?

W: 서점 바로 밖의 계단을 이용할 수 있는데, 좀 한참 내려가야 하죠. 대신에, 서점 밖에서 왼쪽으로 돌아서, 복도 끝까지 걸어가면, 엘리베이터가 보일 거에요. 엘리베이터를 타고 지하 1층까지 내려가세요. 지하층 전체가 카페테리아에요.

option 선택, 선택권   corridor 복도
underground floor 지하 1층

6-11.

Mass communication is one of the most powerful tools we have for spreading information. This includes different media, such as television, magazines and, of course, newspapers. The stories in the media are written by journalists. Journalists are responsible for reporting facts exactly as they happen or happened. The readers or viewers should be given an unbiased view, so that they can form their own opinion. Q11 However, we constantly see journalists and their stories showing their opinion by siding with one side of the story or issue. Why does this happen?

A large part of the problem is caused by culture and favoritism. Everyone is taught and given ideas about certain things in life. So, it might be hard for one person to give up that view easily. Because of this, expressing their personal opinion on how they report the stories might be understandable.

However, there is also another reason, and it's the main reason why the problem has escalated into an ethics issue. Some journalists are getting corrupted by large companies. They are given favors and sometimes even money, to show favoritism to the company's goods or services. They do this because the benefit of getting good reviews in various media is the most effective way for companies to succeed in business. If the journalist and the company get caught, it could mean serious trouble under the law. Q10 But to be fair, not the entire problem lies with journalists.

대중매체는 정보를 퍼뜨리는데 가장 강력한 도구 중의 하나이다. 이것은 텔레비전, 잡지와 당연히 신문 등의 여러 가지 다른 매체를 포함한다. 이런 매체의 기사는 기자들에 의해서 쓰여진다. 기자들은 사실을 일어나거나 일어났던 그대로 정확하게 보고할 의무를 가진다. 독자나 시청자들에게는 편견 없는 관점이 제공되어서, 그들 스스로의 의견을 형성할 수 있도록 되어야 한다. 그러나, 우리는 기자들과 그 기사들이 특정 이야기나 논점에 대해서 한 쪽을 편듦으로써 그들의 의견을 나타내는 경우를 계속 본다. 왜 이런 일이 생기는 것일까?

문제의 큰 부분은 문화와 편애 때문이다. 모든 사람은 일생의 여러 가지 것들에 대해서 배우고, 개념을 얻는다. 따라서, 한 사람에게 있어서 그런 관점을 포기하는 것은 어려울 수가 있다. 이 때문에, 기사를 어떻게 쓰는지를 통해서 그들의 개인 의견을 표현하는 것은 이해가 된다.

그런데, 여기에는 또 다른 이유가 있는데, 그것은 왜 이 문제가 윤리적 쟁점으로 확대되었는지에 대한 주요 원인이다. 어떤 기자들은 대형회사들로 인해 부패되고 있다. 그들은 그 회사 제품이나 서비스에 대한 편을 들어 보이기 위해서 그런 회사들로부터 선물이나 가끔은 돈까지도 받는다. 그들은 여러 매체에서 좋은 비평을 받는 것이 성공하기 위한 가장 효율적인 방법이라는 것을 알고 있기 때문에, 그렇게 한다. 만약 기자와 기업이 잡히게 되면, 그것은 법에 의해 매우 중대한 문제를 의미할 수 있다. 그러나 공정하게 말하자면 기자들에게만 문제가 있는 것은 아니다.

mass communication 매스컴; 대중매체   journalist 기자
unbiased 편견 없는   favoritism 편애   escalate 확대되다
corrupt 부패시키다, 변질시키다

12-17.

T: Bicycles are a great example of how efficiency works, because bikes have been developed to increase efficiency.

M: What do you mean by efficiency?

T: It's a measurement of how something works, with the same amount of power.

W: Does better efficiency mean wasting less energy?

T: Exactly. I'm glad you understood it quickly. Now, bicycle pedals are pushed with our legs. And since we get tired after some time, bicycles must make full use of what we put in.

M: How can bicycles do that? Aren't they all the same?

T: That's a good question. Bicycles can look similar, but their efficiency can be different. One bike might be hard to pedal, while another can be very easy. Let's compare between the old high-wheeled bicycles and modern bicycles.

W: I think I've seen those before in books and television shows. I don't even know how people got up on those things. They look very dangerous.

T: Yes, they were dangerous. Many people fell because they were so tall. But during that time, people just started to understand about efficiency. 🎧 They realized that by using a larger wheel, we could travel a longer distance with one circle of the pedals than a smaller wheel. Since the pedal was directly on the front wheels, people just made the wheel as big as they could. It **didn't make the pedaling easier, though.**

M: Couldn't they do the same thing with gears? My bicycle has so many gears to choose from.

T: No, gears came much later. They didn't even have a chain. Modern bicycles take advantage of the same ideas, but without having large wheels. Because of different gears, modern bicycles have much greater efficiency than older bicycles, even if the new ones are physically smaller.

T: 자전거는 효율을 높이기 위해서 개발된 것이기 때문에, 효율이 어떻게 작용하는지에 대한 아주 좋은 예입니다.

M: 효율이 무슨 뜻이에요?

T: 그것은 같은 힘이 주어졌을 때, 얼만큼 일을 하는가에 대한 측정입니다.

W: 효율이 좋다면 에너지는 덜 낭비한다는 뜻인가요?

T: 정확해요. 빨리 이해하니까 기쁘군요. 자, 자전거 페달은 우리의 다리로 밟히죠. 그리고 얼마 후에 우리는 힘이 들게 되니까, 자전거는 우리가 공급하는 것을 모두 사용할 수 있어야 하죠.

M: 어떻게 자전거가 그렇게 하나요? 그것들은 그냥 다 같지 않나요?

T: 좋은 질문이에요. 자전거들은 비슷해 보일 수 있지만, 각각의 효율은 다를 수가 있어요. 어떤 자전거는 페달을 밟는 것이 힘들 수 있고, 다른 자전거는 아주 쉬울 수 있습니다. 옛날의 바퀴가 높이 달린 자전거와 현대의 자전거를 비교해보죠.

W: 책하고 텔레비전 쇼에서 그런 자전거를 본 것 같아요. 그 위에 어떻게 탔는지도 모르겠어요. 많이 위험해 보이던데.

T: 예, 그것들은 위험했어요. 그것이 높기 때문에 많은 사람들이 떨어졌죠. 그러나 그 시대에, 사람들은 곧 효율이라는 것을 이해하기 시작했어요. 그들은 커다란 바퀴를 사용함으로써 한 번 페달을 밟는 것으로 더 긴 거리를 이동할 수 있다는 것을 깨달았죠. 페달은 앞 바퀴에 바로 달려 있었기 때문에, 사람들은 단지 바퀴를 가장 크게 할 수 있을 만큼 최대한 크게 만들었습니다. 그러나 그것이 페달 밟는 것을 쉽게 만들지는 못했습니다.

M: 기어를 이용하면 같은 일을 할 수 있지 않나요? 제 자전거에는 고를 수 있는 기어가 아주 많이 있는데요.

T: 아니, 기어는 훨씬 나중에 나왔어요. 그들에게는 체인조차 없었죠. 현대의 자전거들은 커다란 바퀴 없이, 같은 개념의 이점을 이용합니다. 여러 가지의 기어 때문에, 현대의 자전거들은 물리적인 크기는 작더라도, 옛날의 자전거보다 훨씬 큰 효율을 가집니다.

efficiency 효율　measurement 측정　gear 기어, 장비
physically 물리적으로

Actual Test ③

p.154

1. (C)   2. (A)   3. (C)   4. (B)   5. (A)
6. (C)   7. (B), (C)   8. (C)   9. (B)
10. Yes: (C), (D) / No: (A), (B)   11. (A)   12. (D)
13. (C)   14. (C)   15. (A)   16. (D)
17. Freeware: (B), (C) / Shareware: (D) /
    Commercial ware: (A)

1-5.

T: 🎧 Hi, Alex. How are you?

M: Fine, thank you. I was wondering if you had a minute or so.

T: Sure. We can talk now. So what's your question?

M: I really like your course and would like to take it. I'm just not sure about the assignments. I'm not used to writing short papers together with my work in other courses. I don't know if I will be able to turn in all the short papers that the course requires.

T: Hmmm ... I see. I designed the course work in order to help the students in the class. I didn't want to put on pressure by asking for a big final exam.

M: Yeah ... I can see that. But I think that it might be better for me to take a big exam or two big exams.

T: OK ... Why don't we do this? I think that you should still hand in a short paper, just so that you get some practice. It's not easy to write a short paper, because you really have to say exactly what you want to say. So turn in a short paper and then two smaller papers. How does that sound?

M: Great. Thank you so much. I really appreciate it. Will you give me the deadlines for the smaller papers next time in class?

T: Sure. Thanks for reminding me. Let me make a note of it. OK, great. I'll see you soon, then.

T: 안녕, 알렉스. 잘 지냈니?
M: 예, 안녕하세요. 혹시 시간 좀 있으세요?
T: 그래. 지금 얘기할 수 있어. 질문이 뭐니?
M: 선생님 과목이 정말 좋아서 듣고 싶어요. 그런데 숙제에 대해서 확실하지가 않아서요. 다른 과목 공부랑 동시에 짧은 보고서를 쓰는 게 익숙하지가 않은데요. 과목에서 요구하는 짧은 보고서를 전부 다 낼 수 있을지 모르겠어요.
T: 음… 그렇구나. 나는 수강생들한테 도움이 되도록 강의 일정을 짰는데. 중요한 기말고사로 부담 주기는 싫어.
M: 네… 그건 잘 알겠습니다만 그래도 저는 큰 시험 한 번이나 두 번을 보는 게 더 나을 것 같아요.
T: 그래… 이러면 어떻겠니? 나는 그래도 네가 연습할 수 있도록 짧은 보고서는 꼭 내야 한다고 생각하거든. 네가 하고픈 말을 정확히 써야 되기 때문에 짧은 보고서를 쓰는것이 쉽지는 않을 거야. 그러면 짧은 보고서 하나를 내고 그리고 더 짧은 보고서 두 개를 제출하거라. 어때?
M: 좋아요. 정말 감사합니다. 다음 수업시간에 짧은 보고서 기한을 알려주시겠습니까?
T: 그래. 알려줘서 고맙구나. 그것에 대해서 메모를 해 놓으마. 그래. 좋아. 그럼 또 보자.

require 요구하다   design 고안하다
put on pressure ~에게 부담을 주다   turn in 제출하다
deadline 기한, 마감 시간

6-11.

T: Let's discuss something called evolution. Evolution means changing according to the surroundings. Just 20 years ago, everybody thought that humans evolved from monkeys.

M: Yes, I heard about that. Didn't Charles Darwin write a book about it? That's why he's so famous.

T: You're right. He wrote a book called *The Origin of Species*. The book talks about how all animals evolved from some different animals. He stated that humans came from apes, a type of large monkey.

W: 🎧 I don't think he was right. I mean, he didn't have any scientific proof, did he?

T: Not really. A lot of people nowadays are wondering about his theory of evolution. Even DNA testing cannot tell us if Darwin was correct. Although DNA still cannot tell us whether we evolved from apes, it did prove some of his other theories.

W: I heard that all he really did was go to the Galápagos Islands and look at different animals. He grouped similar animals together and wrote a book about it. He didn't have scientific evidence to support it.

M: But you cannot say evolution doesn't exist. Even we are changing, aren't we? Animals are designed to adapt to different environments.

W: I see your point, but if there were such big changes due to evolution, there shouldn't be apes anymore. All of them should have evolved into humans. Yet there are still so many types of monkeys and apes around the world.

T: You've got a good point there. It was a rather difficult concept to agree on when Darwin first published the book. It's even harder now that the book is widely accepted as the truth. I don't think that we will really ever find a true answer about evolution.

T: 진화라고 불리는 것에 대해서 토론해 봅시다. 진화란 주변환경에 따라서 변화하는 것을 의미합니다. 20년 전만 해도, 모든 사람들이 인간은 원숭이로부터 진화해왔다고 생각했습니다.

M: 맞아요, 저도 그걸 들었어요. 찰스 다윈이 그것에 대해서 책을 쓰지 않았나요? 그래서 그렇게 유명해졌잖아요.

T: 그래 맞아요. 그는 「종의 기원」이라는 책을 썼습니다. 그 책은 모든 동물들이 어떻게 다른 몇몇 동물들로부터 진화해왔는가에 대해서 설명하고 있죠. 그는 사람들은 큰 원숭이의 일종인 유인원으로부터 진화했다고 했어요.

W: 저는 그가 틀렸다고 생각해요. 그러니까, 그한테는 과학적 증거가 없었잖아요, 그렇지 않나요?

T: 그랬죠. 오늘날 많은 사람들은 그의 진화설에 대해 의문을 품고 있습니다. DNA검사조차 다윈이 맞았는지를 설명해주지 못해요. 비록 DNA가 우리가 유인원으로부터 진화했는지는 알려주지 못하지만, 그의 다른 몇몇 이론들은 증명해줬어요.

W: 제가 듣기로는, 그가 실제로 한 것은 갈라파고스 섬에 가서 여러 다른 동물들을 관찰한 것뿐이래요. 그는 비슷한 동물을 분류해서 그것에 대한 책을 쓴 거죠. 그에게는 그것을 지지하는 과학적 근거가 없었어요.

M: 그래도 진화라는 것이 없다고는 할 수 없지. 우리도 바뀌고 있잖아, 안 그래? 동물들은 다른 환경에 적응하도록 되어 있다고.

W: 일리는 있는데, 만약에 진화로 인해서 큰 변화가 생겼더라면, 유인원이 더 이상 없었어야지. 그들 모두가 인간으로 진화했어야 되잖아. 그런데 아직도 세계 곳곳에 많은 종류의 원숭이와 유인원이 존재하잖아.

T: 좋은 지적이에요. 다윈이 책을 처음 출판했을 때, 진화는 동의하기가 어려운 개념이었습니다. 그 책이 널리 정설로 인정 받고 있다는 점에서 오늘날에는 더욱 어렵죠. 제가 보기에는 우리는 진화에 대한 진실의 답은 언제까지도 찾을 수 없을 것 같습니다.

evolution 진화   surroundings (주변) 환경   evolve 진화하다
origin 기원   proof 증거   group 분류하다   publish 출판하다

12-17.

Downloading computer software from the internet is becoming a normal part of our lives. But is it stealing? It really depends on what sort of program we are downloading. To help us know if we are stealing, let's talk about the three main types of programs on the internet.

The first is freeware. This means that users are free to download and use the program or share it with other people. The makers are usually programmers that make programs for fun or to showcase their talents. However, many companies also offer freeware that can be used with their other programs. Freeware programs are usually very small and simple. Shareware programs are usually demo software for companies. People can use the program, but users should pay if they like the program. Fortunately, shareware programs do not cost a lot. Many of the programs have a limit on how long users can use the program, or only offer basic functions of the program. In some cases, programs are freeware for private users, but shareware if a company wants to use it.

Commercial wares are programs that users must buy to use. These programs are made to make money for the software companies. They are usually very big and complicated programs that users must study to understand. Famous commercial wares are operating systems and designing programs. These programs are so well-known that they do not usually offer any shareware demo programs. A single commercial ware program can cost thousands of dollars.

인터넷에서 컴퓨터 소프트웨어를 다운로드하는 것은 우리삶의 일반적인 부분이 되고 있다. 그런데 그것은 절도인가? 그것은 사실 어떤 종류의 프로그램을 다운로드하느냐에 달려있다. 우리가 절도를 하는 것인지를 알기 위해, 인터넷 상의 프로그램들의 세 가지 주된 종류에 대해서 이야기해보자.

첫 번째는 프리웨어이다. 이는 사용자들이 자유롭게 다운로드 해 사용하고, 다른 사람들과 공유할 수 있다는 뜻이다. 제작자들은 보통 재미로 또는 자신의 재능을 보여주기 위해서 프로그램을 만드는 사람들이다. 그러나, 많은 기업들 역시 그들의 다른 프로그램과 함께 사용될 수 있는 프리웨어를 제공하기도 한다. 프리웨어 프로그램들은 보통 아주 작고 간단하다. 셰어웨어 프로그램들은 보통 기업의 데모용 소프트웨어이다. 사람들은 프로그램을 사용할 수 있지만, 그 프로그램이 마음에 든다면 돈을 내야 한다. 다행히도, 셰어웨어 프로그램들은 별로 비싸지 않다. 많은 셰어웨어 프로그램들이 사용자들이 얼마나 오랫동안 사용할 수 있는지 제한하거나, 프로그램의 기본적인 기능만을 제공한다. 어떤 경우에, 프로그램들은 개인 사용자에게는 프리웨어이지만 기업이 사용을 원할 때는 셰어웨어이다.

상업용 소프트웨어는 사용하기 위해서 반드시 구입해야 하는 프로그램들이다. 이 프로그램들은 소프트웨어 기업들이 돈을 벌기 위해서 만든다. 보통 그것들은 이해하기 위해서는 사용자들이 공부해야만 하는 거대하고 복잡한 프로그램들이다. 유명한 상업용 소프트웨어에는 운영체제와 디자인 프로그램들이 있다. 이런 프로그램들은 매우 잘 알려져서 보통은 어떤 셰어웨어 데모용 프로그램도 제공하지 않는다. 상업용 소프트웨어의 가격이 수천 달러일 수도 있다.

freeware 프리웨어 (누구나 무상 사용이 가능한 소프트웨어)
shareware 셰어웨어 (일정 기간의 무료 사용 후 계속 사용하려고 할 때 요금을 지불하는 형식의 소프트웨어)   function 기능   commercial ware 상업용 소프트웨어   operating system 운영체제

LinguaForum TOEFL® iBT Series eBasic - e - b - b+ - M - M+ - i - Hooked On

Junior Series

*i*BT eBasic TOEFL® Reading / Listening
*i*BT e TOEFL® Reading / Listening / Grammar
*i*BT b TOEFL® Reading / Listening / Writing / Grammar
*i*BT b+ TOEFL® Reading / Listening
Basic Vocabulary

Test Prep.

Intermediate Level

*i*BT M TOEFL® Reading / Listening / Writing / Grammar
*i*BT M+ TOEFL® Reading / Listening
[New Edition] *i*BT i TOEFL® Reading / Listening / Writing / Grammar
Core Topic Guide Series / **Intro Vocabulary**

Advanced Level

[New Edition] Hooked On TOEFL® Reading / Listening / Writing / Speaking
Frequency#1 TOEFL® Vocabulary
TOEFL® *i*BT INSIDER – The Super Guide / TOEFL® *i*BT Test Book I

LinguaForum™

2016 최신 경향을
가장 확실하게 반영한
토플 중급자를 위한
완벽 대비서

링구아포럼

iBT M+ plus TOEFL 시리즈

① **M⁺ TOEFL 시리즈**에서만 제공하는 **TOEFL 최신 경향!**
② **TOEFL iBT** 80~90점 대로 도약하기 위한 **최상의 전략 제시!**

* 무료 iBT TEST 1회 제공
* Actual Test 1회 추가 제공

www.linguaforum.com